Radical Behaviorism for ABA Practitioners

James M. Johnston

2014
Sloan Publishing
Cornwall on Hudson, NY 12520

Library of Congress Cataloging-in-Publication Data

Johnston, James M.
Radical behaviorism for ABA practitioners / James M. Johnston, Auburn University
(emeritus). -- 1 Edition.
pages cm. -- (The Cambridge center-sloan century series in behavior analysis)
Includes bibliographical references and index.
ISBN 978-1-59738-043-0
1. Behaviorism (Psychology) I. Title.
BF199.J66 2013
150.19'434--dc23
2013011710

Cover design by Amy Rosen, K&M Design, Inc.

Sloan Publishing, LLC
220 Maple Road
Cornwall-on-Hudson, NY 12520

Printed in the United States of America

10 9 8 7 6 5 4 3 2

ISBN 13: 978-1-59738-043-0
ISBN 10: 1-59738-043-1

The Cambridge Center—Sloan Century Series in Behavior Analysis

A. Charles Catania, *Series Advisor*

James M. Johnston
Radical Behaviorism for ABA Practitioners (2014)
(978-1-59738-043-0)

A. Charles Catania
Learning: 5th Edition (2013)
(978-1-59738-023-2)

Beth Sulzer-Azaroff, Kathleen Dyer, Susan Dupont, and Dianne
Soucy *Applying Behavior Analysis Across the Autism Spectrum:
A Field Guide for Practitioners, 2nd Edition* (2013)
(978-1-59738-036-2)

G. Roy Mayer, Beth Sulzer-Azaroff, and Michele Wallace
Behavior Analysis for Lasting Change, 2nd Edition (2011)
(978-1-59738-032-4)

Erik Mayville and James A. Mulick, editors
Behavioral Foundations of Effective Autism Treatment (2011)
(978-1-59738-031-7)

Fred Keller
At My Own Pace (2008)
(978-1-59738-017-1)

Jay Moore
Conceptual Foundations of Radical Behaviorism (2007)
(978-1-59738-011-9)

William Uttal
Time, Space, and Number in Physics and Psychology (2008)
(978-1-59738-015-7)

For more information about these titles, visit our website at
http://www.sloanpublishing.com/behavior

Contents

Boxed Features

Dedication
and Acknowledgments

It would be hard to dedicate this book to anyone other than B. F. Skinner. It contains no argument he did not thoroughly explore during his long career, most likely before it had occurred to anyone else. His 1953 textbook, *Science and human behavior*, captivated me as a graduate student. My studies in psychology to that point had not prepared me for such intellectual honesty, unyielding consistency, and downright brilliance. Although Skinner was clear that we cannot escape our personal history, he came as close to doing just that as one could imagine. He fled the confines of his verbal communities to establish a new one defined by the relentless scientific pursuit of behavior as a purely physical phenomenon and free of cultural invention and misdirection. For me and many others, this verbal community has become the core of our professional and personal identities.

Over the years, my repertoire evolved largely through my responsibilities as a teacher. The challenge of preparing for graduate seminars encouraged me to study the field's growing conceptual literature, and leading students to understand the issues and share my excitement gradually shaped my approach to introducing students to this material. Leading students through the intricacies of radical behaviorism and its fascinating implications was always the highlight of my teaching duties, and as is so often the case for teachers, I owe my primary acknowledgment to my students. As I worked on the book, I was also fortunate to have guidance and feedback from colleagues, who found a reference, clarified an issue, evaluated an argument, and generally kept me on the straight and narrow. Among them, Charlie Catania and Bill Ahearn waded through a draft and offered especially helpful advice.

—James M. Johnston

Preface

What Does it Mean to be a Behavior Analyst?

Are you a behavior analyst, or at least studying to become one? What are the characteristics of researchers and practitioners who describe themselves as behavior analysts that differentiate them from individuals who identify with other disciplines? Behavior analysts have considered ways of answering this question since the earliest days of the field, and for good reason. Shared views about the nature of behavior as a scientific subject matter and the methods by which we investigate it greatly influence what the field discovers. In turn, what we learn about how behavior works serves as the foundation of a practical technology for changing behavior in everyday life. Furthermore, how we talk about behavior, study its underlying mechanisms, and change behavior for practical purposes serves as a curriculum in which new members of the field are trained. Their careers drive the field's evolution and preparation of still more behavior analysts, and so it goes.

Over the years, some defining features of the field have emerged on which there is widespread agreement. Perhaps the most fundamental feature of behavior analysis is its focus on behavior as the sole subject matter of the science and the target of practitioner interest. Although this consensus may seem both obvious and simple, it is neither. In fact, it will take the whole of this book to consider the nature of behavior and distinguish it from the implications of a colloquial vocabulary about behavior that we unavoidably bring to the discussion. As we will see, this unwavering focus on behavior sets behavior analysts apart from others who are interested in behavior more as a basis for interpretations about the mental qualities suggested by everyday language.

Behavior analysts are especially interested in **operant behavior**. This focus flows from the central role of operant behavior in an organism's repertoire and the crucial adaptive relation between operant behavior and the environment. Decades of both basic and applied research have provided a remarkably clear picture of how operant behavior works (see, for example, Catania, 2007), and respect for this literature is therefore another key characteristic of the field. Behavior analysts accept this scientifically based understanding of operant behavior as a limiting condition on speculations about behavior. They understand that both general proposals about behavioral phenomena and guesses about particular instances of behavior must be consistent with what our science has already established.

Still another important area of agreement that defines this field is its reliance on a collection of research methods that have proven effective in studying behavior under both laboratory and field conditions (e.g., Johnston & Pennypacker, 2009; Sidman, 1960). These practices emerged from early laboratory experience and are more similar to those of the natural sciences than to social science methods. Direct measurement of the behavior of individual participants is the centerpiece of this approach, and it is complemented by ways of arranging experimental comparisons and analyzing the resulting data that are especially effective at isolating the effects of environmental variables. Behavior analyst practitioners have even integrated these methods into best practice requirements for routine applied interventions.

Finally, what ties these features of behavior analysis together is agreement on a conceptual framework for how we talk about behavior as a scientific subject matter and as a focus of more practical interests. This conceptual approach, which B. F. Skinner labeled **radical behaviorism**, grew out of a scientific understanding of the nature and workings of operant behavior (Skinner, 1945). The ability to explain particular instances of behavior based on sound science has been vital in helping behavior analysts avoid the pitfalls associated with culturally invented causes of behavior. The defining features of radical behaviorism are the focus of this book's chapters and are summarized in Chapter 10.

In sum, the field of behavior analysis is defined by a particular set of characteristics: a predominant focus on behavior guided by an established scientific literature using methods specifically suited to describing how operant behavior works and integrated with a conceptual framework that is consistent with these research findings. The history of behavior analysis has shown that these three characteristics have powerful consequences for the effectiveness of its researchers and practitioners. The pervasive influence of these characteristics in one's professional repertoire is what it means to be a behavior analyst.

Widespread agreement that these features are the foundation of the field's effectiveness means students must acquire a basic mastery of each of these areas. Regardless of a student's interests, core coursework should focus on how operant behavior works, how behavior can most effectively be measured and evaluated, and how we can talk about behavior in a way that is consistent with what research has already revealed. This book addresses the last of these topics.

Why Do Practitioners Need to Understand Conceptual Issues?

Practitioners representing physical science disciplines work at the interface between their science-based specialties and society. For example, physicians bring the fruits of basic and applied research to their patients, who are not expected to understand the scientific findings underlying their medical treatment. In fact, patients' convictions about their medical problems are often rooted in ignorance and misunderstanding, and part of the physician's job is to explain what is really going on and how a proposed treatment will help. Given the encouraging track record of the medical profession, patients are usually predisposed to accept their doctors' explanations and recommendations. Were patients to prefer their own convictions about their medical issues, they would be less inclined to accept or cooperate with recommended treatment regimens and might not benefit from medical technology.

Applied behavior analysis (ABA) practitioners confront a similar challenge. Their job is to bring decades of basic and applied research to bear on behavioral problems presented by individuals who are unlikely to understand how their problems originated and why they seem so difficult to resolve. Unlike medical patients, however, individuals, families, and even other professionals facing behavioral issues are not usually predisposed to unquestioningly accept the ABA practitioner's recommendations and the underlying science. Of course, the field of behavior analysis does not yet have the widespread recognition and acceptance enjoyed by more mature disciplines such as medicine and engineering.

Applied behavior analysts face this challenge because the culture provides a wealth of invented explanations woven into our language about how behavior works. For example, we are used to assigning the causes of behavior to internal, mental processes, as when we say "I made up my mind to lose some weight." Everyone brings these implicit convictions to discussions of behavioral problems, which means that applied behavior analysts must shoulder a burden their physician counterparts are largely able to avoid. ABA practitioners must convince their clients to accept an explanation and course of treatment that is unfamiliar and that probably conflicts with widely held views that otherwise seem obvious and comfortable. Furthermore, the fact that the field of behavior analysis is not yet broadly accepted as the default discipline for addressing behavioral needs means that alternative approaches likely to appeal to uncritical consumers are also available in the marketplace. This competition only adds to the behavior analysts' task of selling their point of view and methods.

Experienced ABA practitioners are all too familiar with these circumstances. For example, an applied behavior analyst holding a contract with a school district to help teachers address behavioral problems with selected students is asked to assist a third grade teacher. The student in question is frequently disruptive in various ways and has often been remanded to the school's alternative classroom and even suspended for periods of time. The teacher is convinced that the student is frustrated by his inability to do assigned school work and that his acting out is a reaction to this frustration. The teacher believes that the disruptive behavior will therefore decrease if his academic skills improve but simply cannot find additional time to devote to this child's academic needs.

After conducting a functional behavioral assessment, the ABA practitioner develops a somewhat different view. She finds that although the student is weak in certain academic skills, these weaknesses are not so severe as to prevent him from doing assigned work. She also finds that the teacher frequently responds to the child when he is acting out but pays little attention to him when he is behaving appropriately. Knowing the considerable research literature pertinent to this kind of situation, the practitioner is confident that changing the **reinforcement contingencies** will result in less disruptive behavior and more academic behavior. She suspects that once the child is spending more time on academic tasks, it will be much easier for the teacher to address his specific skill needs.

The ABA practitioner recognizes that the teacher's focus on frustration as the underlying cause for the problem behavior is a misguided colloquial explanation. At a minimum, the challenge of the practitioner is to guide the teacher toward changing his interactions with the student, regardless of his assumptions. Depending on the teacher's level of cooperation and interest, however, the practitioner may also be able to help the teacher appreciate the general role of operant learning in understanding student behavior.

In this case, the teacher's belief that frustration is the cause of the child's disruptive behavior stems from an explanatory framework that encourages people to refer to an almost limitless variety of **invented mental events**, such as frustration, as causes for patterns of behavior. It is important that the ABA practitioner understand the pitfalls of this kind of faulty reasoning and be able to apply a conceptual framework that offers an alternative explanation about the real causes of behavior that is consistent with the established scientific literature. If the ABA practitioner shares the teacher's convictions about the causal role of invented mental events, she might focus on ways of decreasing frustration instead of selecting procedures that directly address problematic reinforcement contingencies and reduce disruptive behavior. As we will see, attempting to address frustration raises some significant challenges and will probably not decrease disruptive behavior anyway.

In other words, it is important for ABA practitioners to understand the field's conceptual framework because it avoids problems resulting from the **mentalistic** framework implicit in everyday language. This colloquial perspective is endlessly at odds with the way behavior actually works. It explains behavior in ways that are not only incorrect but that suggest solutions that will usually be unsuccessful. Even worse, these apparent solutions are often incompatible with interventions based on the basic and applied science that is the foundation of ABA technology.

ABA practitioners must confront this conflict in their efforts to guide others toward effective solutions to behavioral problems. In order to be an effective interface between science and society, they must not only be able to offer a coherent science-based framework for understanding behavior but be skilled at persuading others to consider, if not adopt, this point of view as it applies to the circumstances of each case. This is an important competency for practitioners to master. In sum, one reason for ABA practitioners to learn about the field's conceptual framework is that it allows them to be more effective in working with clients, families, and other professionals.

Another reason for practitioners to master this material is that it helps ensure consistency between the field's science and the resulting technology. Maintaining close relations among basic research, applied research, and service delivery areas of the field is a long-standing concern in behavior analysis (for example, see Moore & Cooper, 2003). A shared way of looking at behavior as both a scientific subject matter and a focus of practical interventions is a key mechanism for maintaining mutual influences among otherwise diverse interests within the field. It is the glue that binds together the different elements of the discipline.

The risk is that over time the evolution of ABA practice might be influenced less by the findings of basic and applied research and their associated measurement and evaluation methods and more by outside influences such as the demands of the marketplace. There are many ways this could happen. Basic researchers might fail to appreciate the fundamental behavioral questions implicated in daily practice. Applied researchers might focus on issues that gradually drift away from a foundation in the basic research literature. Practitioners might be inadequately trained in the findings of basic research or well-established measurement and evaluation procedures. They might even be seduced by the financial demands of clinical practice and drift away from best practice standards.

A particularly worrisome risk is that practitioners might succumb to the familiarity of everyday language and abandon much of the field's conceptual orientation. This kind of backsliding can be difficult to resist. After all, practitioners must retain their professional dialect and its underlying philosophy while communicating effectively with clients and other professionals in the common parlance that is so often an impediment to understanding the real causes of behavior. Other professionals face a similar challenge. For example, physicians talk with each other about their cases using a technical vocabulary that must be put aside when talking with patients and families. ABA practitioners face an even greater challenge, however, because their professional vocabulary involves more than just some technical terms. It is based on a fundamentally different conception of behavior and its causes than the point of view implicit in everyday language. Furthermore, ABA practitioners continue to speak this everyday language under non-professional circumstances. There is no point in trying to speak in this technical dialect when ordering a meal at a restaurant or chatting with friends, for example.

The only way to be sure that ABA practitioners continue to approach behavioral problems with the full power of the field's conceptual framework is to make sure that they are especially well-trained in this area and have acquired a deep appreciation of its importance to their effectiveness. In effect, their training must "vaccinate" them against the seductions of the familiar and comfortable dialect that otherwise surrounds them. This book offers them a means of beginning to acquire this mastery and appreciation.

What This Book Will Do

This book presents an argument. The essence of the argument concerns why it is important for ABA practitioners to learn how to talk about behavior in a way that is fully consistent with what the science of behavior has revealed about its nature. Laying out this argument involves describing this specialized dialect and its rationale (Hineline, 1980). Part of the rationale is based on the characteristics of behavior and their implications for how we describe and explain it. However, the justification for this science-based dialect is also based on the many problems presented by everyday language, which is for everyone else the default way of talking about behavior. As a result, much of the book's discussion focuses on how we all learn to talk about behavior from our families and other **verbal communities**.

At times, the intellectual challenge posed by this argument may seem much like learning to speak a foreign language—you have to assimilate many new words and linguistic constructions that can replace those you already know. The task is actually even more difficult, however. Putting aside matters of syntax, if you already know French and are trying to learn to speak Russian, there is usually a word or phrase in Russian that more or less substitutes for most French words or expressions. In learning this new way of talking about behavior, however, there are few such simple substitutions. Instead, the vocabulary of ordinary talk contains many terms and phrases for which there is no straightforward translation in technical behavioral dialect. In fact, we will see that everyday conversation about behavior and other purported human qualities is overflowing with meanings and implications that are not supported by scientific evidence.

The analogy to learning a foreign language is weak for another reason as well. Learning to talk about behavior from a scientific perspective, and without allowing the implications of everyday language to intrude, requires acknowledging the fact that talking about behavior is itself behavior. Although this might seem obvious, viewing verbal behavior as fundamentally the same kind of phenomenon as other kinds of behavior (such as driving a car or eating a cheeseburger) has some disconcerting consequences for how we approach it.

For example, when we talk about behavior, such talk, as with other behavior, is the result of a **learning history**. This means that our convictions—our verbal behavior—about how behavior works come from how we have learned to talk about behavior and must therefore be explained in terms of our learning history. This view contrasts with the more familiar colloquial assumption that verbal behavior, unlike most other behavior, originates in our minds and therefore allows explanation from a mental rather than a physical or environmental framework.

The challenge of learning to replace our everyday way of talking about behavior with a technical scientific dialect is accordingly not so much a matter of vocabulary as it is mastering a view of what behavior is and where it comes from that is fundamentally different from commonly accepted views. Unlike the task of learning a foreign language, we cannot use the familiar vernacular as a foundation for understanding this new dialect. In other words, this is truly a journey to places you have never been.

If all this makes your head hurt, rest assured that as one chapter leads to another, everything will fall into place and you will feel better. Generations of behavior analysts before you have made the same journey and discovered the excitement of arriving at a cohesive framework for talking about behavior that is free of the burden of colloquial inventions and their distractions. The revelations of a science-based dialect about behavior are so pivotal, so broadly valuable, so personally meaningful, that senior behavior analysts can relate the story of their own epiphany as if it occurred just the other day.

Given that this book is one big argument, its style is explicitly persuasive. Because the discussion is as much about our own behavior as it is about the behavior of others, the writing is personal and informal. This is not the kind of material that can be mastered merely by studying a carefully outlined exposition and a list of key points at the end of each chapter. After all, this is a retelling of the story of behavior from the perspective of its science. There are far too many issues, details, and implications to wrestle to the ground; the resulting volume would be far too long. Every point unavoidably raises questions and issues that require reflection and discussion. As a result, each chapter's content should be viewed as a prompt for enthusiastic discussion—and not just in the classroom. This is the kind of material that you need to think about as you are driving to a practicum assignment or the grocery store and to argue about with your peers over some brews on a Friday night.

In other words, what happens in class is only the beginning of figuring out what this all means. Yes, this is what teachers always say about a course of study. In this case, however, the task of discovering all of the ways in which our colloquial dialect has infected our understanding of behavior is more daunting than it might seem. As well, your ability to exercise your new technical vocabulary will initially be modest. (Actually, you are going to be pretty lousy at it at first.) The right interpretations and phrases will not come easily. This book will only show you the way, not leave you with mastery. After all, you have had decades of exposure to the colloquial dialect. Learning a different dialect that is based on a fundamentally different perspective about the nature and causes of behavior will take continuing effort and time.

What This Book Will Not Do

This book is primarily written for applied behavior analysts, particularly those who work in some capacity as practitioners, and especially students planning careers delivering ABA services. In choosing what to cover and how to approach each topic, I have favored the interests of professionals who deliver behavior change services, whether as clinicians or in supervisory or administrative capacities, over those of more diverse readerships.

I have already noted that ABA practitioners work at the boundary between the science and society. This interfacing role means they must first understand the conceptual issues that are important to the field, their foundation in the science of behavior, and their implications for efforts to resolve behavioral problems. As well, they need to be particularly familiar with the colloquial assumptions about the nature and causes of behavior brought to them by clients, families, and other professionals. They further need to be skilled at preventing these assumptions from interfering with the consideration of each case. When appropriate, they need to know how to gently persuade others to view particular instances of behavior in terms of environmental variables instead of assumed mental causes.

With these interests, the book does not delve deeply into some topics that might be appropriate for more comprehensive instructional objectives. For instance, it does not review the historical evolution of various versions of behaviorism, nor does it pursue the many connections with philosophical traditions. These are important topics for an in-depth command of this material, but leaving them aside will not prevent practitioners from dealing effectively with the conceptual issues that routinely arise in applied settings. The text also does not succumb to the temptation to probe all of the implications of each topic, which would often lead too far away from more central interests. Nor does it exhaustively engage the considerable literature in this area that has developed over the years, although it will give you more than passing familiarity with it. Although these omissions may seem significant, they will not interfere with readers attaining a coherent, faithful, and useful understanding of the conceptual framework of the field of behavior analysis.

On the other hand, this book does not attempt to reduce its subject matter to a set of simple rules that might guide an ABA practitioner's reactions to different types of conceptual challenges. Such rules would be ineffective in any case. Being able to identify and respond appropriately to conceptual issues concerning behavior, especially those raised by everyday discourse, requires a level of understanding that integrates the various features of this framework into a complex but coherent world view.

Furthermore, this picture must be sufficiently broad and deep to accommodate all conceptual challenges in an internally consistent manner. In fact, one of the most notable features of the field's conceptual framework is its comprehensive and internally consistent reach. It addresses any and all conceptual issues posed by the characteristics of behavior that science has revealed and the conflicting assumptions embedded in everyday language. Furthermore, it does so without exceptions, that is, without violating the core features of its conceptual positions.

Describing the essential features of this conceptual system, but without probing its full complexity, has required countless decisions about what to include and thereby exclude. My choices will likely bother most instructors at one point or another. After all, each will have acquired his or her command of this material in other contexts and can argue why certain topics or points should have been included or even left behind. I share this frustration. I avoided including issues that are interesting to me and arguably important in some ways. My overriding criterion for what material to cover, however, was based on the necessity of describing a coherent conceptual framework that would be not less, but not much more, than ABA practitioners need to know in order to effectively deal with conceptual issues in their daily work. If every topic and implication was fully pursued and every possible confusion was avoided with more discussion, this would be a different book for a different audience—and a much longer one at that.

A persistent challenge in writing this book was to tread a fine line between the conceptual matters of primary interest and the underlying science and technology they support. After all, these topics should all come together in painting a comprehensive and integrated picture of the field of behavior analysis. Again and again, it was tempting to digress from the conceptual agenda toward discussion of related research and practical techniques. It is not that these digressions might not be useful, but at what point would the temptations result in a different (and much longer) book for a different audience? If conceptual discussions sometimes fail to go as far as you might like in pursuing their experimental and practical implications, I certainly sympathize with any disappointment. However, the goal of this book is necessarily modest—to present practitioners with a limited treatment of the conceptual foundation of behavior analysis. Thoroughly integrating this material with its scientific origins and practical implications would require many more pages and more time than a semester or a curriculum offers.

The result of my choices is a book that will be useful not just for ABA practitioners but for all behavior analysts who need something less than advanced training in this area. This book presents the heart of the conceptual framework that underlies behavior analysis. It explains the key elements of this perspective in a way readers can retain as a coherent point of view ready for practical use as needed. However, it avoids expanding each topic to the point that the goal of comprehension is burdened by the challenge of remembering. The goal is to teach you how to talk about behavior in a certain way, not to teach you things you will soon enough forget.

Prerequisites

Compared to other topics in behavior analysis, this material does not require lots of novel terminology and technical phrasing that would prevent unprepared readers from understanding its essential features. Nevertheless, the more background in behavior analysis you bring to these issues, the more you will profit from your efforts. In a coordinated program of study in the field of behavior analysis, this material should therefore come late in the schedule. The reason for this delay has to do with the fact that this conceptual orientation originated in scientific discoveries about the characteristics of operant behavior. You must have a solid understanding of these characteristics and a deep appreciation for the power and pervasiveness of **operant selection** processes in explaining behavioral repertoires. If you lack this background, it will be difficult to accept the role of learning in instances of behavior that convincingly replace culturally invented mentalistic causes.

Another prerequisite is more difficult to arrange because it does not strictly depend on prior coursework. The challenge of understanding this material lies not so much in comprehending the arguments in each chapter as in dealing with the conflict between these positions and everything we have learned from our culture about the causes for behavior. What we learned from our families and our other verbal communities has long since become so familiar that it can be difficult to recognize its shortcomings or even consider alternative points of view. These culturally based explanations of behavior are so thoroughly embedded in everyday language that it can be hard to imagine other ways of talking about an issue. Some of you may be reluctant to abandon familiar terms and phrases and their implied explanations. Even those who are willing may baulk at the initial awkwardness of a new dialect.

This challenge means that you will profit most from this book if you are sufficiently confident in your development as a behavior analyst to question prior convictions and to consider alternative views. It is not clear what training history assures this particular preparation. Some are readied by their experiences to find this intellectual summons exciting and relish the journey. Others need more encouragement along the way. In my experience, however, all students find that this material pulls together what they have learned in other courses and leaves them with a more integrated understanding of the field.

Teaching

Teaching this material requires that instructors take a somewhat different approach than they might in addressing other topics in the field. Presenting and explaining principles of operant learning or research methods, for example, often requires little more than the right reading material, good lectures, and focused discussion. Although some time will need to be spent describing and explaining these conceptual issues, encouraging students to confront seemingly endless instances of mentalism in everyday language is an even more important instructional task.

This challenge can be eased by creating a classroom atmosphere that balances acknowledgment of the shared struggle with high intellectual standards. That is, it is important that students feel comfortable admitting their discomfort with challenging familiar viewpoints. They need to know that speaking out about their concerns is not only acceptable but useful. On the other hand, they should understand that familiarity is not an adequate defense for retreating to vernacular phrasing or resisting new concepts. It is particularly important to establish a good standard of intellectual honesty in examining colloquial explanations of behavior. It should not be acceptable to accept the credibility of an everyday explanation of a particular behavior merely because "it seems right." Defending such a position should require describing the mechanisms of operant selection that are necessary to make it credible. This insistence will often lead away from the colloquial position and toward a science-based explanation.

Of course, instructors cannot require that students pledge unending devotion to the features of radical behaviorism described in this book. They can only insist that students at least understand this framework and be able to explain its details, mechanisms, and rationale. A course of study in this area can only create some new learning history, which, when done well, might begin to supplant the effects of a much longer history of a mentalistic explanatory model. A more fulfilling instructional goal might be that students become excited about how this conceptual system ties together everything else they have learned, which then motivates them to accept the challenge of figuring out these issues and modifying their verbal repertoire accordingly. Some students will get to this place, but others will not make it all the way. The pedagogic approach to this material can have a big impact on the relative size of these two groups.

Organization and Learning Aids

It is customary to begin a book about the conceptual framework of behavior analysis with an historical explanation of how this point of view evolved and how it relates to other conceptual systems. Instead, this book's early chapters introduce you to some assumptions, facts, and arguments that form the foundation of all that follows. The sequence of topics from one chapter to another has been chosen to make this way of talking about behavior increasingly appealing and ultimately convincing. As Chapter 7 recommends, effective arguments begin with easily accepted premises, which are followed by other premises that might be seen as at least reasonable, and then still others that may be less obvious but that should be found plausible, if not appealing, when their turn comes. Conclusions upon conclusions will accumulate to form a coherent conceptual framework. Throughout, the interests of ABA practitioners serve as a touchstone for selecting topics, framing discussions, and developing examples.

This book is primarily written to serve as a text for courses offered by college and university programs focused on training ABA practitioners. It should also be useful for ABA practitioners already established in their careers who want to bring more depth to their clinical skills, as well as for professionals in other disciplines interested in broadening their perspective about behavior and the field of behavior analysis. Whether serving as a textbook or a professional volume, the book includes some features that should make learning easier and more effective.

Perhaps most importantly, each chapter contains a number of text boxes that address specific issues. The topics treated in the boxes are relevant to the chapter's focus but might distract from the flow of discussion if included as regular text. Some raise particular points that supplement the chapter's themes. Others address a topic that might be too specialized to include in the chapter outline. Collectively, these text boxes are an important component of the book's content and should not be neglected or assigned secondary status.

In addition, the chapters end with some useful supplements. A summary of main points is followed by a study guide. Discussion topics and exercises are designed to probe students' understanding of the chapter and encourage them to engage with its issues. Facilitating discussion among peers should be an important component of each class meeting. There is also a list of recommended readings that acknowledge some of the background for the chapter's material, recognize some well-known publications, and help readers find sources for further study. Throughout the book, terms that might benefit from clarification have been bolded and are defined in a glossary at the end of the book. Finally, a bibliography compiles references to all citations and is supplemented by additional references to important publications in this area.

Two Verbal Repertoires

This book challenges you to learn a new dialect of the English language. In contrast to the colloquial dialect we grew up with, this one originated in the science of behavior analysis. As with other scientific dialects, it serves the needs of the science for a way of talking about its subject matter that accommodates what the science has revealed, offers a precise vocabulary devoid of surplus or unintended meanings, and helps scientists develop effective research questions and interpret results clearly. In other words, the function of this dialect is to improve the quality of the science, and that is the standard by which it must ultimately be judged.

By extension, this dialect offers similar benefits to those who apply scientific findings to practical ends. As already argued, speaking the field's technical dialect helps ABA practitioners prevent conceptual misunderstandings embedded in everyday language from intruding on evidence-based decision making about the behavioral problem at issue. The availability of a technical dialect helps practitioners confront everyday misconceptions about the nature and causes of behavior. It also provides an alternative way of talking, especially among colleagues, that reduces the likelihood of practitioners giving in to their long history with vernacular terms and expressions and failing to recognize their sometimes subtle but mistaken implications about behavior.

You should therefore complete this book with a rudimentary command of a new dialect that not only represents an understanding of certain conceptual issues but facilitates professional discussion with your peers. With continued effort, you should grow increasingly skilled at switching from one dialect to the other, depending on the audience. In a discussion with the parents of a child with autism, for example, colloquial dialect will often be appropriate, even though you are aware of its embedded misunderstandings about the child's behavior. However, your familiarity with these confusions allows you to judge how to encourage the parents to appreciate the role of the environment in understanding how to address their child's needs. On the other hand, in discussing the case with a supervisor trained in behavior analysis, the professional dialect will be appropriate, thereby avoiding misleading references and focusing on relevant issues.

Of course, colloquial dialect is always preferred in talking with family, friends, and everyone else who is not trained in behavior analysis, if only because attempts to speak technically in daily social situations are likely to be punished. Scientific dialects are always laborious and awkward for ordinary conversations. After all, they have evolved under the contingencies associated with clarity and precision, not convenience. In other words, as with individuals who are bilingual, different verbal repertoires are maintained by different audiences.

Admitting that the task posed by this book is largely a matter of learning a scientific dialect about behavior may ease the strain of challenging the familiar colloquial dialect. Although it is important to understand the conceptual basis for conflicts between scientific and everyday ways of talking about behavior, it is not as if the objective is for you to speak and write only in technical language or to replace one dialect with the other. The objective in any conversation is to be effective, which in part means accommodating the listener's repertoire.

In fact, even conversations with other behavior analysts involve a certain amount of professional slang as a way of simplifying discussion among participants who all already share the same conceptual point of view. Technically correct phrasings often purchase precision at the cost of wordiness. There is no need for conversations among colleagues to sound like everyone is reading from a textbook. As a practical matter, some sloppiness in technical language may be acceptable as long as it stops short of accommodating conceptual misunderstandings that would otherwise be avoided by scientific dialect. Nevertheless, you should be able to use the scientific dialect appropriately as needed in conversations with professional peers. This includes being ready, if your bluff is called, to replace everyday words and phrases with more technical language that shows understanding and appreciation for the underlying conceptual issues.

What is All This Fuss About?

With all this vague reference to conceptual issues and scientific versus colloquial dialects, you should be pretty curious about the reasons for all the fuss. What I have emphasized so far is that this material is really different from what you are used to and really important as well. How different? Well, you are going to be asked to question quite a lot of things concerning your own behavior and the behavior of others that you have never before thought about. You are going to discover that much of what you, and everyone else, have been taught about the causes of behavior is largely a sham. You are going to be surprised at the pervasiveness of the problem and how powerfully it misdirects us. You are going to wonder again and again how it is that people fail to figure this stuff out, while forgetting that you failed to do so as well. And you are going to get used to being the only one in the room who gets it.

On the up side, you are going to be excited by your new-found freedom from mentalism. Does "excited" seem too strong a word? Well, the satisfaction you get from having a way of interpreting instances of behavior that both avoids even a hint of mentalism and is consistent with sound science is going to be pretty powerful. Even if you think of yourself as a "nuts and bolts" kind of practitioner who is not into philosophical niceties, you will realize that this is going to be a big part of what you have to offer. And as with all who have gone before you, you will discover that this conceptual framework is also a big part of your respect for the field of behavior analysis and for yourself as a member of it.

But Before We Get Started...

Have you ever taken a foreign language course in which the teacher announces on the first day of class that she is going to speak only the new language in class? And that you have to follow suit? You probably joined your classmates in a collective groan.

You will be relieved to know that this approach is not an option in writing a book like this. It is probably impossible, and certainly undesirable, to introduce readers to radical behaviorism and all of the attendant issues without writing in more or less plain everyday dialect. This means that in order to present ideas and argue points in a clear and convincing way, I must often use everyday terms and phrases that may themselves be problematic. For example, a sentence may begin, "Keeping this point in mind, let us go on to..." (Actually, I think I successfully avoided this phrase throughout the book.) As we will see, references to the "mind" are seriously problematic, but such phrases are familiar, comfortable, and unlikely to be misleading in your effort to understand the point of the paragraph.

In a way, this apparent inconsistency only emphasizes the observation that mentalism is inextricably intertwined in everyday language. In any event, the mentalistic allusions of ordinary English should not distract you from the primary focus of what you are reading. You will quickly come to appreciate the necessity of everyday phrasing in discussing the material yourself. The key is to make sure that your inclusion of everyday words and phrases in otherwise technical discussions is based on convenience of exposition, not failure to recognize mentalism and its challenges.

With that, let us begin.

Chapter One

An Unavoidable (but Reasonable) Assumption

Zoey has a consulting contract with a provider agency that serves individuals with various developmental disabilities. She is a Board Certified Behavior Analyst (BCBA), and her contract calls for her to be on site for 10 hours each week. Her activities usually revolve around developing, implementing, and monitoring programmatic interventions for individuals served at different sites, although she is also involved with staff training and management, not to mention troubleshooting systemic problems within the agency's service components.

Today she is attending a meeting with agency staff concerning an individual named Robert. He attends a day program and gets back to his group home around 3:00 p.m. Although the afternoon schedule includes various activities, he typically refuses to participate. Instead, he pesters other residents, and staff have to spend a disproportionate amount of their time dealing with him and the disruptions he instigates.

In addition to Zoey, the meeting includes the usual cast of characters. Liz, the psychologist based in the agency's central office, is there, along with Sharon, a social worker. Of course, the group home manager is present, as is the behavior specialist whose assignment includes this group home, among others. The purpose of the meeting is to consider what to do about Robert's uncooperative and disruptive behavior in the afternoons.

In discussing the fact that Robert refuses to participate in scheduled activities, it doesn't take too long before Liz observes that Robert is free to choose not to participate in activities in which he's not interested, and Sharon agrees. Zoey acknowledges that he should not be forced to participate but tactfully wonders about the reasons for his lack of interest. However, Liz takes the position that he doesn't have to have a reason; he can choose to ignore staff prompts to participate for no reason at all. Zoey counters with the idea that there must be something that makes him prefer bothering his peers rather than participating in planned activities. She even throws out a couple of possibilities based on what might be reinforcing his behavior more or less.

Liz, perhaps feeling that her status as the agency's psychologist is being threatened, doesn't warm to the implication that reinforcement, or the lack thereof, might be at the root of Robert's behavior. She doesn't want to let go of the idea that there doesn't always have to be a reason for his actions. He may simply not want to participate, just as he may simply want to hassle other individuals. Sharon is no more interested than Liz in the notion that reinforcement might be at work. She argues that although Robert is intellectually disabled, he is no less free than she is to choose one course of action over another. She insists that she can choose to have a salad or a baked potato for lunch today and that the choice is solely hers.

At this point, the group home manager and behavior specialist are more than happy to sit back and stay out of the way. Zoey can now see that this isn't the time to debate philosophical issues and that the discussion certainly isn't helping the group figure out what to do about Robert's problems. She backs off any consideration of whether his behavior represents choices that are free of outside influences and instead tactfully shifts to the nature of the consequences for his behavior that the home manager and behavior specialist have observed, thereby bringing them into the now more practical discussion.

FREE OR DETERMINED?

Inside versus Outside

The convictions of Liz and Sharon about the causes of Robert's behavior raise an issue that has been around for a very long time. Their view is that he is free to choose one course of action over another, regardless of the different consequences associated with these choices. Another way of describing their position is that his uncooperative and disruptive behavior is not the result of outside influences but of the choices he makes.

This view implies an "inside" versus "outside" distinction about the causes of behavior. The implication is that the causes for behavior originate from inside the person in some way or at least are internally modulated. Even though there might be obvious external influences, such as environmental consequences that would seem to make one course of action more or less likely than another, this view holds that it is what goes on inside the person that ultimately controls the behavior that others see. We seem to implicitly assume that any outside considerations are secondary to the individual's deliberations, which are what lead to action. When someone has behaved in a way that to others was obviously unwise, for instance, we might ask, incredulously, "What were you thinking?"

In other words, from this perspective some sort of mental activity precedes public behavior and may override any influence that environmental consequences might have. If true, this would mean that behavior can at least sometimes be free of outside influences. Of course, we have no way of directly accessing the mental activity of others, so we can only turn to our own experiences to evaluate the credibility of this argument. Taking Sharon's example, if you are trying to decide whether to have a salad or a baked potato for lunch, it certainly seems that the choice is yours. You might consider reasons for one alternative over the other, but the way you have learned to observe and describe what you are doing leads you to insist that the outcome is yours alone to determine. In fact, you might decide on the salad but, just as the waiter is about to walk away, switch your order to the potato (loaded, of course). You have learned to see yourself making a seemingly free choice.

This apparent ability to change our minds, or to come up with even more options than we started with, makes it seem that we are truly free to choose what we want to do. If someone dares to confront us with an explanation of our choice based on outside factors, we can simply change our minds again, thereby emphasizing the point that we control our own behavior. Under these conditions, denying the role of mental deliberation as the final arbiter of public action is just not credible. After all, we can plainly see that this is exactly what we do much of the time. Right?

Are We Free to Choose?

The assumption that we can make choices that are free of outside influences is the essence of a long-standing philosophical position called **free will**. This position implies that choices are not caused by environmental or even hereditary factors but are free of such influences. In this context, choice is said to be free because it is not determined by physical variables. The assumption that the individual can make decisions that are independent of physical influences leaves only mental deliberation as the source of the resulting behavior.

The expression "free will" means that our will, our ability to control our own actions, is entirely our own, which means that it is not susceptible to other influences. When we talk about our "willpower," for instance, we imply that our capacity to make ourselves do something is the result of something internal, a power that is uniquely our own. That is, what determines whether we can resist ordering a big fat slice of coconut cream pie as dessert is a personal choice controlled by something indefinable that is at the root of who we are as an individual. Although our decision may take our waistline or cholesterol level into consideration, the actual choice may ignore such unpleasantness and is therefore free.

Of course, most people do not think about these matters as they describe or explain their own behavior. We casually say we've "made up our mind" or "changed our mind." We proudly report that we "made ourselves" go to the gym yesterday. We talk about "deciding" to do this or that. Everyday language includes countless phrases that suggest that individuals act in ways that are ultimately the result of mental deliberation, no matter how obvious other possible influences might be. This mental deliberation may be labeled as thinking, deciding, or choosing, but the key is that the outcome is ultimately free of any influences we can identify.

Sometimes there is no reference to a mental process at all. We may explain the actions of ourselves or others without any implication of careful thought or decision making. We may report that we "decided on the spur of the moment" or "simply decided" to do something as a way of tacitly admitting we are not aware of having made a considered choice. Often we simply report that we "don't know" why we did something, which carries with it the insinuation that there was no reason for doing it. We are especially likely to make this assessment for others, given that we are not privy to their thinking anyway. For example, we might describe a friend's behavior as unthinking, capricious, or irrational. However, lack of awareness of a deliberative process involves the same assumption we make when we refer to having deliberately chosen a course of action—that the behavior of interest occurs without influence by known or unknown variables.

This is all terribly familiar. We grew up learning to describe our behavior and the actions of others as if behavior can be free of environmental influences. We are quite comfortable with the idea that we alone decide what we are going to do, overriding the possible contribution of other factors. This does not mean that most people would not be willing to concede that some portion of our behavior is influenced by physical variables. After all, behavior such as breathing is obviously largely controlled by biological processes, and most would admit that many daily activities such as driving a car are influenced by environmental factors. Whether we put our foot on the brake or steer one way or another is certainly not independent of what is going on around us. However, if someone were to argue that we *never* have the luxury of free choice, most people would be offended. In rejoinder, they might point to choices involving the future, such as where to go for dinner, and argue that no matter what realities might intrude (for example, one restaurant could be closed, another too expensive, etc.) we are still free to choose. They might "prove" our point by changing their mind at the last minute. And how could anyone provide convincing evidence that our choices are not free?

Or Is Our Behavior Determined?

To deny that we can make choices that are free of hereditary or environmental influences is to take the position that our behavior is determined by such factors.

This position is called **determinism**, and it is just as much a fundamental assumption as is the argument for free will. Fortunately, assuming that behavior is determined by physical variables does not require knowing exactly what variables are at work in each instance. In fact, it might be wise to concede that just because we are able to point to certain environmental factors as possible causes for our behavior does not mean we are right or that other factors are not also operating. After all, we are often not especially aware of our behavior and its environmental context. Even when we are paying attention to our actions, any convictions about their causes are hardly the result of skilled and unbiased observation.

The assumption that behavior is determined by physical variables is usually interpreted as allowing no exceptions. In this view, all behavior has such causes, even though we are usually unaware of the details. When confronted with this argument, most people seem threatened by what appears to be an unavoidable loss of autonomy. The assumption that we have free will seems to put us in control of our own behavior, whereas the deterministic assumption means this is only an illusion. It means our behavior is fully controlled instead by variables of which we are usually unaware.

Not surprisingly, it is difficult for most people to accept that the choices they make to behave one way or another are not free but are actually controlled by physical variables. This would mean there is no such thing as free choice or free will. After a lifetime of explaining behavior in terms of such apparent freedom, it is understandably difficult to accept what appears to be a helpless or passive role, instead of a controlling responsibility, as we are pushed this way and that by forces we are likely unaware of and might not be able to control anyway. It simply makes sense to us that whether to adopt a puppy from the shelter, for example, is an act that is ours to decide, rather than a behavior that is entirely the result of current environmental variables in tandem with our cumulative learning history.

In spite of any discomfort with the implications of determinism, the assumption that physical events are fully explainable in terms of other physical events has a long and respected position in the natural sciences. After all, if your job is to explain how the physical universe works, it makes little sense to start with the assumption that the phenomena you are trying to explain may sometimes occur or vary for no reason at all. Scientists assume that there are physical causes for whatever they are studying because they have a long track record of finding such causes and because to assume otherwise would mean their work is pointless. If a cause-effect relation discovered today might not hold tomorrow, scientists could not accumulate a body of reliable findings that could serve as the basis for practical technologies. Behavior is a physical event, of course, and there is no scientific reason to assume it should be an exception to this general assumption of determinism.

Competing Assumptions

These beliefs about the nature of behavior are unavoidably assumptions. It is not possible to gather direct evidence proving that behavior can be free of physical causation or that it is always determined by physical variables. Proving free will would require showing that behavior can occur without influence by hereditary or environmental factors. Not only is it impossible to eliminate the role of these variables, we cannot rule out the possibility that we are simply unaware of their possible contributions, even if they are not obvious, and searching for them would require an endless scientific effort.

On the other hand, proving determinism would require demonstrating the physical causes for any behavior, an impossibly exhausting task as well. Even with the advantages of studying behavior in a laboratory setting using non-human species, the challenge is daunting. Although you might be able to show that when a rat will press the right lever versus the left lever depends on a specific training history, the animal's behavior will usually vary somewhat from otherwise regular patterns. In order to show that these variations are themselves determined by other factors, we would have to identify them and their contribution. Trying to identify all of the influences on behavior in our everyday environments is doomed from the start.

The fact that one position cannot be proven over the other gives us the latitude to consider which assumption is the most useful. Perhaps utility should be the criterion guiding our decision about which assumption we should make. The issue comes down to how one assumption or the other affects our ability to understand behavior and live happily ever after. What, then, are some of the implications of assuming that behavior can be free of physical causation versus assuming that it is always influenced by physical variables?

First, consider what it means to say we have free will. It means that we can control our own actions, we can make choices about what we do, and those choices are not influenced by any other factors. If behavior can occur independently of hereditary and environmental variables, it follows that it may be capricious or random and therefore without explanation. Although it might be argued that "you" are the source of control over what you do, in order for your choice to be free, there must not be any factors influencing your decision. "You" must be completely free to choose. If your choice is influenced by similar experiences in the past or by your assessment of the outcomes of behaving one way or another, it will not be free.

The assumption of free will, if true, has other consequences as well. Researchers would not be able to understand all of the factors influencing behavior, no matter how thorough their efforts. No matter what they discovered or how much they learned about operant selection, for example, it would always be possible for behavior to occur for no reason. This limitation means that our ability to resolve behavioral problems is constrained as well. For instance, we might learn from a functional analysis about some of the variables apparently controlling self-injuri-

BOX 1.1

Variations of Free Will and Determinism

In his book, *Understanding Behaviorism*, Baum (2005) summarizes some variations of the free will and determinism positions. Philosophers call the everyday assumption that we can make choices that are free of our past experiences "libertarian free will." It is this position that explicitly conflicts with determinism. Baum suggests that this view evolved exactly to confront the deterministic argument that all behavior has physical causes.

On the other hand, the philosopher Daniel Dennett (1984) views free will as deliberating prior to actions. In Baum's example of Dennett's reasoning, if you think about the pros and cons of eating a bowl of ice cream, your decision is therefore freely chosen. Baum describes this position as compatible with determinism in the sense that such deliberations are themselves behavior that might be influenced by heredity and environmental history. As he notes, however, this is not what people generally mean by free will.

A variation of the deterministic position attributed to the early psychologist Donald O. Hebb (Hebb, 1949) is called "soft determinism." In this argument, free will is the dependence of behavior on heredity and past environmental history. However, this position does not hold that free will involves the individual causing his or her actions and instead implies that free will is just an experience or illusion.

ous behavior in a child with autism and design an intervention that takes advantage of this information. However, the assumption of free will means we must admit our efforts to reduce the occurrence of the target behavior might be unsuccessful simply because the behavior can occur for no reason, regardless of any intervention. In other words, this would be a discouraging assumption for practitioners and those they are trying to help, not to mention our culture in general.

In contrast, the assumption of determinism means there are always causes for behavior, regardless of the characteristics of the particular behavior of interest. Whether it is a life-changing act such as getting married or the seemingly trivial act of combing your hair, the position of determinism assumes that all actions are the result of hereditary or environmental factors. The causes may be multifaceted and complex, and it may be wise to accept that we do not yet fully understand them, but the assumption of determinism allows for no exceptions. No instance of behavior is considered free of physical causation.

It is also wise to admit that we are rarely in the position of being able to explain with any certainty what factors are at work for a particular behavior at a particular moment or to predict what a person will do in a specific instance. This inability is not a weakness in the argument for determinism. In addition to the possibility that we still lack a full understanding of the underlying laws involved, we always lack information about the variables operating in a specific instance. Other sciences face comparable limitations. Even if we were specialists in fluid dynamics, we could not predict the path of a leaf falling from a tree or exactly where it will land, but we do understand the laws of fluid dynamics well enough to bet our lives on the science underlying airfoil design when we get on an airplane. The limitation is simply one of having enough information on the relevant variables in a specific instance.

The assumption of determinism also means that we must steadfastly resist the temptation to assign causal status to a non-physical universe. Eliminating the familiar roster of explanations that specify or at least imply mental causes for behavior is quite disconcerting at first, but it has the advantage of avoiding interpretations that distract us from considering the real variables that might be at work. Avoiding fanciful, unsupported, or unnecessarily complicated explanations of events is an important feature of scientific method. Scientists are **parsimonious** in their approach to explaining how things work because it helps them avoid unnecessary research, wild goose chases, and dead ends. In offering explanations of a phenomenon, they have learned that it is wise to exhaust well-established variables and relations before turning to possibilities that are novel, overly complex, or difficult to evaluate.

Explaining behavior in terms of **mental "events"** that by definition have no physical status clearly violates parsimony as a scientific value. How would scientists investigate such supposed phenomena? How can you measure something that has no physical dimensions? How do you conduct experiments in which you must control the features of mental events as the independent variable? The solution to

---

BOX 1.2

Are Scientists Stingy?

Even though it is not often spoken of, parsimony is one of the most respected attitudes of science. In a word, it means to be stingy. Scientists are parsimonious in their preference for exhausting simple and well-established explanations of phenomena before turning to complex and less well-understood explanations. Scientists follow this strategy because they have learned that it makes science more efficient. It helps avoid wild goose chases and blind alleys, which are always a risk in scientific research. Instead of offering fanciful explanations of some event, scientists cautiously insist on trying to explain the event in terms of empirical evidence that they already understand fairly well because the odds of successful resolution are usually better than with more "far out" notions.

This approach urges us to explain the observable facts of behavior with reference to variables in the physical world, which the natural sciences understand pretty well, before inventing a non-physical world of the psyche, which certainly goes beyond the laws of nature as we understand them. We need to remember the principle of parsimony when we theorize about human qualities and their explanation.

these challenges cannot depend on verbal reports from the person whose mental activity is under consideration. This indirect source of information has weaknesses that have long been documented. The solution is to avoid inventing mental explanations for behavior in the first place.

A Few More Issues

Non-physical causation. In considering free will and determinism, here are a few more issues to think about. For instance, if behavior is assumed to be at least sometimes free of physical causes and susceptible to our choices, what is the mechanism by which our behavior results from these choices? That is, how can non-physical factors (that is, mental qualities) influence physical events such as behavior? We understand different means of physical causation, but it is hard to understand how "events" in a "non-physical universe" can cause events *in* the physical universe. If they have no physical dimensions, they cannot involve the same kinds of causation that apply with physical events; if they do, they would have to have physical dimensions.

Responsibility. Another issue that often comes up when discussing this topic concerns the notion of personal responsibility. Much of our culture is rooted in the idea that each person is responsible for his or her own behavior. We teach

---

BOX 1.3

Talking About Freedom: Freedom From Physical Constraints

Our everyday language includes many ways of talking about freedom. Perhaps the most obvious sense of freedom has to do with the absence of physical constraints on our behavior. We say we are free if we are able to do what we want. If we are prevented from doing something because our actions are not physically possible, we say that we are not free to act in that situation. Someone who is in jail is unlikely to say he or she is free. Other physical limitations may lack bars and locks, but the effect is the same. We are not free to get a dish from the top shelf of the kitchen cabinet if we do not have something to stand on. We cannot drive to the store if we cannot find the car keys.

This way of talking about freedom may be extended to situations in which we are not free to act because of less obvious limitations that are beyond our immediate control. For example, we may lack a required skill, thereby preventing us from acting in some way. Without training, we are not free to walk a tightrope, fly a plane, or solve a quadratic equation. These ways of talking about freedom do not conflict with the position of determinism because they only refer to situations in which some action is not possible.

this value to our children and enforce it in our legal system. If we assume that behavior is determined by outside factors, does this mean that the individual is not responsible for his or her behavior? Could we behave without thinking about the consequences of our actions? Could we plead that we are not in control of our own behavior when our actions cause problems for others? Would not the position of determinism mean that our behavior cannot be blamed on a personal failure to behave in an acceptable way?

Well, yes and no. It is true that the position of determinism means that each person's behavior, including the behavior we label as "making choices," is fully influenced by hereditary and environmental variables. In this sense, we can always point to such factors that might have influenced our actions, and we must acknowledge that there is no inner controlling agent that is independently in charge of our behavior. So, yes, we are not responsible for our behavior in a scientific sense because the individual is not a controlling authority who makes decisions about his or her behavior that are independent of physical variables.

On the other hand, another way of talking about responsibility is in terms of consequences. We cannot avoid confronting the effects of our behavior on the environment, which in turn greatly impacts the kind of behavior that produced these effects. This means we are responsible for our behavior in the sense that we must live with its consequences. If we have too much to drink when out with friends and act out in ways that offend them, they may be less inclined to ask us to join them next time. In this instance, we may not be able to avoid the social consequences of our behavior.

This sense of responsibility is also enshrined in cultural mores and laws, which insist that individuals should consider the possible consequences of their behavior before they act and then deal with these consequences after the fact. For behavior that is especially important to the culture, rules are established that hold individuals responsible for the outcomes of certain behavior. Consequences are also established for abiding by or violating those rules. Sometimes these **behavior-consequence contingencies** are informal and personal, as when a parent requires a teenager to be home by a certain hour at night. Of course, we are all familiar with rules sanctioned by government in the form of laws that prohibit certain kinds of behavior and set out penalties for breaking those laws. These contingencies are important in helping to manage behavior that is especially important to society.

The reality of consequences therefore means that the question of whether we can dispense with the obligation of personal responsibility can also be answered in the negative. Accepting that behavior is determined does not mean we can abandon the everyday notion of responsibility. Although we do not control our behavior independently of environmental influences, we cannot avoid dealing with the consequences of it. By arranging particular consequences for different kinds of behavior, we (both individually and collectively) encourage or discourage others to behave in certain ways. So, when parents tell their teenage daughter she has

---

BOX 1.4

Talking About Freedom: Feeling Free

Another way we talk about freedom has to do with how we feel about constraints on our behavior. If we are threatened into behaving a certain way, we are unlikely to say that we feel free. If someone holds a gun on us and asks for our money, we will certainly not feel free to refuse or walk away. We may feel no less free when the threat is less direct, immediate, and personal. If we are driving to the beach and notice police using radar guns and stopping speeders, we are not likely to feel free to drive above the speed limit.

Sometimes the threat is not about encountering unpleasant consequences but about losing something we enjoy. Social relationships often embody this kind of contingency. A husband may offer social positive reinforcers for his wife behaving in a certain way with the hope that she will feel compelled to comply with his wishes. Even if his enthusiasm does not carry any suggestion that she might lose these reinforcers were she to act differently, our experience in social relationships helps us understand this risk. In other words, the "soft" coercion of positive reinforcement may feel no less constraining than a more obvious risk of punishment. As a more obvious example, just because we might earn a high salary in a job does not mean that we may not feel trapped doing work we do not enjoy.

---

to be home by midnight or she will be grounded for a month, this contingency is likely to affect her behavior, given a history of her parents following through on similar contingencies in the past. Although we may describe the parents as holding their daughter responsible or the daughter as being responsible for her behavior, it is the past and current contingencies that are responsible for her compliance.

That is, in accepting that behavior is determined, we assign the responsibility for behavior not to the individual but to sources of control in the physical environment. From this perspective, holding individuals responsible for their behavior by specifying the consequences for certain actions remains an important contingency because it helps manage those tendencies to act in one way or another. The outcome—behavior that complies with cultural values—results not from choices by each individual but from a history of consequences for behaving appropriately. (Chapter 7 considers the topic of responsibility further.)

Choice.   Another outcome of assuming that behavior is fully determined by physical variables is that it conflicts with everything we have been taught about our ability to make choices. As already pointed out, determinism unavoidably means that the idea that we can make choices that are free of environmental influences is an illusion. The decisions we make are not our own in the sense that they are free from outside influences. When we cast our vote for a particular political candidate,

BOX 1.5

Choice versus Preference

If someone asks you to make a choice or state your preference, it seems they are asking the same thing because the terms choice and preference are often used interchangeably in daily discourse. This chapter argues that both terms purchase a serious conceptual problem if they imply that the origins of the behavior involved in choosing or preferring lies in mental deliberations. Although we do not typically characterize a preference as "free," as we might a choice, we seem to mean the same thing when we refer to a "personal" preference. If describing preferences as personal implies the same mental origins as free choice, the same conceptual problems arise.

In spite of these similarities, everyday dialect also seems to allow for a distinction between the two terms. For example, we say someone has a preference when he or she is more likely to choose one alternative over another. Our reference to this preference is merely a tact of a behavioral tendency, whether transient or relatively stable. Although we may allow a role for mental deliberation in explaining the origin of a preference, we may at least acknowledge the influence of different consequences in a history of choosing from alternatives. In fact, this history is all that is necessary to explain a preference. The way we behave when faced with alternatives comes from our previous experiences with those alternatives. Any mental attributions are gratuitous.

In contrast with the idea of an existing preference, the everyday notion of choice—the behavior of choosing—implies a decisive action, presumably based on a preference. However, if preference is taken as no more than a behavioral tendency rooted in our experience with the alternatives, there is no reason to view the act of choosing as having different influences. That is, making a choice (an instance of preferring) may be viewed as behavior fully explained by the past consequences of such behavior under similar circumstances. Of course, this view conflicts with the idea that the behavior of choosing can be free of environmental influences.

we may believe this is a free choice, but we are simply unaware, or unwilling to acknowledge, all of the factors that influence our voting behavior. By seeming to put the cause for action inside the person, the language of choice conveniently avoids the need to specify outside influences.

At the least, this way of talking is efficient; it is much simpler to describe ourselves merely as agents for an action than to list all of its possible influences. The price of this efficiency is that we fail to appreciate the factors that are actually responsibly for our behavior. In learning the language of our culture, we satisfy the grammatical necessity of specifying a noun associated with a verb by identifying ourselves as the cause for much of our behavior ("I decided to go to the movies"). In doing so, however, we fail to consider the implications of putting causes for our

BOX 1.6

Talking About Freedom: Making Choices

Our vocabulary of freedom is often based on having choices. If we can identify alternatives when facing decisions, we are more likely to talk in terms of our freedom to choose a course of action. Conversely, if we see only one course of action available, we would probably not say we are free to act as we wish. The more choices we have, the more we might describe the freedom of our situation.

Problem solving is often seen in this light. As Chapter 5 explains, problem solving involves situations in which someone is not able to act in a way that resolves a condition of deprivation or aversive stimulation (Skinner, 1953). Put another way, we have a problem when we cannot choose a course of action that will solve the problem. Even one choice may do the trick, but more than one option may provide what we describe as even greater freedom. So, if you misplace your apartment key and cannot open the door, you would not say you are free to get into your apartment. If you do not have a spare key available, live on the second floor, and the apartment complex office is closed, you may have no reasonable way to get in. If you left a key with a neighbor, or live on the first floor and can (worse case) break a window, or the office is open, you have choices that might encourage you to say you are still free to get in your apartment.

behavior in a mental or non-physical universe. What does it mean to say that the behavior occurred because "I decided," or "I made up my mind," or "I chose"?

If we are interested in a science of behavior, we cannot ignore this question or its implications. I have already mentioned the methodological complications of studying events that cannot be directly measured. Nevertheless, the physical sciences successfully address this challenge when there is empirical evidence supporting the existence of the events in question. The field of physics spends huge sums of money to identify and understand various subatomic entities, even though they might never have been observed. Although their existence might be theoretical, the depth and precision of the supporting evidence is such that this investment is deemed worthwhile. What physicists do not do, however, is pursue purported phenomena that apparently do not have physical dimensions at all and for which there is no empirical evidence of their existence.

This is the case when we specify ourselves as the cause for behavior. The mere fact that it seems obvious we make decisions or choices that are entirely up to us does not constitute scientifically credible empirical evidence for the existence of free will. We talk about making decisions or choices and defend this perspective because that is how we learned to describe our behavior as we were growing up. In the Renaissance and Elizabethan times, you would have learned that there were four humors (sanguine, choleric, phlegmatic, and melancholic) that were responsible for both medical conditions and personality. This view no doubt seemed perfectly obvious at the time, although in light of modern scientific knowledge, it now seems quite naive.

Even if you understand and appreciate why it is not a good idea to assume we can make choices about our actions that are free of outside influences, it is difficult to let go of the notion that we have free will. This view is so pervasive in our culture and language that putting it aside is more than a little bit disconcerting. At first, you will find that avoiding phraseology that implies freedom of choice makes it more difficult to talk about behavior because you have not yet developed a more appropriate way of talking. You will develop this facility as you read the following chapters. For now, focus on identifying those words and phrases that place causes for behavior in a non-physical, mental universe. Try replacing that language with simple descriptions of actual behavior and past and present environmental factors that might be responsible for it. For example, instead of saying "I made up my mind" as a way of both describing and explaining some action, identify the behavior that actually occurred (going to a particular movie) and consider its possible influences (similarity to other movies you have enjoyed, a review you read, a friend's recommendation, and so forth).

BOX 1.7

Talking About Freedom: Spiritual Freedom

We may sometimes talk about a kind of spiritual freedom. This sense of freedom is not about having religious choices but about freedom from material or worldly attachments or from social pressures or pursuits. This kind of freedom is often expressed in terms of liberation from things and experiences that may be strong reinforcers, such as expensive houses and furnishings, nice clothes, fine cars, eating at fancy restaurants, taking far-flung vacations, or achieving lofty social status. Pursuing such reinforcers is likely to be constraining for most because it may require sacrifices in the kind of work we do, how much time we spend working, and how we allocate our time. Spiritual freedom tends to connote release from chasing social reinforcers or approval.

Spiritual freedom is said to be available when our behavior is more influenced by non-material reinforcers such as helping others, especially to the point of self-sacrifice. Such actions benefit particular individuals or society at large and not, apparently, ourselves. If the consequences for our actions benefit us in some obvious way, we (and others) may be less inclined to say they lead us to an experience of spiritual freedom. If helping others seems to depend on a history in which we have learned this social value, especially if such behavior is stronger than more materially motivated behavior, we may be more likely to talk about experiencing a kind of spiritual freedom.

Yes, Your Assumption Is Itself Determined

It may have occurred to you by now that if our behavior is determined, it means your "decision" concerning where you stand regarding free will versus determinism is not your choice but is determined by various influences. Of course, the arguments in this and succeeding chapters are likely to be one such influence, as will be the discussions you have about these issues in class and with your friends. In any event, how you talk about free will and determinism is, after all, just verbal behavior. The way behavior works will not be changed by how you talk about it. However, the position on this issue taken by you and other behavior analysts will greatly impact the effectiveness of our science and our technology.

Just remember, you cannot have it both ways. It is either possible that our behavior can at least sometimes be free of outside influences, or it is always the case that whatever we do is determined by hereditary or environmental factors, although we should acknowledge that such influences are complex and usually not fully appreciated in individual instances. People who are most comfortable with the idea that we have free will may admit that our behavior may often be controlled by physical variables but insist that they can still make choices that are independent of outside influences. A conviction that our behavior is fully determined allows no such equivocation, however. This position means that choice is an illusion. In other words, if you want to decide moment by moment whether particular actions are susceptible to physical influences or available for your free choice, you do not accept the assumption that behavior is determined.

CONSEQUENCES FOR PRACTITIONERS

So why does it matter what practitioners think about this issue? As the preface emphasized, practitioners talk with clients, families, and other professionals every day. The ordinary dialect of these conversations is rooted in a causal model in which individuals are assumed to be able to control their own behavior at least some of the time. This assumption that we are free to choose to behave one way or another is at least implicit, and often explicit, in discussions about the behavior of both clients and caregivers. Because such behavior is seen as originating from within the individual, it complicates ABA practitioners' efforts to convince all concerned to focus on environmental factors that may be important in changing the behavior of interest.

The vignette at the beginning of this chapter highlights this challenge. The view held by Liz and Sharon that Robert's disruptive behavior may be the result of his free choice, rather than environmental factors, quickly gets in the way of Zoey's effort to generate a discussion focusing on those factors. Her ability to lead the group toward possible environmental interventions depends on her familiarity with this issue. She must be able to recognize the underlying philosophical issue, have already figured out her position based on her professional training, and know how to lead others to see that focusing on environmental variables is likely to be useful. If Zoey was unfamiliar with this issue, she would be less likely to be able to lead the discussion in a clinically beneficial direction. Worse, she might wind up agreeing with Liz and Sharon and fail to consider constructive environmental options for intervention planning.

Consider the approach to treatment that might follow from an assumption that Robert's misbehavior is the result of his choices, which are free of outside influences. The focus of intervention would likely be on Robert's behavior of choosing, not his disruptive behavior. If this behavior were truly free, there is nothing anyone can do that will impinge on his decisions. Caregivers may try presenting choices differently or teaching him to choose one course of action over another when presented with the opportunity, but these approaches imply that his choice is not free but can be influenced by the learning experiences arranged for him.

A focus on the behavior of choosing is not necessarily a problem, however, as long as we reframe the way we approach choosing. If we recognize that Robert's choosing behavior is merely the result of different contingencies for cooperative versus disruptive behavior, then a focus on choosing *per se* is merely misleading. He does not choose in the sense of having the option of selecting behavior A or behavior B independent of his history and the present contingencies. He simply engages in one or the other because of the history of consequences for each alternative. Describing this as choosing is gratuitous, tends to focus on the individual rather than the environment, and comes from how we have been taught to label his actions. If he engages in behavior A, we are taught to say that he chooses to behave this way instead of the other way, though we do not observe any private behavior of choosing. Even if we formally present both options ("Robert, would you like to do A or B?"), describing his response as belonging to a particular response class called "choosing" can be misleading if we attribute characteristics to it that are different from any other behavior.

In other words, the assumption of free will makes a focus on the behavior of choosing pointless. A deterministic assumption accommodates a focus on choosing as long as it is seen as a behavior like any other—that is, fully influenced by environmental variables. This perspective quickly leads to consideration of why Robert engages in ("chooses") disruptive behavior instead of more desirable behavior, which leads to an analysis of the past and present consequences for both ways of behaving. Out of this comes ideas for ways of changing behavior-environment contingencies that will change his behavior at the day program.

There is much more that can be written on the issue of free will and determinism, a topic that has occupied philosophers, psychologists, and other ne'er-do-wells for ages. Because we cannot prove either position, debating the issue might be taken as a pointless exercise, and in a sense it is. Intellectual calisthenics aside, however, there are real consequences that follow from each assumption. Moreover, this is not a matter on which one can have no conviction. The nature of the two assumptions ensures that everyone takes one view or the other, even if they are unaware of their philosophical posture. Absent reflection, most people probably follow the implications of everyday dialect and assume that at least some behavior is free of physical causation. You are now aware of some of the consequences of this perspective, and the assumption that all behavior has physical causes should therefore be more appealing.

Have you arrived at this point? Are you reasonably comfortable with the deterministic assumption? Are you willing to accept this assumption as the foundation of a philosophy of science and behavioral technology? Your answers to these questions are important as this first chapter comes to a close. If you find it too difficult to let go of free will and its implications, you will struggle mightily with the content of the remaining chapters. Worse, you may be tempted to retreat to the argument that particular instances of behavior under discussion do not have hereditary or environmental causes, thereby enabling you to speculate about mental possibilities. The material in upcoming chapters may bring you around on this issue, but the going will be much easier if you can appreciate at this stage that it is possible that all behavior has hereditary or environmental causes, even though we may often be uncertain what they are. Where do you stand?

CHAPTER SUMMARY

1. Assuming that one is free to choose how to behave implies that causes of behavior may lie both inside the person and outside in the environment. The notion that we control our own behavior means that some form of mental activity may precede public behavior and that our behavior can at least sometimes be free of outside influences.

2. The assumption that we can make choices that are free of outside influences is a philosophical position called *free will*. This position implies that choices are not caused by environmental or even hereditary factors and are therefore assumed to be free of such influences. The assumption that the individual can make decisions that are independent of physical influences leaves only mental deliberation as the source of the resulting behavior.

3. To deny that we can make choices that are free of hereditary or environmental influences is to take the position that our behavior is instead determined by such factors. This position is called *determinism*, and it is just as much an assumption as is the argument for free will. The assumption that behavior is determined by physical variables is usually interpreted as allowing no exceptions. In this view, it is assumed that all behavior has physical causes, even though we are usually unaware of the details. The assumption that physical events are fully

explainable in terms of other physical events has a long and respected position in the natural sciences.

4. It is not possible to gather direct evidence proving that behavior can be free of physical causation or that it is always determined by physical variables. Proving free will would require showing that behavior can occur without influence by hereditary or environmental factors. It would be impossible to eliminate the role of these variables. On the other hand, proving determinism would require demonstrating the causes for any behavior, an impossibly exhausting task as well. Practical utility should be the criterion guiding our decision about which assumption we should make.

5. Assuming free will means we can control our own actions, we can make choices about what we do, and those choices are not influenced by any other factors. It means behavior may occur without physical causation. If behavior can occur independently of hereditary and environmental variables, it follows that it may be capricious or random and therefore without explanation. This position would also mean that researchers would not be able to understand all of the factors influencing behavior, no matter how thorough their efforts.

6. Determinism means there are always causes for behavior, regardless of the characteristics of the particular behavior of interest. This position assumes that all actions are the result of hereditary or environmental factors. The causes may be multifaceted and complex, and it may be wise to accept that we do not yet fully understand them, but the assumption of determinism allows for no exceptions. No instance of behavior is considered free of physical causation. The assumption of determinism also means that we must resist the temptation to assign causal status to a non-physical universe. This has the advantage of avoiding interpretations that distract us from considering the real variables that might be at work.

7. One challenge for the assumption of free will is to explain the mechanism by which our behavior results from those choices. That is, how could non-physical factors influence physical events such as behavior?

8. A second issue is to rationalize the notion of responsibility. If we assume that behavior is determined by outside factors, does this mean that the individual is not responsible for his or her behavior? In one sense, we are not responsible for our behavior in a scientific sense because the individual is not a controlling authority who makes decisions about his or her behavior that are independent of physical variables. On the other hand, we cannot avoid confronting the effects of our behavior on the environment, which in turn greatly impacts the kind of behavior that produced these effects. This means we are responsible for our behavior in the sense that we must live with its consequences.

9. A third issue concerns choice. Determinism unavoidably means that the idea that we can make choices that are free of environmental influences is an illusion. It

is much simpler to merely describe ourselves as agents for an action than to list all of its possible influences. However, the price of this efficiency is that we fail to appreciate the factors that are actually responsible for our behavior.

10. Practitioners talk with clients, families, and other professionals every day. The ordinary dialect of these conversations is rooted in a causal model in which individuals are assumed to be able to control their own behavior at least some of the time. This assumption that we are free to choose to behave one way or another is at least implicit, and often explicit, in discussions about the behavior of both clients and caregivers. Because such behavior is seen as originating from within the individual, it complicates practitioners' efforts to convince all concerned to focus on environmental factors that may be important.

TEXT STUDY GUIDE

1. What does it mean to say that being free to choose one course of action over another implies an "inside" versus an "outside" distinction about the causes of behavior?

2. If mental activity of some sort precedes public behavior, why would that mean behavior can be free of environmental influences?

3. If someone challenged your view that you can change your mind, how might you defend your conviction?

4. Explain the philosophical position called free will.

5. Identify some common expressions that imply a belief in free will.

6. Explain the philosophical position called determinism.

7. Why can the position of determinism allow for no exceptions?

8. Explain why in each case the positions of free will and determinism can only be assumptions.

9. List some of the practical consequences of assuming that we have free will.

10. List some of the practical consequences of assuming that our behavior is determined.

11. What is the problem of explaining non-physical causation presented by the assumption of free will?

12. How can you answer the question of whether the individual is responsible for his or her behavior if we assume behavior is determined?

13. How might you defend the argument that there is no such thing as choice?

14. If assuming free will versus determinism is just verbal behavior, why does it matter what view one holds as a behavior analyst?

15. Why is it important that practitioners understand this issue?

BOX STUDY GUIDE

1. Distinguish among libertarian free will, Dennett's version of free will, and Hebb's soft determinism.
2. Explain the scientific attitude of parsimony. Why is it an important value in science?
3. Distinguish among the following everyday uses of the term freedom: a) freedom from physical constraints, b) feeling free, c) having choices, and d) spiritual freedom.
4. What is the problem in explaining instances of behavior in terms of preference or choice?

DISCUSSION TOPICS AND EXERCISES

1. List some everyday phrases you hear as a practitioner that imply free will.
2. Pick some of these phrases and make reasonable guesses about environmental factors that might be influencing behavior.
3. There are important legal ramifications for the conflict between the everyday notion of personal responsibility and the assumption that behavior is always determined by physical causes. Discuss this issue in the context of different examples of criminal behavior.
4. Choose some examples of situations in which it might seem that you can make free choices and then consider alternative explanations of your behavior in terms of environmental factors.

SUGGESTED READINGS

Hayes, S. C. (1984). Making sense of spirituality. *Behaviorism, 12(2)*, 99–110.
Skinner, B. F. (1961). Freedom and the control of men. In B. F. Skinner, *Cumulative Record* (pp. 3–23). New York: Appleton-Century-Crofts.
Skinner, B. F. (1971). *Beyond freedom and dignity*. New York: Alfred A. Knopf.

Chapter 2

It's Just Verbal Behavior

Sarah was ready for Friday night. It had been a tough week, but it seemed they all were. She was halfway through a Master's program in applied behavior analysis, and the work sometimes got the best of her. Tonight she was meeting some of the other students at their favorite hangout, and they had earned some beers.

Carrie and Matt were already into the first pitcher when she got there. Jenny soon showed up with her new boyfriend, Chad. They ordered a second and then a third pitcher. They had sworn not to talk shop, but that went out the window soon enough, as usual. Besides, their professors encouraged them to make what they were learning part of their everyday life. It seemed as if the program was their life, so it was hard to avoid talking about school. Carrie was talking about a discussion they had in class and said she hadn't made up her mind yet about the subject.

Matt sat upright, eyebrows arched. Using his best professorial manner, he asked, "What do you mean, 'made up your mind'? You think that's like making up your bed?"

Carrie saw the game and grimaced. "Alright, one point for the boy."

Sarah and Jenny cackled. Chad, who was trying to fit in, frowned. "I don't get it. What's wrong with saying that?" he demanded.

The students glanced at each other, wondering if they should continue. Jenny tried to rescue Chad, hoping to avoid getting into a real discussion. "There's no such thing as a mind," she said casually. "It's just the way we learn to talk growing up."

This didn't help Chad at all. "How could we not have a mind?" he said. "That's how we decide everything. It's what makes us tick."

The waitress brought another pitcher, which should have been a sign to talk about something else. But Sarah couldn't help it. "How do you know there's such a thing? No one has ever seen one," she said.

"What about when they show how different parts of your brain light up when people are asked to think of certain things?" Chad countered.

"But that's just your brain responding to stimuli," Carrie insisted. "That's not your mind."

"But how does your brain know how to react to different things? Something has to tell it what to do," Chad said, as if that should be obvious.

Jenny knew this wasn't going to end well. Chad seemed to have some pride on the line, and she was a bit worried about the rest of her evening. Matt saw her concern and tried to help her out.

"From a scientific point of view, the mind is just made up. It's fine to talk about your mind in everyday conversations, but it gets in the way of trying to study what's really going on. We're supposed to practice talking about behavior strictly in terms of what's really there."

Sarah and Carrie saw what was happening and took Matt's lead. Sarah jumped in and said, "Food! I'm ready for some eats!"

SOME QUESTIONS ABOUT VERBAL BEHAVIOR

Do You Agree...?

It may already be obvious to you that everything we say or think or write is learned. After all, no one is born knowing how to talk. If you accept this, are you ready to acknowledge that all verbal behavior comes from the same kind of environmental experiences and is not fundamentally different from other forms of behavior? Does it follow that we should explain verbal behavior in the same way that we explain other behavior?

The questions get more challenging. If you are still with me, would you agree that the meaning of what we say—our verbal behavior—should be explained no differently than the meaning of other behavior? Would you go further and concede that verbal behavior does not have meaning in the everyday sense, that when we speak or write we are not communicating ideas, concepts, intentions, or beliefs? That dictionaries do not tell us the meaning of words? Are you okay with admitting that your most strongly felt convictions are "just verbal behavior" and had you grown up in a different family in a different culture you would likely hold very different views?

The way that behavior analysts answer these and other questions about that most cherished human quality—the ability to learn an elaborate verbal repertoire—are rooted in how we approach behavior as a scientific subject matter. A behavior analytic view of verbal behavior took form as basic research began to reveal the details of how **operant shaping** works. As this literature grew, B. F. Skinner focused this emerging understanding of verbal behavior in a book-length treatment (Skinner, 1957), which he viewed as his most important work. In it, he described a conceptual framework for analyzing verbal behavior that was consistent with what was even then a well-established science of behavior. What was most impressive about his approach was that it was free of cultural preconceptions about the nature of our verbal repertoire. Over the years, a sizable research literature has accumulated (see, for example, the journal *The Analysis of Verbal Behavior*), as well as extensive clinical applications consistent with this framework.

Verbal behavior is a fascinating feature of the human repertoire, but that is not why this chapter explores the topic. It is important for you to understand the nature of verbal behavior in order to ease your consideration of the remaining chapters. After all, this book is about how we talk about behavior, so understanding your own verbal repertoire is the key to appreciating how the way we talk can cause problems for a scientific, as well as a practical, approach to the subject matter of behavior. Absent this background, it will be difficult for you to grasp the arguments in upcoming chapters.

Verbal Behavior is Learned

The most fundamental fact about verbal behavior is that it is learned. Most people would probably agree with this statement, at least after some reflection. It is easy to concede the point if you observe babies and young children over a period of time. At less than six months of age, they show only some preverbal skills such as babbling and non-word utterances. Parents hear their first words when children are about 11 months old, but by the time they are three years old, their vocabulary exceeds 800 words and they are well on the way to acquiring the other basic features of a useful verbal repertoire. By the time they are teenagers, their verbal abilities are impressively developed.

It should also be obvious that we learn to talk from the people around us who have already acquired this repertoire. Early on, a child's verbal community is comprised of parents, siblings, extended family, and others they interact with daily. Of course, a child's verbal community gets much larger as he or she grows up, spends time with friends and teachers, and encounters an expanded social world. A child who had no access to a verbal community would simply not learn to talk. This tragedy is borne out in those rare instances when a child has been reared under conditions of extreme social deprivation. Depending on the extent and kind of contact they have had with others, they tend to have little verbal repertoire at all, regardless of their age (Newton, 2002).

Although few would deny that children can learn to talk only by being around others who already do so, it is more challenging to admit that *all* the human behavior we call language or communication—whether speaking, writing, or signing—has been learned. It is difficult to understand how the complex verbal repertoire of an adult can be explained in terms of a simple reinforcement history. What we say and think and write seems so complicated, flexible, spontaneous, and creative that there must be more going on than just years of differential reinforcement. What about reasoning and argument, poetry, self-expression, conversation, and all of the other features of mature verbal abilities? How can we explain such complex forms of verbal behavior?

Well, there is more than a simple reinforcement history at work here; our biology plays a necessary role, to be sure. However, it is hard to overstate the role of operant selection in creating a verbal repertoire. In making the leap from basic principles of operant behavior to verbal behavior, it is important not to get trapped by the challenge of explaining fully developed verbal capabilities as if the task is no more difficult than explaining how you taught your dog to sit on command. Deconstructing any complex performance that has a long history into a brief explanation of how it was acquired can easily come off as superficial, inadequate, and unconvincing. The challenge is best met by starting at the beginning, understanding how rudimentary features are acquired, and following the emerging performance over time—never forgetting to give fair weight to the natural contingencies of endless practice.

What is Verbal Behavior?

How should we differentiate verbal behavior from other behavior? Skinner (1957) defined verbal behavior as operant behavior that requires the presence of another person for its reinforcement. The person emitting the behavior is the speaker, and the person reinforcing that behavior is the listener. He qualified his definition by requiring that the listener must be responding in ways that have been learned because they reinforce the behavior of the speaker. Of course, such reinforcement contingencies are typically intermittent, which means that the speaker's behavior is not reinforced on every occasion, and the nature of the reinforcer may not be obvious. Take notice that Skinner added no special qualifications suggesting that verbal behavior is fundamentally different from other kinds of operant behavior.

Although verbal behavior is often vocal, it need not be. It can be written, of course, and gestures frequently fit the definition as well. Sign language is a formal set of gestures that requires specific training, but we often participate in informal speaker-listener exchanges involving gestures. For instance, you might be in a noisy bar with a friend who is talking with someone else nearby, and you catch her eye and point to the exit with raised eyebrows. If she nods and you both separately make your way to the exit, your gesture, together with your friend's reaction, qualifies as a bit of verbal behavior.

Is verbal behavior uniquely human? We certainly like to think so, but it helps to distinguish between operant behavior and **fixed action patterns**. Alarm calls in various species seem to be like verbal behavior in that the behavior of a "speaker" (the animal sounding an alarm) has an effect on the behavior of "listeners" (others in the herd). However, this type of behavior is usually a fixed action pattern,

---

BOX 2.1

What is Behavior Anyway?

This might seem an easy question, but simple answers often seem inadequate, which can lead to chapter-length discussions (see Johnston & Pennypacker, 2009, Chapter 2). Whatever its particulars, behavior is a characteristic of living organisms and is unavoidably rooted in their biology. Drawing a line between behavior and biology can be tricky at the margins, but one trap that must be avoided is assuming that the skin provides a useful demarcation between the two. Although it is true that most behavior of interest in daily life and to practitioners involves actions that are obvious to others, behavioral phenomena also include movements that are subtle, brief, or occur inside the skin.

An important result of behavior's biological foundation is that it occurs only at the level of the individual organism. This fact suggests that we should measure behavior separately for each individual in order to get a clear picture of what is happening. It also suggests that the notion of group behavior can be confusing if it leads us to think that such measures refer to anything other than the collected actions of individuals (see Box 9.2).

Perhaps the most obvious defining feature of behavior is that it involves movement. Given the "hand-in-glove" relation between behavior and environment, this also means that behavior cannot occur without having effects on the environment, however small they might sometimes seem. The reciprocal character of the relation between behavior and environment is critical as it underlies the adaptive character of behavior. Behavior is not merely movement but actions that are directly affected by the organism's interactive interface with its environment and that result in changes that enhance the individual's effectiveness in diverse circumstances.

ABA practitioners use science and technology in describing these reciprocal behavior-environment relationships to design contingencies that lead to preferred behavioral outcomes. In doing so, they do not usually face difficult questions about the nature of behavior. Their interest typically lies in its most obvious features, and scrupulous avoidance of mentalism is otherwise sufficient to avoid the confusions suggested by everyday dialect. As upcoming chapters will show, however, the temptations of mentalism are pervasive, and fully understanding the nature of behavior is only possible when they can be identified and resisted.

---

which is a relatively invariant behavioral sequence that depends on specific sign stimuli and is largely genetically mediated (Catania, 2007), for example, the mating dances typically performed by male birds of certain species in the presence of a female bird of that species. Human verbal behavior is operant behavior, however, and is gradually acquired through the mechanism of reinforcement contingencies and very malleable in the face of changing environmental conditions.

Do some non-human species also acquire this kind of operant behavior in the wild? Possibly, although the answer is not entirely clear. We often read that

BOX 2.2

Communication, Language, or Verbal Behavior?

Although communication, language, and verbal behavior might seem synonymous, it is important to make some distinctions. Perhaps the broadest of these references is communication, which implies that something is communicated and therefore has mentalistic connotations (see Chapter 3). What is it that might be communicated? An idea? A message? An understanding? Information? How is a communication understood or decoded? Is there a process of translation from one party to another? These might seem tempting questions, yet they are not so much prompted by facts to be explained as implicit assumptions about what is no more than operant behavior. The term is too vague to be scientifically useful.

Language is also a pretty broad term. It has the sense of a tool used for communication, though there is no "thing" to point to. As something we supposedly use, we talk about language as if it is acquired and thereafter possessed. As usually described, it requires a mental system to address what people know and say, as well as a mental lexicon and a system of rules about the syntax and morphology of sentences (Hart & Risley, 1999). These implications are fundamentally mentalistic as well. Once again, there are those awkward questions: What are the dimensions of this tool? Where do we keep it? How do we use it? How does language get turned into speech?

In contrast, there is no pretense that verbal behavior is anything other than operant behavior. As such, it is a natural phenomenon with fully physical characteristics that can be directly measured and related to other physical events. This conceptualization hardly makes it simple to explain the human verbal repertoire, but at least it makes it possible to use scientific methods to undertake the task. One advantage is that this approach allows us to see the fundamental similarities among different forms of verbal behavior, such as speaking, gesturing, writing, and so forth. It also encourages us to understand the interplay between speaker and listener in terms of environmental contingencies, thereby avoiding the temptation to invent mentalistic alternatives. These are some of the reasons why behavior analysts avoid references to communication and language in favor of a focus on verbal behavior.

researchers have discovered some form of communicative behavior in certain species, but the mainstream media is not a credible source of scientific information. Even reports in scientific journals require careful examination of methods and theoretical bias. One reason for such caution is that research on animal communication often runs afoul of many of the conceptual problems detailed in this book.

If we bring our own verbal repertoire into the picture, however, there is a possibility that we might serve as a verbal community for other species (see Catania, 2007, Chapter 15). For example, it has been shown that chimpanzees can be taught to communicate with their trainers using sign language. This ability to hold a conversation of sorts involves both parties being able to exchange speaker and listener roles, that is, to be a verbal community. Some interactions with non-human animals that might otherwise appear to involve verbal behavior may not meet this requirement, however.

For example, if your dog brings you his leash and you often take him for a walk when he does so, is his behavior of bringing you the leash verbal behavior? Certainly his bringing you the leash is operant behavior that has been acquired from a history of your reinforcing this response by taking him for a walk, and you must be present for this behavior to produce reinforcement. Does this make your dog the speaker and you the listener? The problem with this perspective is that you and your dog are not a verbal community because you cannot switch speaker-listener roles. Yes, you may give commands that your dog (occasionally) obeys, but that may be stretching the sense of a verbal community. More about our pets later.

How Do We Learn Our Verbal Repertoire?

At first, a baby's vocalizations are more properly described as vocal rather than verbal behavior. For the first month or so, this vocal behavior is in the form of crying, which does not vary much with different reasons for any discomfort. From about the fourth through the sixteenth week, the baby will make particular sounds, including cooing, laughing, and some vowel sounds. Crying begins to vary in tone depending on the circumstances. Babbling begins at about 20 weeks and involves the baby stringing together sequences of one-syllable, often repetitive sounds. An important advance develops from six to nine months as babbling turns into making imitative sounds. The child will initially repeat his or her own sounds but then begins repeating sounds that adults or other children make. Eager parents will often identify a child's first words between 10 and 12 months, although these responses are usually just imitations of sounds the parents have made.

At this point, parents may say that their child is talking, but there is a long way to go before they have to tell the little tyke to be quiet. The interplay between the child and a gradually expanding verbal community over the next few years is complex and the subject of a large research literature. Not surprisingly, most investigators approach this subject matter from the conceptual perspective shared by the larger culture. As we will see, this framework is burdened by the conviction that verbal behavior can only be understood as part of a mental world in which it occupies a special place. In the absence of contrary and irrefutable evidence, behavior analysts approach verbal behavior as nothing more than operant behavior. As a physical rather than a mental phenomenon, its features can usually be directly measured and studied with experimental methods that long ago proved their effectiveness.

For example, some years ago, Betty Hart and Todd Risley (1995, 1999) undertook the daunting challenge of documenting and analyzing the utterances of children and those around them over an extended period. They recruited 42 families that had a young child and audiotaped monthly, hour-long samples of verbal behavior that involved the child. They started when the children were seven months old and continued until they were three years old, logging 1,300 hours of observations, coding 30,000 pages of transcripts, and documenting more than 175,000 child utterances.

Hart and Risley revealed what they called a social dance in which the verbal interchanges between a young child and others had a powerful effect on the child's eventual verbal repertoire. Their data showed that about half of the talk the children heard was spoken to them and that they progressed from utterances containing words to longer interactions and eventually to talking as much as the parents. Much of the parent's talk initially involved prompting and encouraging the child's speech. The interchanges gradually changed so that by two years of age the child was holding the floor more often than the parents. Not surprisingly, the child's talkativeness was related to the amount of verbal behavior in the family. Hart and Risley estimated that the total language experience of the children in their study ranged from 10 million to more than 30 million words by the time they were three years old. While these are impressive numbers, imagine how big they are by the time a child reaches adolescence!

The Hart and Risley study did not address the nature of the learning contingencies children experienced moment by moment during these three years. In order to understand how a child learns the full variety of customary verbal skills, we need to know the details of everyday verbal interchanges. How do children learn to label and describe events and experiences? How do they develop the ability to describe private events such as a stomach ache to which others are not privy? How do they learn relational concepts such as inside and outside or near and far? How do they learn syntax and grammar? Argument and reasoning?

These are challenging questions, and we do not yet have an adequate scientific foundation for answering them fully. However, researchers have looked closely at the kinds of moment by moment experiences that ever so gradually lead to a complex and seemingly unexplainable verbal repertoire and have documented shaping processes we might expect to find (see, for example, Moerk, 1983, 1990). The key is focusing on the contingencies between a child's utterances and surrounding environmental events without resorting to mentalistic explanations of what we see. Unfortunately, our cultural history has not prepared us for this task. Our everyday dialect includes endless mentalistic blind alleys that discourage us from making sense of what is otherwise plainly evident.

For instance, in watching a child say *doggie* when the family pooch comes in the room, it is natural to say that the child knows what that word means. Embedded in this seemingly obvious assessment is the notion that words are useful units of behavior and that they have meaning in that they refer to objects or events. This further implies that verbal behavior is different from other behavior in that it can only be explained in terms of a non-physical lexicon. Do not feel badly if you fail to see anything wrong with this perspective, but it is filled to the brim with serious conceptual problems for a science of behavior.

It helps to appreciate that all behavior, even unexpected or novel behavior, comes from the accumulation of many learning experiences over time, as the Hart and Risley study suggests. Verbal behavior, like other operant behavior, grows more complex and functional one instance at a time. No one knows how many millions of learning trials occur along the way to a typical adult verbal repertoire, but there are surely enough to provide the basis for explaining how it is acquired. Just because verbal behavior is complex does not mean its explanation must be mysterious.

Most people do not appreciate the contribution of a learning history because they do not understand the mechanisms and power of **operant learning**. This limitation is exacerbated by the fact that we cannot see a history of behavior-environmental interactions laid out before us in some recognizable form. What if we could observe a complete set of video clips of the interchanges between a child and family members associated with learning to label dogs and cats? Aside from the fact that it would take forever and a day to watch them, would it then be obvious how this discrimination is acquired? How much longer would such a video have to be to show all of the episodes necessary to teach pronouns, proper syntax, reasoning, and all the other features of a mature verbal repertoire?

The point of emphasizing the role of operant shaping and the literally countless learning moments accumulated in gradually building an adult verbal repertoire is to help explain how its complexity can be understood in a non-mentalistic conceptual framework. This perspective should not be taken as minimizing the role of biological preparedness in learning to talk. Acquiring this repertoire requires not just responsiveness to the social contingencies of a verbal community but other features of brain development. However, the role of operant selection is no less a prerequisite, and it implies a particular conceptual approach to understanding and explaining our verbal performance. From this perspective, the adult verbal repertoire is acquired very gradually from one verbal interchange to another, and we must give this process a pre-eminent role when we try to explain verbal behavior, not just in general but in individual instances. It is especially important that you take this approach in understanding your verbal behavior as you consider the issues in this book.

ORGANIZATION OF VERBAL BEHAVIOR

The Concept of Response Classes

Skinner (1957) eased the challenge of explaining where each bit of verbal behavior comes from and what it means by proposing that different utterances otherwise sharing the same kind of relations with the environment should be described as belonging to the same **response class**. He had realized some years earlier that one of the keys to understanding behavior was to recognize the natural structure underlying the limitless variety of an organism's responses (Skinner, 1935). Although differences in the way we do a particular thing from occasion to occasion are what we tend to notice, it is the similarities that are most important.

For example, the responses involved in the behavior of opening a door vary a good bit from one instance to another. Differences in the physical features of individual doors and how they work, the details of our actions, and their varying outcomes mean that no two door opening responses are exactly alike. There are differences in what we do depending on the characteristics of the door and the outcome that will be reinforcing. We may push, twist, pull, turn, and so forth, and our actions may involve one hand or the other, a foot, a shoulder, or even our backside, all with varying degrees of effort. Regardless of these differences, all responses that open the door produce a reinforcing state of affairs, as long as it is open a sufficient amount in each instance. The shared relation between these responses and both the antecedent features of the door and the consequences of opening it define the different responses as belonging to the same class. All of the included responses are what we describe as the behavior of opening doors.

This concept of individual responses falling into particular classes is important because they represent the organizing effects of natural contingencies. The fact that different actions produce the same reinforcing outcome in similar situations, thereby falling into the same class, allows us to make sense of what would otherwise appear as endless and confusing variety, both within and across individuals. Those responses that share the same kind of relations with the environment are functionally the same, even though they may sometimes look somewhat different. They serve the same function in an organism's repertoire and are therefore called **functional response classes**.

Understanding how response classes work is also important because it helps us understand operant behavior in terms of the contingencies that control and therefore explain it. Practitioners depend on the concept of response classes when they are called on to develop an intervention to ameliorate a problematic behavior. One of their first tasks is to determine the characteristics of the target behavior. What actions under what circumstances lead to the same kind of outcome for the individual? Not only does this information help them define the target behavior and design measurement procedures, it helps explain the occurrence of the behavior and suggests environmental changes that may resolve the problem. The focus on response classes is no less relevant when the assignment involves teaching a new skill. The task then is to figure out the characteristics of the intended class (both the responses and the surrounding environmental events) that will be supported by natural contingencies in the target setting.

Consider this scenario. Clint, a BCBA, is asked to figure out why a middle-aged woman living in a group home for intellectually disabled individuals sometimes gets upset and to develop an intervention that will resolve the problem. From talking with caregivers and observing the woman's behavior, Clint learns that under certain conditions she throws objects, kicks things, strikes out at staff and her housemates, and curses. She seems to act this way when she is asked to do things she apparently does not want to do, such as participate in scheduled activities. When she gets upset, staff clear the area, stop making their requests, and leave her alone for a while. Clint also notices that she curses when she is not being disruptive in other ways and that staff mostly ignore this. With this information, he reasons that throwing, kicking, and hitting may function as a single response class but that cursing might not be part of this class. Clint's suspicion is that throwing, kicking, and hitting tend to produce the same consequences in terms of the staff's reactions (possibly serving as negative reinforcers) but that cursing does not usually produce these consequences. He then goes about developing a definition of the response class for staff to use in counting occurrences. He also takes his hypothesis about the variables that might be prompting or maintaining the behavior into account in considering intervention procedures.

Verbal Response Classes

The reason for discussing the concept of response classes is that it is especially useful in understanding verbal behavior. Skinner (1957) identified a number of verbal response classes that have withstood decades of experimental and clinical scrutiny. These classes bring valuable structure and clarity to any discussion of verbal behavior, but it is important to appreciate that they are justified by research evidence, not merely conceptual preference or convenience. These response classes represent different kinds of operant contingencies and help explain how our verbal abilities are learned. They should therefore be used in explaining any particular instances of verbal behavior.

Let us briefly consider a couple of verbal response classes that are extensively involved in our daily talk, as well as a common focus of training efforts by ABA practitioners who work with children diagnosed with autism spectrum disorders. We often say things in which there is a characteristic relation between the form of the response and the reinforcers received from listeners. This kind of verbal response is called a **mand**, which is sometimes described as a response that specifies its own reinforcer. More loosely, we often mand for things or circumstances we want (or, more properly, under certain conditions of deprivation or aversive stimulation), whether it is an object or a change in someone's behavior. "Water!" is more likely to be followed by receipt of water than other events, just as "Stop!" is likely to get someone to cease what they are doing at the moment. There are a number of variations of simple mands, and they are clearly an important facet of our verbal skills. Children learn to mand early on, and when the skill is absent, as with some individuals with intellectual disabilities, it is one of the first communication skills to teach.

Unlike mands, for which there is no specified relation with a prior stimulus, **tacts** are operants whose form is evoked by a certain object or event or a property of an object or event. Whereas the reinforcers for mands are closely related to the form of the response, the reinforcers for tacting objects or events vary widely but are narrowly related to features of the object or event tacted. The early steps in developing this type of verbal operant involve teaching children to simply label things or events. The role of the verbal community is to assure consistency in the correspondence between the tact and what is tacted. This can be challenging for young learners. Think about all of the physical differences among dogs, for example, yet a child must learn to accurately identify all kinds of dogs as dogs, as well as differentiate between dogs and cats.

A comprehensive analysis of verbal behavior requires additional kinds of verbal operants, including **echoic, textual, and autoclitic operants**, as well as other variants. However, you might notice what is missing in this list of terms are some structural elements of language with which we are all familiar—words and sentences. Their shortcoming for a behavioral analysis is that they are not behaviorally functional units. The same word (response topography) can serve different functions depending on the circumstances. The utterance "stop," for example, has different effects on a listener in sentences such as "Please stop doing that!" versus "When can I stop?" The same limitation applies to sentences, which can be structurally the same but functionally different. For example, the sentences "I went to a movie yesterday" and "I went to a concert yesterday" have the same structure, but the one word that differs between them may result in different effects on the behavior of a listener. We recognize the value of focusing on **behavioral functions** in analyzing behavior when we acknowledge that other kinds of behavior must also be understood in terms of its function rather than its form. For instance, we view the behavior of running differently in different contexts, such as running in a race versus running from the police.

Reconsidering Conventional Concepts

The idea of verbal response classes acquired through learning experiences is only the beginning of learning how to approach verbal behavior from a scientific perspective, free of cultural preconceptions. Many conventional concepts underlying the way we have been taught to view language must be reconsidered as well. For example, our verbal repertoires offer many regularities, such as their grammatical structure. These regular patterns are called rules, as in the rules of grammar. Many linguists view these rules as existing inside the mind of the speaker and give them a role in generating verbal behavior.

Behavior analysts, however, view these regularities as no more than learned patterns of responding. In fact, most behavior exhibits some degree of patterning or organization. Although most people do not often notice these patterns, they are not difficult to identify when we study behavior closely. The basic research literature on operant behavior is a description of such regularities (see Catania, 2007), many of which have attained the status of empirical generalizations or even scientific laws. When grammatical or other kinds of rules are viewed as merely descriptions of behavioral regularities, there is no temptation to argue that they are entities that must have a mental existence. The rules of grammar are not in our head. They are just summaries of the observations of grammarians, which they tact in their verbal behavior.

Another common conviction underlying how we have learned to think about language is the view that words and sentences have meaning and that conversations communicate or transfer this meaning from speaker to listener. The assumption that words and sentences have meaning is based on the idea that we "use" them to refer to things and events. The word *car* is said to "refer to" a large wheeled conveyance that we can drive from one place to another. As a reference, the word is therefore taken as a symbol of the thing itself. Of course, there are many differences from one car to another, so *car* represents not just an object but a category or concept. These representations are said to be in a lexicon or collection of objects or events— a kind of personal dictionary. The idea is that speakers and listeners communicate by looking up representations in their lexicon and relating them to symbols in order to understand what is being said. But where is this lexicon and where do these processes take place? Lacking physical dimensions, the required assumption is that the lexicon and its consultation are mental phenomena. As always, this is a serious constraint because it places the explanation of our verbal abilities beyond the reach of natural science.

Criticism of reference theories of language begs what might appear to be a fair question: How do behavior analysts handle the notion that our talking and writing seem to have meaning to listeners? First, understand that this notion is inherently mentalistic. The idea that words mean something goes beyond the observable fact of an utterance and its effects on a listener and invents a mental entity for which there is no evidence. Behavior analysts avoid this problem by recognizing that the meaning of words and sentences lies in their impact on the listener's behavior, which in turn affects the speaker's behavior. In other words, behavior analysts approach the meaning of verbal behavior no differently than they do the meaning of any other behavior—as a matter of the environmental function of the behavior.

How do we deal with the meaning of any behavior? What does a driving response mean? An eating response? Put this way, the idea of meaning seems, well, meaningless. We do not consider non-verbal operant responses as having meaning in the sense that we conventionally attribute to verbal responses. Pressed to come up with the meaning of other behaviors, we turn to their function. The meaning of a response or pattern of responses lies in the effects on the environment. Take the example of running mentioned earlier. Absent context or function, running is just a physical event or action. In context, however, running in a race differs from running from the police because the surrounding environmental events—antecedents and consequences—allow us to see that the action serves different functions in each instance. Running alongside others along a prearranged route leads to a finishing time and congratulations from friends and family, if not an award, and has a different function than running that leads to being tackled by a police officer, handcuffed, and taken to jail.

In applying this approach to the meaning of our verbal behavior, we look to the circumstances under which we emit a particular verbal response. The meaning of an utterance, whether a word, phrase, or sentence, can be found not by looking it up in a dictionary, which only offers more words, but by discovering what set the occasion for emitting the utterance and what effect it had on the listener. Skinner made this argument in a seminal paper titled, "The operational analysis of psychological terms" (Skinner, 1945). He explained that we can only understand the meaning of psychological terms and constructs by examining the conditions under which we "use" (emit) them. (See Box 9.4. for discussion of Skinner's view of **operationism**.) What we mean when we "refer to" anxiety, for example, lies in the stimuli that prompted the emission of that utterance and the effects of the utterance on the behavior of a listener. If we say that our friend seems anxious, and others respond with sympathy or helpful reactions, the meaning of the utterance is no more or less than those environmental events. After all, the spoken word *anxious* is just a sound we make. If we had grown up in a different country and were speaking a different language, we would emit a different sound, but it would have the same "meaning" or relation with surrounding environmental events, including the behavior at issue.

Here, then, is the approach to understanding the "meaning" of a word, phrase, or sentence. Ask yourself what environmental events occasioned and followed the utterance. The answer will not usually be simple, but it will be revealing. If we comment to a friend that Jules seems happy today, what we mean by *happy* can be discovered using this analytical approach. Upon reflection, we might realize that we noticed she was being more talkative than usual, smiling to others frequently, and making jokes. It is our reinforcement history associated with emitting this or similar responses ("Jules seems happy today") in the past that leads us to emit it again now. Our friend, in contact with these same stimuli, might have a similar history and agree with our assessment, thereby reinforcing our verbal response and increasing the likelihood that we will emit it again under similar conditions in the future. If our friend disagreed, it might have the effect of making us less likely to emit this verbal response (describing Jules or even others as happy) in the presence of such stimuli. In other words, what we mean when we say Jules is happy lies in the relation between this verbal response and its prompting and reinforcing conditions. If enough people in our verbal community share a similar history in their role as speakers and listeners regarding the verbal response *happy*, then this is all there is to the "meaning" of the word.

GIVEN THAT VERBAL BEHAVIOR IS LEARNED...

Just Verbal Behavior?

Perhaps it is not too difficult to concede that everything we say is learned. After all, persuasive argument aside, the scientific evidence for this position is overwhelming. We have seen, however, that accepting this proposition leads to some disconcerting corollaries. The idea that we do not "use" words and sentences to "refer to" things and events and that they therefore do not have "meaning" in the colloquial sense takes some getting used to. And yet, understanding why we must view verbal behavior as fundamentally the same as other operant behavior is the key to understanding your own verbal repertoire.

In pursuing this interest, the focus of this chapter is somewhat narrow. Although it briefly introduces some of the conceptual issues underlying the behavior analytic approach to verbal behavior, it does not go on to address the more substantive and technical features of this perspective. Instead, the chapter's primary objective is helping you come to grips with the arguments in the remaining chapters. By virtue of your long history in the verbal community of our culture, it would be natural for you to read, think about, and discuss the issues in upcoming chapters without appreciating the impact of your own verbal history. Not only has this history fully determined your reactions to the issues, it has given you a certain view of verbal behavior in general, including your own. It is that conventional account of your own verbal behavior you must put aside in order to understand and reconsider the long-standing views you bring to this discussion. In order to ease your transition from a colloquial to a scientific point of view, it is necessary that you appreciate what it means to admit that what you are accustomed to saying about these issues is "just" verbal behavior.

Of course, scientific talk about these issues is also "just" verbal behavior. Our talking, thinking, and writing is not fundamentally different from other forms of operant behavior, and we must therefore approach verbal behavior within this constraint. This does not mean what we say is unimportant, however. Just because our verbiage does not have meaning in the conventional sense should certainly not imply that what we say is trivial in terms of its consequences. How we talk about the conceptual issues addressed in this book is important because our verbal behavior has effects that are often important.

To consider this point further, remember that any behavior we emit is a physical event that changes the environment. Sometimes these effects involve only momentary environmental outcomes. For example, when we nod to someone in greeting as we walk by and they respond in kind, this result of our action is brief and leaves no physical trace. Once the interchange is over, there is no evidence of either our behavior or how it changed the environment. Other things we do produce more enduring environmental effects. If we turn off the lights when leaving a room, the room remains dark until someone turns them on again. Sometimes these more-than-momentary effects do not last all that long. The effects of cleaning the car windshield at a gas stop while on a trip never seems to last long enough once you are back on the road. However, sometimes these environmental changes are quite durable, as when we paint a lawn chair, the effects of which might last at least a few seasons.

What about the effects of our verbal behavior? When we say something, the immediate physical effects disappear with the speed of sound, although if we write something, the written product might be around for a long time. But what about their effects on behavior, whether the behavior of others or our own behavior? As environmental events, what we say in the presence of others frequently induces changes in their behavior, as when we ask someone to close the door and they do so. Indeed, it is these changes in the behavior of listeners that maintain our verbal behavior. Can our verbal behavior affect us in the same way? Does it make sense to consider ourselves as listeners for our own verbal behavior?

In a word, yes. When we make a grocery list, for instance, what we have written serves as a prompt for what to buy when we are in the store. Just as we often comply with rules given by others, we may also state them "to ourselves" as a way of helping to control our own behavior. So, if you are trying to lose weight and tell yourself (either silently or out loud) at a restaurant that you must not order dessert, this instruction may increase the likelihood that you decline when the waiter offers to bring the dessert menu. Sometimes we say things to ourselves that increase the likelihood of solving a problem, such as when we have lost our keys and systematically review where they might be or where we last saw them. We also say things to others that have the effect of controlling our behavior, as when we publicly announce our intentions to go to the gym, which may arrange social consequences for going or failing to go. We may argue a certain point in class in a way that leads us to take a position we might not have previously held, just as our argument may change the views of classmates.

There are endless examples of how our verbal behavior may influence our behavior as listeners, although it is important to acknowledge that there may often be more going on than just verbal behavior (see Box 2.2). Even simple instances of behavior are often influenced by multiple factors, and there is nothing simple about verbal behavior. But there is no question that what we say can affect what we do.

What is a Conviction?

You will better understand the impact of your colloquial verbal repertoire as you consider the conceptual issues discussed in the following chapters. The way we learned to talk about behavior from our family, friends, teachers, and the larger verbal community—whether we are talking to others or to ourselves—is important because of how this kind of talking affects other behavior. The present task is to

BOX 2.3

What Else Might Be Going On?

Skinner emphasized the multiple determinants of behavior, especially verbal behavior, in a discussion of complexity in the analysis of behavior (1953). Our behavior as speakers and listeners results from more than just simple reinforcement contingencies. He pointed out, for example, that humor often depends on multiple sources of strength. Puns are a good example. There was a sign at the drug rehab center that said, "Keep off the grass." The humor, such as it is, comes from multiple sources of control over the response "grass."

Skinner also noted that sustained verbal behavior is always multiply determined. His example is that it is impossible for us to call out random numbers because we have a history in which certain sequences of numbers have been reinforced in different contexts. Learning to count by multiples, recite multiplication tables, and give telephone numbers means that each number we say alters the probabilities of the next number we call, thus preventing us from offering truly random sequences.

There are also practical uses of the multiple sources of control over our verbal behavior. As Chapter 6 explains, for example, when we try to persuade someone to agree with us, we often emit propositions in a particular sequence that are more likely to be accepted in order to increase the likelihood that our conclusion will also be accepted. These examples of ways in which our verbal behavior is multiply determined highlight its complexity and the challenge for researchers.

appreciate how your colloquial repertoire can get in the way of your learning the new dialect introduced in this book.

For example, as you read upcoming chapters, you will certainly find that you have been holding convictions about how behavior works and can be explained that are contrary to the arguments presented here. As you examine your existing views, appreciating that everything you have to say has been learned from your verbal community, consider what it means to "have a conviction." When we describe someone as having a conviction, we are labeling or tacting some aspects of their behavior. Although the word *conviction* is a noun, it is not a physical thing that can be picked up, turned over, or directly measured. This limitation should not encourage us to assume that it is a mental "thing" either. The word "conviction" is just an utterance, and we have been taught to emit it under certain stimulus conditions. (See Chapter 7 for further discussion of convictions and beliefs.)

Keep in mind that describing someone's behavior is fundamentally no different than describing their other features, such as their clothes or hair. We learn to label behavior while we are learning to label other aspects of the environment, and we learn to label our own behavior in the same way. Just as our parents teach us to say "dog" when we see a dog, they teach us to say "crying" when a sibling is crying or when we are. Of course, it gradually gets more complicated than this, especially with reference to our own behavior, and upcoming chapters will explain more about this learning process.

When we say that someone has a conviction about something, we are tacting their behavior, typically multiple examples of it observed over time. If we report that a friend does not like to eat meat, for instance, our description is probably based not on a single observation but on numerous instances of her behavior. She may say that she does not eat meat, refuses to eat meat when offered, criticizes others who eat meat, and so forth. When we say that she does not like to eat meat, we are emitting what is called an extended tact under the control of these observations, in effect summarizing our observations of her behavior with respect to eating meat.

This is the same thing we are doing when we say that we hold a certain conviction. We are tacting our own behavior, most often our verbal behavior. Here is the part that may be hard to grasp: We do not "have" a conviction in the sense of possessing something. Remember, a conviction or belief is not a thing in either a physical or mental sense, and we do not "report" its status. When we make statements such as "I am convinced that..." or "I believe that..." or "I hold the view that..." we are typically saying what we have previously said in other ways on other occasions. We are, in effect, saying that "I have a history of making these kinds of statements about such and such" or "I am likely to say these kinds of things" or "I often emit this kind of behavior." We are doing no more than tacting some of our behavior.

So, when you find yourself wanting to argue with positions described in upcoming chapters in order to defend a point of view with which you are already comfortable, remember that "it's just verbal behavior." Everything you are arguing for, the point you feel so strongly about, the position you want to preserve—these are all "just verbal behaviors" that you learned from your verbal community along the way. Although you may want to focus on the "content" of your argument, you should first examine the sources of control over what you are saying. Are you saying things that come from your colloquial verbal history? Are they consistent with established scientific findings about how operant behavior works? Is your position based on and consistent with directly observable facts? Does it involve unsupported or unprovable assumptions, especially assumptions that depend on the existence of a mental universe?

If researchers based their questions on your viewpoint, where would their methods and findings lead? Would such studies be a wasted effort or would they result in discoveries that will improve our understanding of behavior? The ultimate criterion for evaluating a philosophy of science, after all, is how well it serves scientific discovery. The views described in this book cannot be legitimately defended by reference to authority. Just because they largely originated with B. F. Skinner may be reason to consider them carefully, but it is not a sufficient reason to enshrine them as true or beyond improvement. If talking a certain way about behavior helps researchers ask better questions and leads to results that improve our ability to control and predict behavior, that perspective might be deemed useful. Even then, such status may be temporary. By this criterion, better arguments may emerge, and the history of behavior analysis reveals examples of such advances (see Box 2.4).

You might raise the same question about the implications of your existing views for ABA practitioners. If they adopted the convictions about behavior you grew up with, would they be more or less effective in providing services than if they adopted the point of view described in this book? How would these two different perspectives affect their selection and assessment of target behaviors and the nature of interventions designed to change them? True, ABA practitioners must always interface with the general public, who require plain English for effective communication. Physicians, lawyers, engineers, and other professionals face the

---

BOX 2.4

Speaking of Antecedent Events

An example of the importance to both our science and professional practice of how we talk about behavior involves a proposal offered by Jack Michael (1982) about how we talk about antecedent events. He realized that the traditional assignment of discriminative stimulus functions betrayed a failure to appreciate a distinct motivational role for many antecedent events. By reintroducing the concept of establishing operations (originally defined by Keller and Schoenfeld, 1950), he called attention to a broad array of motivational stimulus functions that exceeded the definitional limits of discriminative stimuli. In doing so, he advanced our understanding of behavior and the ways in which it is tied to environmental events.

Michael reminded us that the effectiveness of reinforcers depends on some degree of deprivation or satiation and that there is a similar relation involving aversive stimuli. He proposed that we view establishing or motivating operations as events, operations, or stimulus conditions that share two functions. One is to alter the effectiveness of other events as reinforcers or punishers. The other is to alter the frequency of behavior associated with these reinforcing or punishing events. This latter effect is especially noticeable, though it can be confused with a similar effect of discriminative stimuli. The distinction, he pointed out, is that discriminative stimuli concern the differential availability of a reinforcer for a certain behavior, whereas motivating operations concern the differential reinforcing efficacy of a certain environmental event (Michael, 2007).

The technical vocabulary of science should always be at the mercy of its utility. By this standard, Michael's proposal has already proven its worth. Both researchers and practitioners enthusiastically adopted not just a set of terms, but their implications. For instance, a review by McGill (1999) reveals how the concept of establishing/motivating operations has influenced the assessment, treatment, and prevention of problem behavior, especially in developmentally disabled individuals.

BOX 2.5

The Translation Trap

The exercise of translating everyday terms such as convictions or beliefs into the technical dialect of the science of behavior has a certain appeal. It seems reassuring to find what appear to be thoughtful substitutions for conventional terms that now appear to be prohibited. To some extent, such translations are a necessary part of explaining why behavior analysts insist on avoiding vernacular references in favor of what is obviously a more laborious alternative. These translation exercises identify an everyday term concerning some aspect of behavior, explain why it is misleading, describe what is really going on with behavior instead, and offer an alternative term or expression that avoids the original problem. The desired result is that the reader will appreciate how colloquial terms and expressions misdirect our interests in understanding human nature and be motivated to focus on behavior and its environmental context instead. Upcoming chapters will offer many examples of these translations, just as Skinner often found it necessary to do (e.g., Skinner, 1953, 1974).

This practice contains a trap or two, however. As argued in the Preface, for example, the act of translating assumes that a term or expression in one language has a matching term or expression in another that serves the same function for speakers and listeners. For example, "dog" in English and "chien" in French mean exactly the same thing. This is certainly not the case with everyday terms and expressions that appear to describe or explain behavior, however. Vernacular references often require relatively long-winded interpretation in the language of behavioral science precisely because there is no simple one-for-one substitution of terms that works. Other sciences face this same challenge of translating everyday references into technically correct dialect. Everyday terms are generally superficial, conversationally efficient, and do not require special training, which is the basis for their appeal. Scientific language requires considerable preparation and gives more weight to precision than convenience.

A more troublesome implication of this exercise is the implicit assumption that the availability of a term in one dialect warrants a matching term in the other dialect. That is, it is tempting to believe that the existence of a vernacular term means that its referent is real, or at least important, and that it therefore deserves a translation. This position is especially problematic for mentalistic terms, many of which serve as nouns in our grammar and therefore seem to be "things" that should not be dismissed without a proper substitution in a scientific dialect. Routinely attempting to translate such terms may encourage this conviction and imply that a complete alternative scientific lexicon is required.

Because of the limitations of mentalism, however, such a lexicon is neither possible nor would it be satisfying. A complete set of matching English and French words may make a dictionary, but a dictionary that translated mentalistic terms into proper behavioral terminology would not serve as the foundation for a scientific philosophy. As Chapter 3 will show, understanding the "meaning" of everyday words in a behavioral framework is not a matter of substituting one definition for another. The real challenge is to understand how we must talk about behavior so that vernacular phrasing is no longer tempting because our dialect is fully consistent with the underlying science.

same challenge, but they also maintain a specialized technical dialect that is part of the basis for their effectiveness. Such a technical dialect may be even more important for ABA practitioners, given that it is the very foundation for how they look at behavior.

Is Something Missing?

Well, all of this certainly changes things, does it not? We have grown up thinking that we possess things called convictions or beliefs, that they are non-physically held somewhere inside us, and that we express or report on them. Furthermore, when we talk about someone's convictions or beliefs in common parlance, the connotation is often that they are especially important and fervently held. The point of view described in this chapter leaves all of this behind. Are you now feeling as if something is being taken away from you? That something is missing in all of this? If so, it is a common reaction at first. Other scientific advances such as the discovery that the earth is round, that it rotates around the sun, or that diseases may be caused by germs produced similar reactions. Sometimes even otherwise well-educated people have great difficulty coming to grips with sound scientific findings, such as the theory of evolution. It should not be surprising that it has proven difficult to sell the discoveries of well-established behavioral analysis science as well.

Of course, we cannot lose what we never had. The only thing being lost here is our ignorance. Once past this apparent loss, you may become excited about learning a way of talking about behavior, including your own behavior, that is consistent with what science is teaching us. Consider that instead of losing something you are discovering a way of looking at behavior that reveals relations and complexity you did not see before. You are learning how to look past the implications of a misleading colloquial dialect and see a powerful and compelling world of possibilities based on scientific discoveries. What remains is learning a new dialect that allows you to talk about those aspects of behavior that are really there. That will come with the rest of this book.

CHAPTER SUMMARY

1. All verbal behavior is learned from a verbal community. Although a biological foundation is required, so is an extensive and ongoing learning history.

2. Verbal behavior is operant behavior that requires the presence of another person for its reinforcement. It is often vocal but can also be written and gestural. It is maintained by intermittent positive reinforcement contingencies involving a speaker and a listener.

3. Verbal behavior may not be uniquely human, but most of what the behavior we call communicative behavior in non-human species is not verbal behavior.

4. The human verbal repertoire is initially learned through countless interchanges between child and parents or caregivers. Initially the baby's responses are vocal rather than verbal, but repeated interchanges lead to verbal responses of increasing frequency and complexity.

5. Most people fail to appreciate the power of operant selection and the countless learning moments that gradually build the adult verbal repertoire. In explaining this process, it helps to focus on the early history that underlies a young child's limited repertoire.

6. The concept of response classes is key to making sense of the complexity of verbal behavior. Skinner proposed a number of verbal response classes, including mands and tacts, that serve well-researched functions. Traditional structural elements such as words and sentences are not behaviorally meaningful units.

7. In light of the behavioral approach, conventional linguistic concepts must be reconsidered. Regular patterns in verbal repertoires include what are usually called the rules of grammar, though they are no more than learned patterns of responding. The notions that words and sentences have meaning and that we use them to refer to things and events are especially problematic convictions.

8. Behavior analysts deal with meaning in terms of the function of a behavior. What any behavior means, including a bit of verbal behavior, lies solely in the circumstances under which we emit it. We can identify the meaning of an utterance by discovering the conditions under which we emit it, thereby avoiding the mentalistic trap associated with the idea that words have meanings that are stored in a mental lexicon.

9. The point of clarifying the nature of verbal behavior is to appreciate that what we say is "just verbal behavior." Our views, opinions, convictions, and so forth do not have a physical existence and are solely the result of a learning history. They would be different if we had a different history. The concern about our verbal behavior should not be its "content" but its sources of control.

TEXT STUDY GUIDE

1. What is the definition of verbal behavior? How is it different from and yet the same as other operant behavior?

2. Explain why verbal behavior is largely limited to human beings.

3. Describe the Hart and Risley project.

4. Why do people often fail to appreciate the role of operant selection in explaining verbal behavior?

5. Why is the concept of classes of response classes important to understanding verbal behavior?

6. Why are the conventional structural elements of language—words and sentences—not key features of a behavior analytic approach to verbal behavior?

7. How do behavior analysts view rules of grammar?

8. Explain how behavior analysts view the concept of meaning.

9. Describe the tactic for understanding the meaning of a word, phrase, or sentence.

10. For behavior analysts, what is a conviction?

11. What are the implications of the view that our convictions are "just verbal behavior"?

12. How might the arguments in this chapter affect the behavior of practitioners?

BOX STUDY GUIDE

1. What are the key definitional features of behavior?

2. What are the problems that conventional ideas of language and communication pose for a scientific understanding of verbal behavior?

3. What does it mean to say that verbal behavior is multiply determined?

4. How did Michael's proposal for better distinguishing between the discriminative and motivational functions of stimuli illustrate the importance of how we talk about behavior?

5. What is the trap involved in simply translating vernacular terms into behavioral terms?

DISCUSSION TOPICS AND EXERCISES

1. Discuss the various forms of behavior that might be considered verbal. What examples of behavior might seem to be verbal but are probably not?

2. Consider examples of verbal behavior a young child learns (such as the use of pronouns) and speculate on the contingencies that might explain how they are acquired.

3. Using the tactic for understanding the meaning of a word or phrase, select some examples and consider their sources of control.

4. Discuss a current "hot button" issue, such as abortion or gun control. Avoid consideration of the conventional substance of the issue and focus instead on the origin and sources of control over peoples' views.

5. Discuss the sources of control over our verbal behavior concerning love. What does it mean in behavior analytic terms to say "I love you."

SUGGESTED READINGS

Catania, A. C. (2007). *Learning.* Cornwall-On-Hudson, NY: Sloan Publishing. (Chapter 14: Verbal Behavior: Language Function; Chapter 15: Verbal Behavior and Nonverbal Behavior)

Hart, B. & Risley, T. R. (1995). *Meaningful differences in the everyday experience of young American children.* Baltimore, MD: Paul H. Brookes Publishing Co.

Hart, B. & Risley, T. R. (1999). *The social world of children learning to talk.* Baltimore, MD: Paul H. Brookes Publishing Co.

Moore, J. (2000). Words are not things. *The Analysis of Verbal Behavior, 17,* 143–160.

Skinner, B. F. (1948). *Verbal behavior.* New York: Appleton-Century-Crofts.

Skinner, B. F. (1945). The operational analysis of psychological terms. *Psychological Review, 52,* 270–277.

Skinner, B. F. (1953). *Science and human behavior.* New York: Basic Books. (Chapter XIV: The analysis of complex cases)

Chapter 3

Nevermind

Anne had begun her career as a therapist by working as an assistant trainer at an agency that provided services to children diagnosed with autism. She majored in psychology in college but wasn't interested in more costly years in school to get her Master's degree. After a few years with this agency, which offered a wide range of service models, she got a job with another agency as a therapist. In this position, she worked with families in the home, training parents and providing direct services to children with autism. After a couple of years, she was tired of someone else controlling her schedule and making all the decisions, so she started her own consulting practice. Anne had taken a course in applied behavior analysis during her junior year and had attended a workshop or two in the subject along the way, so she felt that she had a pretty good idea about what ABA offered.

Anne was prepared for this meeting with Penny and Michael, the parents of Scott, the cute little three-year-old boy she had been getting to know. They were both eager to be involved in his treatment, just the kind of parents she always hoped for when starting down this long road. Scott had been diagnosed by a child psychologist as having autism spectrum disorder, and he presented the classic features. From her limited time with him, Anne felt that he might respond well to the intervention program she usually recommended. The family was fortunate the local public school had a good special education program, and Anne was going to propose that she be in charge of coordinating with the school and conducting home-based treatment activities.

Anne was aware from previous meetings with the parents that they had already picked up some ideas about autism from the Internet—par for the course, in her experience. As she talked about what would be involved in the home-based treatment and the role the parents would need to play, she was pleased that they seemed receptive to her approach, which involved teaching the child how to behave appropriately. Anne was discussing situations in which Scott often got upset and giving examples of intervention procedures they would need to learn.

*"So, when you are working with him and he starts his **self-stimming** routine, it will be important to refocus on the training task," she explained.*

"Shouldn't we explain to him what we're doing?" Penny asked. "If he is going to learn not to flap his hands and stuff, he needs to understand that he mustn't do that."

"Oh yes," Anne agreed. "We need to teach him what is acceptable behavior and what is unacceptable, so he can learn to make better choices. In fact, we want him eventually to be able to tell you how he should be behaving."

Penny seemed relieved at this clarification. "Good. We feel that he needs to understand the difference between appropriate and inappropriate behavior."

"Yes, especially as he learns to communicate better, " Anne added. "Our training efforts will be more effective if he understands the reasons for what we are asking him to do." She then moved on to go over more details about how the home-based activities would work.

CAUSE AND EFFECT

Anne's assumption that Scott must understand or be able to describe his behavior suggests that she believes that mental processes are required to enable or modulate it. In fact, much of the trouble stemming from our everyday way of talking about behavior comes down to our speculations and convictions about its causes. From the earliest days of recorded history, humankind has not been reluctant to propose entertaining possibilities about where behavior comes from. A seemingly endless array of gods, the position of the planets when we are born, spirits of various sorts, and a miscellany of fascinating forces out there somewhere have long been elaborately detailed. Many of these fanciful explanations are still with us today, though in more contemporary form. For example, a book by Jacobson, Foxx, & Mulick (2004) addresses a number of controversial therapeutic approaches in developmental disabilities that are based on invented causes of behavior.

Perhaps the most persistent explanation for what makes us who we are is that the answer lies within each of us. We do what we do, it is said, because each of us is guided by phenomena that can only be described in a non-physical or mental universe. This kind of explanation suggests that we do not merely respond to environmental events. Before we act, mental processes intervene and influence what we do, even if we are often unaware of this step. (In this chapter's vignette, Anne seems to be comfortable with this reasoning because she believes that Scott must understand what is going on so he can make choices about how he will behave.) Psychologists and others of that ilk have spent a century attempting to explore these mental processes, and it has been a good business. The resulting literature is undeniably impressive in size and scope, perhaps not surprisingly in light of the truly limitless possibilities offered by a non-physical world.

Mentalistic explanations for behavior are understandably tempting. They require no uncomfortable adjustment of the way we have already been taught to look at behavior. Attributing the causes of behavior to a mind is consistent with the way we talk, for example. The grammar of English and many other languages requires an agent for every action, and it is often convenient to assign that role to ourselves. So, it is "I" that is implicitly given causal status, as in "I decided to go to the movies." This personal pronoun stands in for many of the mental processes psychologists have so diligently invented and catalogued. The familiarity of this kind of reference seems to be an important criterion for an explanatory model. As paradigm shifters have again and again ruefully discovered, trying to get people to think in entirely new ways about how the world works is more than a little bit challenging.

One of the conveniences of putting the causes of behavior in our minds is that they are always available for a guiding role just before we act. It seems so obvious that we should look for the causes of behavior in events that immediately precede action. After all, we are accustomed to proximate causation in our daily lives. Thanks to the physics of our world, the most conspicuous kind of causation we experience is mechanical in nature. Sir Isaac Newton laid it all out for us in his studies of classical mechanics. We do not have to understand the mathematical formalities to learn about simple mechanical relations, however. Newton's First Law of Motion (the law of inertia) roughly says that unless acted on by another force, an object at rest tends to stay at rest, and an object in motion will remain in motion. Even if you were absent the day you were supposed to learn that in school, it takes only a little experience to appreciate why driving with a cup of hot coffee in your lap is a really bad idea. Our interactions with gravity alone are convincing. When a glass slips from our grasp and falls to the floor and breaks, it is hard to avoid concluding that the cause of the glass falling was our clumsiness, which immediately preceded the outcome. We are never more than a moment away from examples of mechanical causation.

Our unavoidable and very personal history with the immediacy of mechanical causation leads us to look for causes for behavior that are also temporally proximate to our actions. Mental events are convenient because we assume they are almost always going on and are therefore endlessly available for causal assignments. Even when we may not be aware of specific thoughts immediately leading to our actions, we are comfortable with offering phrases such as "I was thinking..." or "It occurred to me..." as causally implied explanations.

Extended to our everyday explanations of behavior, this requirement for temporal proximity based on a mechanical or push-pull causal model turns out to be especially problematic. Not only does it force us to invent proximate mental causes for behavior in the absence of obvious physical candidates, it specifically discourages us from noticing the possible role of environmental events that occurred a bit further back in time. Although we may point to accumulated experiences as a factor in behavioral outcomes, we often give them no more than a contributing influence on more convenient and important mental causes. So, in explaining why we insert our front door key a certain way to get a recalcitrant lock to work, we might be able to describe some learning history with the failing lock that helped us learn to make it work. However, we are likely to limit the contribution of this history to helping us "figure out" what worked. The implication is that prior experience only facilitates a mental process, which we offer as the proximate and real explanation.

With this kind of causal history, is it any wonder that we would look for explanations of behavior from this same perspective? Our everyday verbal repertoire encourages us to point to apparently causal internal events as easily as we identify external influences. Just as a child learns to admit under parental questioning that the cookie jar broke because it fell when he was getting a cookie, he also learns to explain why he was getting a cookie by simply saying, "I wanted a cookie." To most people, the proximate cause of the jar falling (because he knocked it over) would seem not fundamentally different from explaining the behavior of trying to get a cookie in terms of some form of private motivation. Note that our scientific understanding of the physical evidence for why a cookie jar might fall contrasts with the complete lack of physical evidence for the mental events (wanting a cookie) supposedly causing the child to try to get a cookie.

Most parents would find their child's implication of a mental cause for his or her behavior fully acceptable, though they might continue the discussion with a reminder about obeying rules. After all, it is hard to argue with explanations of behavior that appeal to mental events because by definition only the behaving individual has access to them. The private nature of mental explanations of behavior is convenient because it enables us to offer mental causes for whatever we do without fear of factual contradiction. Others might complain we are not being honest in explaining our actions, even pointing out other possible motivations, but they cannot prove that what we propose as the private causes for our behavior are false. So, we may say that we did not mean to be rude to a friend in making a comment, though others may argue we did so intentionally. However, they cannot know for sure why we made the comment.

In fact, science has shown that the appropriate causal model for behavior is historical, not mechanical. Although an organism and its behavior are physical events and obviously abide by the laws of motion, a live organism behaves in ways that cannot be fully explained by Newtonian mechanics. This is the origin of Ogden Lindsley's Dead Man's Test: "If a dead man can do it, it isn't behavior" (Johnston & Pennypacker, 2009). He developed this simple rule to help teachers be sure they are targeting actual instances of behavior. Ignoring the macabre implications, what this rule implies is that any movements of a dead person (a corpse falling down stairs, for example) can be explained by the laws of physics. When a very much alive organism moves, however, the resulting changes in the environment, no matter how apparently trivial, have an effect on the organism's biology that, for reasons not yet fully understood, can affect the organism's behavior in the future. Behavior is the result of this contact or interface between a live organism and its environment, and it is a phenomenon that can only be fully explained with the benefit of the laws of operant learning (see Box 3.1).

Unlike temporally contiguous physical events (mishandling a glass and its subsequent crash on the floor), historical relations are difficult to discern. A particular kind of action immediately followed by a characteristic change in the environment can occur again and again over time without our noticing. Even if we do see the relation, we are unlikely to appreciate its potential to change behavior, whether ours or someone else's. For example, parents often fail to notice that occasionally giving a fussy child a cookie in the grocery store creates a history that explains

---

BOX 3.1

Molecular versus Molar Analysis

Even though all behavior analysts agree about the central role of learning history in explaining behavior, there is some disagreement about how we should examine its role. The most widely held view emphasizes the role of temporal contiguity between responses and surrounding environmental events. This molecular perspective focuses on momentary contingencies in explaining responding, and it is a key feature of the applied research literature and practical interventions. For example, if you are shaping a new performance, you must pay close attention to the timing of prompting stimuli, responses, and reinforcers in each training trial. Everyone certainly appreciates the importance of the timing and distribution of reinforcers in modifying or explaining patterns of responding.

On the other hand, it is also the case that behavior depends not just on current contingencies but on contingencies going well back in our histories. These past contingencies may continue to influence behavior in an aggregate way and encourages a more molar perspective to analyzing behavior (Baum, 2002; Rachlin, 1994). The behavior of fixing a pot of coffee is the result of a long history of such episodes that have a cumulative effect. Furthermore, we could view behavior as not just momentary occurrences of one response class or another (fixing a cup of coffee, drinking coffee, checking our emails) but as related activities that extend over long periods of time. For example, what do we mean when we say that Tim loves football? What is the behavior of loving football? If we observe Tim's repertoire, we might see a variety of distinguishable response classes under different circumstances over time (watching football on TV, reading about a favorite team on line, talking with friends about football, etc.) that we could collectively call "loving football." When Tim is not engaging in any of these behaviors, we would not say he does not then love football, however. The key is how often Tim engages in any of these football-loving activities. If these episodes occur sufficiently often over time, we might say Tim loves football.

why the child tends to be fussy in the grocery store. Instead, parental explanations are likely to be in terms of proximate mental events on each occasion, such as the child being hungry or tired or feeling grumpy.

Scientific advances might someday be able to describe what is going on at a physiological level in the brain when a certain form of responding produces a certain kind of consequence and therefore becomes more or less likely to occur in the future. However, these discoveries will not explain behavior any better than physics explains our actions. Both the physics and biochemistry of behavior are necessary for a comprehensive explanation of behavior, but they cannot explain why each of us does exactly what we do at every moment that makes each person unique. Their limitation is the inability to take into account the processes of learning underlying interactions between organism and environment.

What makes each of us—even identical twins—unique is our behavior, which results from unavoidably unique histories of response-consequence contin-

---

BOX 3.2

Causes and Gaps

Our tendency to look for temporally proximate causes of behavior complicates our appreciation of the role of influences that lie in our history. If this history is only moments old, we seem to have no difficulty in appreciating the possibility of a causal relation between environmental events and behavior. When the microwave bell sounds signaling that our food is done, it is easy to see the relation between the bell and the action of retrieving our dinner. Even when the temporal gap between the bell and our response to it is a minute or two, we seem comfortable with the notion that an event in our past can influence our behavior in the present. If the gap is much longer, say an hour or more, we often seem less confident about attributing a causal role to the bell. And when gaps between environmental events and behavior involve days, weeks, months, or even years, we tend to reference apparently immediate mental causes for our actions, such as memory, for example.

In fact, there is very little about behavior that does not rely on historical influences, which may obviously go back quite some time. Any behavior we emit is the result of its entire history, though as time passes more recent aspects of this history may be more important than earlier features. There is no point in the historical timeline for a behavior at which the nature of causal variables requires a different sort of explanation, however, whether the units of time are in seconds, minutes, hours, days, or longer. Experiences in our childhood can play a significant role in current behavior in the same way as experiences that occurred yesterday or even a few moments ago. As Baum (2008) points out, the notion of causal actions at a distance was initially hard for people to accept, and the concept of gravity was slow to be accepted. Popular culture may have a similar problem with the idea of causal influences on behavior over gaps of time.

gencies. Their influence accumulates in small but complex ways, instance by instance, to explain any moment of our behavior, however distant in time the history might lead. Such analytical precision is difficult to achieve even in a laboratory with non-human species and careful control of the environment, but enough has been learned over decades of research that there is no longer debate about the natural aspects of behavior. The processes of operant shaping, now quite well understood, are always operating and are fundamentally historical in how they explain behavior.

IS MAKING UP YOUR MIND LIKE
MAKING UP YOUR BED?

What is Mentalism?

The tendency to look for the causes of behavior not in the physical world but in a mental universe that has no physical dimensions is called **mentalism**. This conceptual approach is a form of philosophical dualism that says that neither mind nor matter can be reduced to the other in any way, that they are irrevocably distinct. Mind-body dualism has long been recognized by the natural sciences as an unacceptable philosophy of science because of the mischievous and insurmountable problems it poses.

Mental explanations often take a piece of behavior as the basis for creating a fictional entity of some sort, which is in turn offered as a cause for the behavior. If Anna votes for conservative political candidates and argues that the country needs smaller government and lower taxes, she might be described as having conservative beliefs. Her friends may explain her complaints about government regulations as being based on or caused by these conservative beliefs. Her belief, however, is fully inferred from her behavior, which is all there is to observe. One of the problems with this kind of reasoning is that we now must explain not only why Anna talks about politics and votes as she does but what her beliefs are and where they come from.

The Mind-Body Problem

Inventing a mental "force" called beliefs also requires an explanation of exactly how it is that beliefs cause particular behaviors to occur. This is called the *mind-body problem*: How can something lacking physical dimensions affect physical events such as behavior? This is a fundamentally unsolvable problem because it first requires assuming a mental universe, a position for which there is no supporting evidence. However, the solution that is sometimes offered is to assume that beliefs, along with other mental events, actually exist in some sense and therefore can be the causal origin of behavior. There is no supporting evidence for asserting that beliefs are physical events, and it is unlikely there ever will be. Although science continues to learn about how the brain works, these advances cannot reify mentalistic concepts. We may come to understand what is going on in the brain when we behave in certain ways, but that will not explain the nature, origins, and environmental causes of the behavior. It is more likely mentalistic concepts will eventually be replaced by a scientific understanding that relates real events in the brain to behavior and its environmental context.

Do Mental Explanations Explain?

Another problem stemming from the fact that this mental world is entirely invented is that attributing the causes of behavior to mental "events" does not actually explain anything. Instead, it invites endless inventions of supposed causes that cannot be directly investigated or falsified. If someone asks why you did something and your explanation—"because I wanted to"—relies on a mentalistic rationale, how might researchers study that kind of explanation? Could they show that such explanations are not valid? How could they disprove it? What does it mean when we say that we *want* to do something? What is wanting? Is it a physical phenomenon that can be directly measured? What kind of experimental manipulations would researchers arrange to investigate such a phenomenon directly? How would they know they are systematically varying wanting as an independent variable?

What we do know is that saying "because I wanted to" is behavior, which is a physical phenomenon. We also know about the learning history that spawns such verbal behavior and the variables that modulate it. But where is the wanting? The colloquial assumption is that wanting is a mental state that causes our actions and that we are able to identify and describe this mental state, albeit only in ourselves. Scientists, however, have to put aside everyday preconceptions and work with what is really there. Although they might try to vary the degree of wanting across experimental conditions to see how behavior changes when it is present versus absent, how can we know that wanting varied as required? Some might find measures of brain activity using imaging technology when participants are exposed to a "wanting" condition an appealing result, but such imaging data do not constitute a direct measure of wanting. The only way to know the status of wanting from one condition to another is to obtain some kind of report from participants. Unfortunately, this report can only be taken as indirect evidence of the wanting itself and therefore raises the challenge of showing that the indirect measure (a statement about wanting) is unambiguously related to actual wanting, the real focus of interest. If wanting exists only in a mental universe, no such evidence can be found. For this reason, it is impossible to conduct experiments that allow researchers to directly measure and study wanting or even show that it exists. This protection against falsifiability violates a key feature of scientific methods.

By seeming to provide explanations of behavior, mentalism interferes with our efforts to understand why we do what we do. Mentalistic explanations appear to answer our questions about behavior and thereby distract us from considering more useful explanations. Well-trained behavioral scientists can avoid these distractions, although mentalism has proven too tempting for many scientists trained in other areas. Our tendency to be satisfied with the mentalistic explanations embedded in colloquial dialect also takes a toll in everyday life. When we fail to identify and appreciate how behavior really works, we miss opportunities to be more effective in our daily lives. Parents who give a fussy child a cookie pay the price of more fussiness (as does the child) when they explain the fussiness in terms of grumpiness instead of recognizing the role of intermittent positive reinforcement.

Inventing Inside "Causes"

Mentalistic explanations of behavior tend to place causes inside the organism. This practice is so common we may fail to notice the endless examples in our everyday dialect. For example, Skinner (1953) discussed three general types of inner causes that may help you appreciate the breadth of the problem. He noted that some inner causes are seemingly *neural* in nature, such as when we say that our nerves are on edge or that our brain is tired. We have been taught to offer these explanations of our behavior under certain circumstances, such as when we screw up in some way. We may sometimes be tacting real physical variables in our body we can directly sense, but the relation between what is actually going on in our nervous system and our description of it in these phrases is vague at best. When we say that our nerves are on edge, we are not really describing actual neural conditions because we cannot detect their status in any meaningful way. In other words, we are inventing these apparently neural phenomena. Of course, when we explain the behavior of others in this way, we have no direct evidence about the condition of their nervous systems. Contemporary behavioral neuroscience might seem to offer more sophisticated options, but its interpretations of what may sometimes be interesting findings remain fundamentally mentalistic (Uttal, 2000, 2011). For example, it may be proposed that a particular area of the brain is related to a certain kind of behavioral activity, but this does not justify concluding that mentalistic qualities colloquially associated with such activities reside in or are explained by physiological processes in the brain.

Explanations of behavior in terms of *psychic* inner causes are even more common. This type of explanation refers to inner agents lacking any physical dimensions. All references to mind and its apparent products fall into this category. In addition to explicit attributions to the mind in any form, examples include ideas, wishes, impulses, thoughts, and much more. Skinner noted that this practice is hardly limited to lay people. Psychologists and others who address behavioral issues tend to formalize such dependence on psychic causes with psychological

---

BOX 3.3

Corrrelation or Causation?

Behavior analysts tend to view the underlying physiological events associated with any action as correlates rather than explanations of behavior. When an environmental event occurs and is followed by some action, it is tempting to assume that the unavoidable biological effects of the environmental event are responsible for the ensuing action. For instance, if we are about to cross the street and hear a car horn, we will probably look around quickly and stay on the sidewalk for the moment. Of course, the sound of the horn and our actions involve our physiology in various ways. Even when the biological underpinnings of our behavior are generally clear, however, it need not follow that they should be seen as the cause of our behavior. Both physiological and behavioral events may best be interpreted as the result of the environmental event to which they are both related. That is, our physiological reaction to the environmental event may be necessary for the behavioral reaction, but giving biological variables causal status over behavior is misleading.

Behavior analysts take this explanatory approach because it is important that our explanations of behavior extend beyond correlated physiological variables to the preceding environmental variables of which they are also a function. If our attempts to explain behavior stop at a biological level (saying that behavior is caused by related physiological events), we will fail to understand the contribution of environmental variables to both behavioral and biological reactions. An interpretation of an action in terms of its neuromuscular requisites may be true, but it is invariably incomplete. The same environmental event can result in different behavioral outcomes at different times for any individual and certainly across individuals. (The same sound of a car horn can lead to quickly jumping back on the curb or waving to a friend.) A search for causal relations underlying these behavioral differences requires going outside of the organism to the environment. In particular, it requires factoring in the role of learning processes to describe why our behavior, and its underlying biology, occurred.

---

theories and technical terminology. Sigmund Freud's concepts of id, ego, and superego are examples that long ago became everyday terms.

Finally, *conceptual* inner causes, which Skinner suggested is the most common type of mentalistic attribution, have neither neurological or psychic dimensions. These causal references are to personal qualities or conditions of some sort, such as intelligence, abilities, instincts, habits, or temporary inner circumstances. When we say that someone does well because of her intelligence, is a great pianist because of his impressive musical ability, tends to argue because he is feisty, smokes because of a tobacco habit, or eats because she is hungry, we attempt to explain some action in terms of inner causes. In doing so, what we miss is that there is only one set of facts underlying such causal statements. We see that Liz

---

BOX 3.4

You and Your Homunculus

We often talk as if we are not alone. We seem to share a private life with our very own homunculus—a kind of inner person or source of control that determines our actions. If we are watching a TV show, it is common to explain that the images are reflected on the retina and that the brain then sees these images via the optic nerve and tells you what you are seeing. This reasoning involves creating a little person or homunculus inside the brain that does the inside work. This explanatory fiction does not help us explain how seeing occurs, however. Instead of you doing the seeing, we have merely moved the seeing from you to your brain, aided by your homunculus of course. The question of how the brain sees remains unanswered.

Colloquial dialect seems to give our homunculus an expansive role in explaining our behavior. This little inside person—we often refer to it as our "self"—seems to process input from the environment and determine the output, our behavior. This casual approach to explaining our actions is obviously bogus and begs the question of what controls the "behavior" of the homunculus. Failing to ask that question means we accept the notion that the homunculus is autonomous, a view we discussed in Chapter 1 in the context of free will. Trying to answer the question is pointless, however, because this little person, whether we call it a homunculus or a self, is entirely fictional and beyond explanation.

---

always gets the highest grade on tests and explain this by saying that she is intelligent, but there is only one set of facts (her test performance) available to support both statements. All we observe is that someone behaves in a particular way, but we make up a general quality or condition that is supposed to cause the behavior. There are no separate facts about this quality or condition; it is merely invented to provide a momentary explanation. At the least, this kind of explanation is merely redundant. Worse, it implies that we have identified the cause and need not pursue other possibilities.

WHAT IS REALLY INSIDE?

Public vs. Private

In order to answer this question, we first need to consider what we mean by "inside." When we refer to our thoughts, feelings, emotions, and the like, we understand them as private or not accessible to others. Unlike public events, which can be detected by others, private events are by definition not public. Your toothache, for example, is private. No matter how loudly you complain or how thoroughly you describe it to others, they cannot share your sensation.

BOX 3.5

Is There Such a Thing as Intelligence?

This may seem a strange question. It seems easy to appreciate that each person has a certain amount of intelligence, which apparently helps explain differences among us throughout our lives. It is almost as if we each have a Mason quart jar somewhere inside us that is filled from the outset with a certain amount of a stuff called intelligence. Of course, no one believes that, but we do seem to reify intelligence as a noun and give it causal status in explaining behavior.

There is no scientific basis for talking about intelligence as a thing or even a vague quality of some sort, however, and this mistake is easily avoided. Even turning it into an adjective by referring to "intelligent behavior" is problematic because it still suggests a special quality that may influence or characterize behavior. It is more useful to simply refer to the effectiveness of behavior when assessing circumstances in which responding varies in its environmental outcomes. This encourages a search for what might make behavior more or less effective.

Might certain features of our brain play a role in how we learn and respond to environmental situations? Of course, but instead of inventing the concept of intelligence to explain behavioral effectiveness, it is more useful to identify the real variables that underlie why we behave more or less effectively under different circumstances. Instead of saying that a child does well in school because she is highly intelligent, which is not a meaningful explanation, we should look for environmentally based reasons she gets good grades, such as established academic skills, parental support, and good teaching. (We presumably could not do anything about the associated physiological variables, even if we understood them.) What we discover will likely be valuable in helping those who do not do well.

ABA practitioners often work with individuals diagnosed as intellectually disabled and long ago learned the practical limitations of the concept of intelligence. Although scores on intelligence tests continue to be used diagnostically or administratively, they mean little to those charged with helping individuals learn a new skill. A particular intelligence quotient says very little about an individual's behavior or what he or she might be able to learn. Practitioners know the only way to discover what someone can do is to arrange conditions that will lead to a desired outcome. Even more importantly, if those procedures are not successful, the most useful course of action is to try to improve the procedures, not to draw conclusions about the individual's capabilities or intelligence.

Although this public-private distinction seems straightforward, it is not really behaviorally meaningful. Skinner made this point when he wrote, "The skin is not all that important as a boundary. Private and public events have the same kinds of physical dimensions" (Skinner, 1969, p. 228). What he meant is that there is no reason to assume that private events are fundamentally different from public events just because private events are less accessible. The difference between private and public events is merely the number of people that can directly observe them. This distinction, which only arises because of how we are taught to label private events, should not lead us to assume they are different from public events in any general way. Such a view would violate the scientific strategy of preferring parsimonious explanations of phenomena (see Box 1.2).

Our overriding concern should be that a science of behavior focuses only on events that are real or natural as opposed to fictional or invented. Natural events that occur inside the skin may sometimes raise methodological challenges, but limited accessibility should not be the basis for defining them as outside the bounds of a behavioral science. The status of private events has been one of the defining issues in the evolution of behaviorism over the years, and we will return to it later.

For now, it may help to appreciate just how tenuous the private-public distinction is. For example, some events are private only because no one else is around. If you are eating alone at home and let out a loud burp, it is private, unless you are exceptionally talented and your neighbor in the adjacent apartment overhears you. In contrast, some events, such as thinking, may appear to be irrevocably private, although it is always possible that advances in measurement technology could change their status. The field of medicine has driven the development of many techniques that make it possible to directly observe much of what goes on inside the skin. Who knows what lies ahead? Might we someday be able to measure what we are thinking? If so, what we now view as a private event would then become public. In the meanwhile, just because we cannot directly observe someone else's thoughts, we need not rule them ineligible for scientific investigation. Scientists in other fields routinely investigate events that cannot be directly measured (such as some subatomic particles) as long as they are confident of the empirical basis for their physical existence.

What About Thinking?

Let us consider thinking, the prototypical private event, a bit further. Although we cannot directly measure anyone else's thinking, we assume most everyone does it. We typically consider thinking something like private verbal behavior. We wonder, remember, have ideas, reason, solve problems, make decisions, and daydream. Some of these things we also do out loud or in some other verbal form. We talk to ourselves as we do to others and even carry out conversations with ourselves, all without making a sound. We also call it thinking when we hear a tune in our head, recall the smell of our favorite food, or see something "in our mind's eye." This kind of private behavior is not necessarily verbal but is more like the experience of sensing things, although they may not be present.

Is thinking behavior? Skinner defined it as "behaving which automatically affects the behaver and is reinforcing because it does so" (Skinner, 1957, p. 438). Thinking is behavior that has automatically reinforcing effects on the person who is engaging in it. When you talk to yourself privately, the consequences are, at least immediately, private as well. The effects of such self talk are reinforcing without the ongoing intervention of others. Merely engaging in this behavior is reinforcing. Of course, how such behavior becomes automatically reinforcing unavoidably involves our learning a verbal repertoire from our verbal community.

There is nothing about this viewpoint that suggests that this behavior and its effects on behavior need be private. As behavior, it may fall anywhere on a covert-overt continuum. We may think privately, or we may think out loud, just as we may think verbally or non-verbally. For example, covert verbal behavior seems to be on a continuum with overt verbal behavior. We may say something loud enough for others nearby to hear, we may whisper the same words so that we may be the only ones who pick it up, or we may "say" the same thing "in our heads." In fact, studies have now made it clear that distinct physiological processes are involved when we say something to ourselves (Schlinger, 2008). Covert verbal behavior certainly has some advantages over overt behavior. For example, it is less effortful to think something than to say it out loud. In part, this is because it is quicker as well, inasmuch as we do not have to accommodate someone else as a listener. We can leave out some of the grammatical formalities without any social penalty, for instance. Talking privately can also avoid social punishment in other ways. Sometimes we may think things instead of saying them out loud because we are unsure of what we are saying. For instance, we may think we recognize someone at another table in a restaurant but not say it out loud to our friends because we are uncertain. We may also think rather than speak when our thoughts might be unacceptable to others. So we might comment to ourselves about an atrocious outfit a friend is wearing rather than pay the social price for saying so out loud.

This expansive conception of thinking as including both covert and overt, as well as verbal and non-verbal, behavior may exceed the boundaries of everyday definitions, but the challenge for science is to look for similarities, not differences. This approach pulls together ways of behaving that share common features and ignores misleading or irrelevant connotations associated with our vernacular dialect. Whether thinking is covert or overt may not be important to our definition because the matter of how accessible it is concerns only matters of measurement, not the fundamental nature of the phenomenon. Similarly, whether the behavior is verbal or non-verbal may be interesting in one instance or another but seems to fall short of a standard for defining critically different events.

Whatever the form and accessibility of such behavior, there is no reason to view it as anything other than behavior, and not a special form of behaving at that. We have already articulated Skinner's position that because thinking may often be private this should not disqualify it from being considered a form of behaving. We certainly do not want to argue that a science of behavior should ignore thinking just because we are not always able to measure it directly. An obvious advantage of viewing thinking as behavior is that it brings quite a lot of established science

BOX 3.6

Does Everyone Think?

Given that the behavior of thinking is only accessible to the person doing the thinking, how do we know that everyone does it? It does not seem that we can answer this question as clearly as we might like, though we can at least propose some limiting conditions. The phenomenon we call thinking mainly involves verbal behavior, so we might argue that individuals lacking a verbal repertoire do not engage in this kind of thinking.

For example, individuals with profound intellectual disabilities are unlikely to have acquired much, if any, verbal repertoire. Some may respond to limited verbal prompts or even respond vocally in limited ways, but it is usually clear that they have not learned even a rudimentary verbal repertoire. It is therefore unlikely that these individuals engage in the behavior we call thinking. For the same reasons, we have no reason to suppose that babies who have not yet acquired much of a verbal repertoire engage in this behavior either.

This requirement also means we should assume that non-human species also do not think. This will be a crushing blow to many pet owners because we routinely attribute human qualities to our pets and other animals. Lacking any other way of describing and interpreting their behavior, this anthropomorphizing is understandable. As our faithful dog sits by the door and whines, we say he wants to go outside and implicitly assume that is what he is thinking. We say that our dog understands he did a bad thing in messing on the carpet as he slinks away from us, head held low and tail between his legs. Of course, we have no direct evidence of these mentalistic attributions. The most parsimonious assumption is that they do not engage in thinking behavior because there is no means by which they could have learned such a verbal repertoire in the first place.

The ease with which we are seduced into reading human qualities into the behavior of non-human species is illustrated by the Columban Simulation Project (Epstein, 1981). This research set up complex experimental conditions for pigeons (genus Columba) that simulated behavior that in humans and other species such as chimpanzees might be called insightful. Watching videotapes of the pigeons' final performances seeming to demonstrate insight and self-awareness, it is difficult for most observers to draw any other conclusions. However, when the training procedures underlying the performance are revealed, the apparent magic disappears, along with the temptation to explain the pigeons' behavior as insightful.

to bear. Instead of viewing thinking as a mental phenomena, we can extend what we know about operant behavior in general to this particular aspect of the phenomenon. Practiced with caution, this kind of empirically grounded interpretation helps investigators develop good research questions and keeps us from wandering too far away from what science has already taught us about behavior.

There are good reasons to take advantage of a scientific framework when talking about thinking. Among the many problems associated with colloquial views is the assumption that thinking causes, and therefore explains, our subsequent actions. True, we may "follow" instructions we give to ourself in the same way we might if they were spoken to us by someone else, but the explanation for our behavior must be somewhat different in these two circumstances.

When we comply with someone else's suggestion that we carry an umbrella because it is likely to rain, we might argue that such advice has acquired the properties of a discriminative stimulus as a result of our reinforcement history associated with following rules given by others. If we privately say the same thing to ourselves, and subsequently take an umbrella, this explanation is not sufficient. When the advice comes from someone else, we do not have to pursue the origins of their behavior in order to explain our behavior of taking an umbrella. As the speaker, they are merely part of our environment, and their verbal responses are just stimuli for us. When we are both the speaker and the listener, however, we must explain where our behavior as speaker comes from. In doing so, we must avoid the temptation of saying that our thoughts (in this case, the observation that it might rain and that we ought to take an umbrella) somehow originated inside our head. That position would be a *prima facie* example of mentalism.

Aside from its physiological foundation, behavior results from our interactions with the environment, and any explanation of particular instances of behavior, especially covert verbal behavior, must be traced back outside the organism to its environmental origins. When we do this, we find that the environmental events underlying overt behavior also seem to explain related covert behavior. In other words, in spite of the fact that our thinking something may immediately precede a related action, suggesting a cause-effect sequence, both kinds of behavior must be explained in terms of environmental history and present circumstances, which are both external causes. In our weather example, stimuli associated with the weather forecast or just looking at the sky might contribute to both thinking that it might rain and that we should carry an umbrella, as well as to picking up the umbrella and putting it in our backpack. In fact, the overt actions might well have occurred even if we did not give ourself the covert advice.

And Emotions and Feelings?

Our emotions and feelings (we often use the terms interchangeably) are an important part of our lives. It is not surprising that we have a large everyday vocabulary describing feelings apparently going on inside of us that have become important as a result of our cultural background. Moreover, we give these private events causal status. Some environmental events we experience seem to result in some kind of genuine private reaction, which we describe as then influencing our behavior. Consider what we might call a patriotic feeling. We stand for the national anthem at a football game as military jets make a low pass over the stadium, and we feel a tingling sensation on the back of our neck, perhaps a sensation in the pit of our stomach or our heart beating strongly, and maybe we notice our eyes getting misty. We hold our hand over our heart as we sing the words.

In the psychological literature, this sequence of environmental and physiological events is abbreviated with the letters **S-O-R**, standing for environmental *stimuli*, which lead to events inside the *organism*, which then lead to overt *responses*. In this model, the environmental stimuli are taken as causing the internal events, which are in turn assumed to cause the organism's public responses. The problem with this approach is that the invitation to invent what might be going on inside the organism leads to speculation about endless mental qualities that cannot be directly studied or falsified. With our newfound caution about how we talk about inner events, let us consider what might really be going on instead.

What happens when we experience a certain feeling? When we feel hungry, for example, we might describe actual physical sensations in our stomach, such as stomach pangs. These sensations are relatively obvious and even fairly specific in location and character. Other feelings may be less clear, though no less real. When we feel angry, research has shown that a number of physical changes occur that are summarized as autonomic nervous system arousal. These include changes in heart rate, digestion, respiration rate, salivation, perspiration, and more. Were we not so angry, we might be able to crudely identify at least some of these physiological changes. Sometimes, however, what we feel is vague at best. When we feel sad or happy, it is more difficult to identify actual physiological variables that might be operating.

Although usually private, the physical correlates of what we call feelings or emotions are quite real. However, we do not always focus on the actual sensations for three reasons. First, we are simply not wired to be able to detect much of what is going on inside our skin, so our emotional vocabulary is weak in this regard (Skinner, 1974). We may not notice changes in heart rate or blood pressure, particularly at the moment, so we are unlikely to give them a central role in our emotional dialect. As we will see in a following section, we also suffer from limitations in how we learn to describe these private events.

Second, we have a long learning history in our verbal community that teaches us to talk about our emotional life in ways that go well beyond any underlying physical sensations. We learn that certain emotional talk is appropriate under certain environmental conditions and inappropriate under others. For instance, we learn to talk about crying as an emotional reaction, but we are likely to describe crying when we win a lottery as involving a different emotion than crying when we have to euthanize an aging pet. In one instance, we may say that we are crying because we are happy, whereas in the other we may say we are sad. Part of what we are labeling when we describe how we feel are the environmental conditions apparently prompting our physiological reactions, not just the reactions themselves. In other words, the nature of the environmental circumstances is likely to influence how we describe our emotions because of how we have been taught to label different circumstances. We are "supposed" to feel happy when we win a lot of money but sad when a pet dies, even though we may engage in the same crying behavior on both occasions.

Third, that same learning history overlays specific physical sensations with countless experiences that individualize our emotional reactions to environmental events. Although there is sufficient commonality among us for conversational purposes, each of us learns somewhat different emotional reactions to otherwise similar events. Although there may be some biological differences from one person to another underlying our individual emotional reactions to events, our different learning histories guarantee that people exhibit varying emotional behaviors under similar environmental circumstances. You are likely to experience and describe your emotions somewhat differently than would your friends or even family members.

In sum, although our emotional vocabulary is vague and varied, emotions and feelings are based on real, though largely private, events. As such, it is important that behavior analysis acknowledges the role of feelings in human behavior,

---

BOX 3.7

Gilbert Ryle's Problem with Mentalism

The perspective described in this book toward behavior and how it should be studied has often received attention, both positive and negative, from philosophers. Gilbert Ryle was a philosopher who shared Skinner's antipathy toward mentalism, although he approached his concerns somewhat differently. As described by Baum (2005), Skinner focused on the practical problems with mentalism, while Ryle was concerned with its logical problems. For instance, Ryle argued that we make a semantic error called a category mistake when we say that Susan plays the piano well because she has musical talent. The category mistake, in his view, lies in seeing piano playing and musical talent as separate or implying that musical talent causes skilled piano playing. For Ryle, the musical ability is the piano playing, as it is also singing or other musical performances. That is, the category of "musical talent" is the musical performances themselves. Making music in one or more ways is what we mean by musical talent.

Ryle argued that the reason we confuse the category and its instances is the idea that "category labels refer to ghostly things in some ghostly space (the mind), and that these ghostly things somehow mechanically cause behavior" (Baum, 2005, p. 45). Ryle called this the para-mechanical hypothesis, although this is what Skinner referred to as mentalism. Whereas Skinner wanted to eliminate mentalistic terms from our professional vocabulary, Ryle was content that we only use mentalistic terms as labels for categories of behavior, not as separate entities than can cause behavior (Baum, 2005).

even though the physical sensations associated with how we talk about feelings are often not publicly observable outside of medical or laboratory settings.

Unfortunately, the colloquial view of emotions and feelings serves us badly. While acknowledging the bodily sensations underlying feelings, our everyday way of talking about emotions often imbues them with mentalistic qualities. For example, we may say something rude to a friend and experience a physical reaction we describe as feeling guilty or ashamed. We may notice our face getting flushed, and were we trying to be observant, we might detect other physiological changes. However, saying that we feel guilty or ashamed or embarrassed most often references a mental state, which we take as leading us to offer an apology.

This tendency to interpret private sensations as mental states is exacerbated by giving them a proximate causal role in how we respond to environmental circumstances, as the previous example suggests. In the traditional S-O-R model, real or imagined internal events are assumed to be responsible for the individual's reactions to environmental situations. When a long-term relationship falls apart, for example, we learn to say that this makes us depressed, which in turn makes us cry a lot, changes our eating habits, and makes us turn down offers to go out with friends. Even though the failed relationship is admittedly a necessary precondition, it is depression that is taken as the proximate cause of changes in our behavior.

Whether the presumed causes are real sensations or invented mental qualities, explaining behavior in terms of inner causes leads to scientific dead ends. It is especially problematic when the inner causes are invented and therefore lack any physical dimensions. There is no way to investigate such mental qualities, much less disprove their proposed causal role. Furthermore, by implying a satisfactory explanation, they tend to discourage looking for better accounts of behavior.

The risk of attributing the causes of behavior to inner variables is only marginally lessened when they are physical sensations we can privately detect. Even though the sensations are real, we must still explain their origins, and this search must lead us outside the organism to the environment. What distracts us from doing this is our preference for describing the private events as preceding our reactions. With our bias toward viewing causation in terms of mechanical principles, we take this private event-public event sequence as causal. However, this assumption begs the question of what causes the private event. For example, it may indeed be that experiencing stomach pangs after going hours without eating leads us to announce, even if only to ourselves, that we are hungry. We have simply been taught by our verbal community to respond in this way to such stimuli. Even so, if we leave the question of what caused the stomach pangs unanswered, or if we assume that they are caused by other private events (for instance, that our private sensations are somehow generated by our mind), we limit our ability to explain behavior by creating an insurmountable barrier to scientific progress.

In fact, both the physical sensations at the root of what we call feelings and our responses may be explained in terms of the same environmental events. Going for a run on a hot summer day leads to both the feeling of being thirsty and the behavior of saying that we are thirsty and other behavior such as looking for a water fountain. There is only one set of facts: running in hot weather, followed by the sensation of thirst *and* the behavior of trying to find some water. Both outcomes result from the same environmental operation. Just because one outcome (the sensation of thirst) is private and seems to precede the other (looking for water) is not a sufficient basis for concluding that the behavioral outcome may be fully explained in terms of the private sensation.

Learning to Respond to Private Events

One of the basic procedural requirements for training a new skill is the timely occurrence of the reinforcer. The trainer must deliver the reinforcer immediately after the learner emits a correct response. Of course, this means that the trainer must judge whether each response meets performance requirements. Under typical training scenarios, this is not usually difficult. The trainer should have already decided what constitutes a correct response, even in shaping procedures for which the criteria for reinforcement gradually change across trials.

What makes a response correct is that it serves the function of increasing the likelihood of reinforcement. A functional response must not only take a useful form, it must occur under appropriate conditions. If a trainer is teaching a child with intellectual disabilities to say the name of presented objects, correct responses must not only be understandable to listeners, they must occur only in the presence of appropriate objects. The child must say "spoon" only when the spoon is presented, for example. Because the trainer is presenting the spoon, there is no question about when saying spoon is a correct response.

This is all quite straightforward, but how does this work when the trainer cannot know whether a response is being emitted under the appropriate conditions? If the trainer could only hear the child say "spoon" but could not see whether the response was being emitted in the presence of a spoon, how would the trainer know whether to deliver the reinforcer? If the child earned reinforcers for saying "spoon" regardless of whether a spoon was present, the resulting performance might be correct in form (others could understand the word) but incorrect in context (spoken when there is no spoon or when the response is otherwise inappropriate). If it occurred in the wrong context, saying "spoon" would be unlikely to produce reinforcers. In technical terms, this kind of training scenario makes it difficult to establish good stimulus control, and the presence of the spoon is not a reliable discriminative stimulus for correct responses.

It might have already occurred to you that this is the challenge of teaching children to respond appropriately to private events. As trainers, parents may know the form of the responses they want to teach their child (describing private sensations in particular ways), but they cannot know when those responses are being emitted under appropriate private stimulus conditions. Without access to the child's internal sensations, it is difficult to know when to reinforce verbal responses that are supposed to describe those sensations. Parents may reinforce what they hope are tacts of bodily sensations but that are not occurring in the presence of the appropriate private events. The risk of training errors is considerable, and a child's self-descriptive repertoire is likely to be slower to develop and under weaker stimulus control than their behavior of describing public events.

Consider the task of teaching a young child to report when she has a stomach ache. The parents notice that the child does not seem to be well. Perhaps she is quiet, pale, or may not be interested in eating a favorite food. Under these conditions, the parents may prompt what they hope are appropriate descriptive reactions, such as "Does your tummy hurt?" If the child responds affirmatively or makes a similar statement, the parents will probably respond with comforting words, physical affection, and intended remedies, all of which are likely to be positive reinforcers. Sometimes the child may not be experiencing any stomach discomfort, but with the benefit of supplementary evidence (vomiting), the parents will often deliver reinforcers appropriate for correct descriptions. Over repeated trials, in spite of variations in the actual sensations that may be present when saying that her tummy hurts, the child learns to tact stomach aches. With further training, more refined stimulus control may develop, allowing differential responding to nausea versus abdominal pain, for instance.

The stimulus control over verbal descriptions of private sensations remains weak for all of us for reasons already mentioned. Physicians are especially likely to see this shortfall. They necessarily ask patients to describe physical sensations in detail. Differences in our individual learning histories result in widely varying reports from one person to another, which limits the usefulness of this kind of information. For example, people are likely to describe pain sensations quite differently. Some may have an elaborate pain vocabulary, and others may not be nearly as responsive.

Worse, such reports may occur under other sources of control. For instance, a child may describe a tummy ache and thereby avoid school or gain access to reinforcers when no such sensations are present. Even as adults, we sometimes reference bodily conditions for the same reasons—to avoid aversive unpleasant circumstances or to obtain reinforcement. So, we say we have a headache in order to avoid an unwanted social obligation or to get sympathetic reactions from others. Of course, lacking access to our private events, others can only suspect inappropriate stimulus control, but the possibilities make us cautious about how we respond to descriptions of each other's private events. We might even assess the contingencies and believe the person is lying.

The means by which we learn to discriminate private events, given that no one else can identify them, requires explanation. In general, the most common instructional approach involves the verbal community having access to features that are more or less consistently associated with what the learner is experiencing privately. For example, there are often public accompaniments of the private event or collateral responses associated with it (Skinner, 1953). If parents notice their child scratching a reddish spot, they are likely to say something like "That itches, doesn't it?" Over a number of trials involving varied public evidence likely to be associated with the sensation we call itching, the child learns to tact the private sensation consistent with practices in the verbal community. The key is that the parents can take advantage of public accompaniments and collateral responses to a presumed private event to guide their delivery of social reinforcers. Even if there is no evidence on the skin that might suggest an itching sensation, the mere fact that they observe the child scratching is likely to prompt parents to teach the child that what they are feeling is called itching.

Again, this method is not foolproof. If the public event (scratching) occurs in the absence of the private event (itching sensations), such discrimination training can go awry. Furthermore, the task itself is complex because our ability to detect exactly what is going on in our bodies is pretty limited. In addition, these physical sensations vary from occasion to occasion, as well as across individuals. When these challenges are added to the difficulty others have in knowing when responses are under appropriate control by private stimulation, the training contingencies for teaching us to identify and describe our private events can only be described as inconsistent. Nevertheless, we eventually learn the culturally sanctioned repertoire, though our ability to "know ourselves" is weak compared to our skills in describing public events.

It may by now have occurred to you that if our verbal community did not teach us to discriminate our private events, we would not even be aware of them. It is the verbal community that makes private sensations important to us through its reinforcement practices. Although it is commonly assumed that we know ourselves better than others do, it is actually others who teach us about ourselves. As we will see in Chapter 4, the social contingencies required to teach us to describe our sensations have effects well beyond merely labeling aches and pains. They give us what we call awareness and a sense of self. If we did not experience such contingencies, or were unable to profit from them, we would fail to acquire a self-descriptive repertoire. As already noted, we see this shortcoming in children who have been reared under conditions of extreme social deprivation, as well as in individuals who are severely intellectually disabled.

Traits, Attitudes, Moods, and All That Other Stuff

The list of human qualities identified by our verbal community seems nearly endless. Most seem to have private dimensions and are seen as existing in a mental world. The general assumption is that the individual possesses various inherent qualities that may on occasion be reflected in his or her behavior. Although we may grant

BOX 3.8

The Private Life of Your Dog

Box 3.6 points out that there is no reason to assume that non-human species, including our pets, engage in the behavior we call thinking. They simply do not have access to a verbal community from which they could learn a verbal repertoire. Although they respond to at least some of our commands, what they hear are sounds, not words. In fact, you can modify your "words" by changing all but their key features (typically the vowel sound and tone of voice) and they will still be effective in getting your dog to do what you want. (Just say "It" the same way you usually say "Sit," and you will probably get the same result from your faithful beast.) In fact, other stimuli such as your posture, facial expression, and features of the situation that usually accompany the command may be as effective as what you say in producing the desired outcome.

Our dogs and cats are no different than other animals, but our familiarity with them makes it especially difficult to imagine them simply responding to their environment in a non-sentient manner. We are used to talking about them and to them as if they were human. We assume they are aware of their own behavior and environmental circumstances in the same way we are. As we will see in Chapter 4, however, we learn to observe and describe our own behavior from a verbal community, an advantage our pets do not share. As a result, they do not respond to their own behavior in the same way we do. They merely respond to what is going on around them.

When you open a can of yummy seafood dinner with the electric can opener and your cat comes running, switching his tail and meowing frantically, he is not anticipating a treat. His behavior is controlled by biological variables and learning history, not mental processes. Although we might operationalize anticipation as a coordinated set of biological and behavioral changes under certain environmental conditions, it would be a grave error to reify the term or give it causal status. All that is really there are stimuli and responses connected by a complex history of learning processes. As humans, what our verbal community gives us is the advantage of learning to respond to our own behavior.

that these qualities can be influenced by experience, they are often assumed to have an immutable character rooted in each individual's personality, however much it may evolve as we go through life. Furthermore, our colloquial dialect often assigns these qualities a causal role in our behavior. We say that a friend is upset with a store clerk because she has a domineering personality, that a child is being fussy because he is in a bad mood, or that we apologized to a friend because we were ashamed of something we said. These verbal practices are examples of mentalism.

Behavior analysts face the challenge of translating this colloquial dialect into the parsimonious language of science. This exercise necessarily begins with abandoning mental fictions in favor of the physical reality of behavior. Although it may at first be difficult to confront what might seem to be the loss of cherished human qualities, all that is discarded is the way we were taught by the culture to talk about behavior. For behavioral scientists and science-based ABA practitioners, behavior is all there is to talk about anyway, aside from its biological underpinnings. Let us work through a few of these "qualities" to see what is really there and how to talk about behavior instead.

Traits, for example, are taken as more or less enduring characteristics of an individual. Traits have to do with variations in our behavior over time and are ways of characterizing features of an individual's repertoire. They are, in effect, merely summary descriptions of many samples of a person's behavior. When we ascribe a trait to someone based on our experiences with them, we are doing no more than tacting many particular observations of their behavior. If we say that Charles is argumentative, what we probably "mean" is that we have often seen him disagree with others, that he often tries to convince others of his position, that he does not let a topic die until he has had the last word, and so forth. What we imply by describing his behavior as a trait is that we have seen him act like this often and over an extended period of time and that this characterization should therefore be a decent predictor of his behavior. Of course, there is nothing wrong with summarizing our observations by assigning such a label to Charles. It certainly saves a long-winded recitation of his argumentative history each time such a reference is called for, and this shorthand may be sufficient for casual conversational purposes. Then again, summarizing a portion of someone's repertoire in terms of a trait is often too general to accurately predict specific behavior across different circumstances.

The real problem with talking about people in terms of traits, however, is assuming that they are real entities in a mental universe and serve as causes for behavior, rather than just summaries. Instead of adjectives—introverted, happy-go-lucky, disorganized—we tend to make traits nouns, which encourages us to imply that they are real phenomena, at least in a mental sense, and can therefore be causes for the labeled behavior. Colloquial phraseology is replete with such implied causal status. Roberto keeps to himself *because* he is introverted. Sarah is always ready with a smile *because* she is happy-go-lucky. Brian is often late *because* he is disorganized. Assigning traits causal status is both unwarranted and problematic. Although we like to think we understand why people act in certain ways, making the tendency to behave in a particular way its own cause obviously fails to advance our understanding of that same tendency. Inventing an underlying force that is supposed to drive our actions only distracts us from wondering about the true origins of behavior, which lie largely in our history of environmental contingencies.

Attitudes seem similar to traits and share the same problems. When we describe someone as having a certain attitude toward a topic, we are again summarizing a number of samples of behavior over time. Perhaps the major difference between attitudes and traits is that attitudes are usually acknowledged as more transitory than traits. The connotation of the terms suggests that traits are more fundamental to someone's personality, whereas attitudes may change with experience. You may

BOX 3.9

Predicting From Effect to Effect

Skinner (1953) pointed out a number of issues involved in using tests of various sorts as a basis for predicting behavior under particular circumstances. These tests are often verbal exercises in which the respondent answers written questions by choosing from alternative answers or filling in blanks with a written response. They may even involve performing in some way, such as when a dentist must fill a patient's cavity as part of a licensing examination.

Tests are designed to predict a kind of performance that is not fully observed under typical conditions or even not observed at all. In the case of a performance exam, such as that required of dental candidates, the behavior sampled may be quite similar to the behavior the test results are supposed to predict. However, tests most often require only a sample of verbal behavior, even though other kinds of behavior will be predicted from this sample. For example, the MMPI (Minnesota Multiphasic Personality Inventory) is composed of hundreds of true-false statements to which the test taker responds. Although MMPI results are supposed to assess personality structure and psychopathology, there is at least an implicit prediction that observed behavior will be consistent with these features.

Test results are usually aggregated in some way. They may be summarized as one or two scores, which is common on tests designed to predict academic capabilities. Results on the Graduate Record Examination are reported as scores on verbal reasoning, quantitative reasoning, and analytical writing. Tests administered to assess personality variables may be summarized in terms of scores on various traits or personality characteristics.

Skinner's concern is that the behavioral prediction involved in most tests is not from cause to effect but from effect to effect. To understand his point, consider that the implicit assumption underlying most tests is that they measure personal qualities than can be assumed to cause the behavior that test results are supposed to predict. If valid, this assumption would mean the prediction is from cause (the sampled quality) to effect (the result of that quality operating under future circumstances). Further complicating this kind of prediction is that the specified qualities that are supposedly playing a causal role are often created by statistical processes, given labels consistent with underlying theoretical models, and assigned mental status.

Skinner argues that the problem with this causal assumption lies in ignoring the variables that explain both the behavior on the test and the behavior of predictive interest. The prediction involved in testing is actually from effect to effect because both the test performance and the predicted performance are the effects of environmental variables, which are not usually evaluated in testing.

It is not that tests may not sometimes be useful in predicting behavior. It is often easier to sample behavior in a convenient format rather than observe the behavior of ultimate interest under realistic conditions, and the predictive performance of some tests may suit limited purposes. However, we should admit we do not usually

> learn anything about the influences on the predicted behavior from approaching it this way. Merely knowing that a certain score predicts good job performance, for example, does not tell the employer what makes an employee effective or how to remediate any performance problems that may emerge over time. For this, we would need to know the factors that actually affect work behavior in context.

have a certain attitude toward a political issue, for instance, but your views might change as you learn more and debate the topic with friends. As with traits, there is nothing wrong with characterizing someone's behavior with reference to particular attitudes as long as those attitudes are not assumed to cause the very behavior they summarize.

Moods are similar to traits and attitudes, except that they suggest even more short-lived behavioral tendencies. When we describe someone as being in a bad mood, we are labeling behavior just as we label other events. Reference to a bad mood involves both a summary characterization that saves specifying behavioral details and an implicit prediction about the kind of behavior we might expect to see in the immediate future. All this works moderately well for everyday discourse but is again problematic when we imply that "being in a bad mood" is the cause of the behavior that leads us to such a description in the first place.

In sum, traits, attitudes, moods, and similar references involve verbal behavior about behavior, whether ours or someone else's. Such statements may function as tacts, **intraverbals**, or mands. As such, they are established and maintained as social behavior under control of verbal communities (Guerin, 1994). Their conversational convenience should not mask the fact that they are only crude summaries of past behavior and weak predictors of future actions. Most importantly, they are not mental entities and do not serve as causes for behavior.

WHAT TO DO ABOUT MENTALISM

This discussion of mentalistic terms could go on and on, but there are obviously too many invented mentalistic causes of behavior in colloquial dialect to review and rephrase each of them here, nor is such an exercise necessary. With practice, it is not difficult to learn to catch mentalistic terms and phrases in daily language that slip by everyone else unnoticed. This is the first step on the road to recovery—to recognize mentalistic talk and its implications, even when they are subtle. You will quickly discover that it is hard to talk about behavior in ordinary language without being mentalistic again and again. This should suggest that there is no point in trying to convince others of the error of their ways; you will only damage your social life and confirm their worst suspicions about behavior analysis. However, it is important that you learn to root out mentalism in your professional dialect. You should get to the point that you can switch from colloquial to professional dialect in the middle of a sentence just as easily as bilingual speakers go back and forth between languages.

The second step is to learn how to rephrase "mentalisms" in a way that focuses on what can be observed about the behavior at issue in its past and present environmental context. The general approach is to ask, "What do we 'mean' when we say _____?" As discussed previously, the best way to answer this question is to begin by considering the sources of control over our verbal behavior. That is, when we reference a personal quality and imply that it may serve as a mental cause for behavior, what about behavior are we actually observing? If we describe Anna as being irritable, implying that this is an internal quality that underlies her behavior from day to day, we are not actually observing a quality of irritability as we would a physical phenomenon. All we can actually detect is Anna's behavior, some of which our verbal community has taught us to label as "irritable" behavior.

So, what do we mean when we say that Anna is irritable? What about her behavior prompts us to describe her that way but not someone else? The pertinent behavior probably includes her frowning a lot, complaining, starting arguments, and so forth. Although we all act this way some of the time, we are likely to emit the verbal response "irritable" if someone acts this way much more than usual. Of course, making the adjective a noun (irritability) invites the implication that irritability is at least a mental entity, if not a physical quality. In the absence of supporting physical evidence, most people are content to place irritability in a convenient mental realm. The further step of inventorying such mental qualities with psychological tests, documented with various statistical exercises, lends an aura of scientific legitimacy to this sort of reasoning. It is a short and seemingly obvious step to assigning these qualities a causal role for the very behavior that prompted us to invent the underlying quality in the first place.

Third, with a newfound understanding of the sources of control over our mentalistic talk, the challenge is to systematically replace it with more appropriate scientific vocabulary, at least under professional circumstances. It is not enough merely to insist that you now understand the problem of mentalism. If you do, then you understand how important it is to replace your colloquial dialect about behavior with a professional dialect rooted in the science of behavior. This transition is important because how we describe and explain behavior cannot be separated from how we address behavior on the job. As suggested by the vignette at the beginning of this chapter, a practitioner who is comfortable speaking about behavior in everyday terms in his or her work is unlikely to offer employers and clients the full capabilities of the science and technology. In contrast, a practitioner who approaches behavior with a ready professional dialect is unlikely to be misled by vernacular language, has already figured out what is really going on with behavior instead, and is in a position to guide others to his or her point of view and clinical judgments.

In sum, addressing the challenge of mentalism in daily practice involves (1) recognizing mentalistic terms, phrases, and reasoning in professional situations;

(2) figuring out what about the behavior we actually observe underlies mentalistic talk and how to bring this understanding to the forefront while restricting mentalistic language to more social circumstances; and (3) incorporating a science-based dialect about behavior into professional interchanges, at least with other ABA professionals. As always, we must judge how to balance the use of professional and colloquial dialects with different audiences, taking into consideration what will make us an effective speaker in each situation. In some instances, technically correct language may alienate a listener who is unprepared for the practitioner's approach. In other instances, rephrasing vernacular phrases into appropriate behavioral terms may help convince a listener to support the practitioner's agenda.

What need not be part of this challenge is trying to develop the perfect behavioral translation of various mental entities. The examples of traits, attitudes, and moods are briefly considered in the previous section only to show the general nature of this kind of exercise, but there is a subtle trap in taking the task of rephrasing mental terms into behavioral explanations too seriously. Just because our colloquial dialect seems to distinguish particular mental qualities is not sufficient justification for assuming that they thereby require distinctive behavioral explanations. Even though behavior analysts reject the implicit reification of the many mental referents in our everyday vocabulary, it is tempting to accept the challenge of explaining what they might mean in behavioral terms. This is something of a fool's errand, however. Not only are vernacular references to such mental qualities uselessly vague and inconsistent, the attention they have received from the social sciences has not imbued them with clarity and utility. It is not that there are no interesting behavioral phenomena underlying these casual references to human nature, but that these mental concepts are unlikely to provide good guidance to researchers about exactly what should be studied. As with much of the way we talk about behavior, they are useful in daily discourse because they are flexible and can thereby accommodate the considerable limitations of our observations and understanding of behavior. The question, "What does _____ mean in behavioral terms?" can prompt entertaining discussion among behavior analysts, but it should not imply that the mere existence of the term should define certain boundaries or even require a behavioral translation.

CHAPTER SUMMARY

1. It is common for people to believe that our actions are controlled by events that take place in our mind, a view we learn from our culture. Our grammar requires an agent for every action, and we typically assume that our mental processes serve this function.

2. Because we are so familiar with proximate causation in daily life, we are comfortable with assuming this causal model for behavior. We are taught to view mental events as the proximate cause of our actions.

3. The proper causal model for behavior is historical. Behavior results from interchanges between an organism and its environment over time. This kind of causation is not obvious and often goes unnoticed.

4. Mentalism is the tendency to look for the causes of behavior in a mental rather than a physical universe, which is a form of mind-body dualism. Mentalistic explanations often use a sample of behavior as the basis for creating a fictional entity or process, which is then proposed as a cause for the behavior.

5. One problem with this approach is the mind-body problem, which asks how something lacking physical dimensions can affect physical events. Another problem is that attributions of behavior to mental events does not explain the behavior, instead inviting inventions of supposed causes that cannot be directly investigated or falsified. Mentalism interferes with efforts to understand behavior by seeming to provide explanations.

6. Mentalistic explanations place the causes of behavior inside the organism. Skinner suggested three types of inner causes: neural, psychic, and conceptual.

7. Unlike public events, which can be detected by others, private events are by definition not public. Skinner argued, however, that there is no reason to assume that private events are different from public events merely because they seem less accessible. His concern is that the science should focus only on events that are real, as opposed to fictional, regardless of any observational challenges.

8. It appears that humans who have a verbal repertoire all engage in the behavior of thinking, though no one can directly observe this behavior in others. It has been useful to view thinking as behavior because it allows us to extend what we already know about verbal behavior and discourages mentalism.

9. Although our thinking behavior may influence our other actions, it is important that we explain thinking behavior in terms of environmental influences so that we avoid the trap of giving it autonomous status. In other words, both thinking and any apparently related actions should be explained in terms of common environmental factors.

10. Although our feelings are private, they may involve real events inside the skin and should not be ignored in a full account of behavior. Our verbal community teaches us to talk about emotions and feelings in problematic ways, often giving them mentalistic features, tying them to certain environmental situations, and giving them a causal role with regard to behavior. Both the physical sensations at the root of what we call feelings and our responses may be explained in terms of the same environmental events.

11. Training children to respond appropriately to private feelings is challenging because parents do not know if a child's verbal behavior is occurring in the presence of the correct sensations. Parents often use public accompaniments of the private event as criteria for when to reinforce the child's statements. This is why our self-descriptive repertoire is weak. The verbal community makes private sensations important to us through its reinforcement practices.

12. Traits, attitudes, and moods are ways of describing more or less enduring characteristics of an individual's repertoire. Such references have a crude summary utility but are especially troublesome when offered as explanations for the behavior they summarize.

13. Addressing the challenge of mentalism in daily practice involves (1) recognizing mentalistic terms, phrases, and reasoning in professional situations; (2) figuring out what about the behavior we actually observe underlies mentalistic talk and how to bring this understanding to the forefront while restricting mentalistic language to more social circumstances; and (3) incorporating a science-based dialect about behavior into professional interchanges, at least with other ABA professionals.

TEXT STUDY GUIDE

1. Describe the reasons why mentalistic explanations of behavior are so appealing.
2. How does our experience with mechanical causation influence our use of mentalistic explanations of behavior?
3. What is the appropriate causal model for behavior?
4. What is mentalism? How is it dualistic?
5. Explain the mind-body problem.
6. Explain why mentalistic explanations of behavior do not really explain anything.
7. Describe Skinner's three types of inner causes.
8. Distinguish between public and private events. Why is the distinction not really meaningful for the study of behavior?
9. Defend the view that thinking is behavior. Why is it useful to consider thinking as behavior?
10. Explain whether thinking should be considered as a cause of behavior and why.
11. Why should feelings be viewed as real, though private events?
12. Describe three reasons our everyday references to feelings can be misleading.
13. Explain why it is a problem to view feelings as causes of our behavior.

14. Explain the challenges the verbal community faces in teaching children to respond to their feelings.

15. Describe both common and distinguishing features of traits, attitudes, and moods. Why is it problematic to give them causal status?

16. Explain how behavior analysts address the challenges of mentalism in daily practice.

BOX STUDY GUIDE

1. Describe the distinction between molecular and molar perspectives in explaining behavior.

2. Explain why the neurological events associated with any action might best be viewed as correlates rather than explanations of behavior.

3. What is a homunculus?

4. What is wrong with saying that someone is showing their intelligence when they score well on a test?

5. Why do ABA practitioners working with developmentally disabled individuals pay little attention to IQ scores?

6. Defend the argument that organisms that lack a verbal repertoire do not think.

7. Who was Gilbert Ryle and why is he often referenced by behavior analysts in discussions of mentalism?

8. Explain why talking to or about our pets (or other animals) as if they were human is conceptually problematic.

9. Explain the difference in predicting behavior from effect to effect versus cause to effect.

10. Why do tests involve predicting behavior from effect to effect?

DISCUSSION TOPICS AND EXERCISES

1. Consider how the cultural practice of explaining behavior in terms of mental events causes problems in our legal system.

2. When we say that someone feels guilty and that their actions are motivated by this feeling, what do we mean? How might we talk about what is going on without buying into the mentalistic implication that guilt is an underlying cause of behavior?

3. Select a few terms or phrases that raise issues of mentalism and analyze the sources of control over such verbal behavior. Specify how you can talk instead about the behavior of interest in each instance.

SUGGESTED READINGS

Guerin, B. (1994). Attitudes and beliefs as verbal behavior. *The Behavior Analyst, 17*, 155–163.

Moore, J. (1980). On behaviorism and private events. *Psychological Record, 20*, pp. 459–475.

Moore, J. (2008). *Conceptual foundations of radical behaviorism*. Cornwall-on-Hudson, NY: Sloan Publishing. (Chapter 14: Opposition to mentalism)

Skinner, B. F. (1953). *Science and human behavior*. New York: MacMillan. (Chapter III: Why organisms behave; Chapter XIII: Function versus aspect; Chapter XVII: Private events in a natural science)

Chapter 4

Seeing Yourself

At the agency where she worked, Julie shared an office with a colleague, Adam, whom she really liked. He was casual and friendly and had a sly sense of humor. He was the psychologist for the agency and had different duties than she did. As a BCBA, she worked with children with autism, their families, and school systems, while he focused on adults who had mental health and substance abuse issues.

Adam had a bit of background in behavior analysis, but he was the first to acknowledge he was no expert, and he did not overstep the implicit boundary. She found it easy to reciprocate and not pretend she was trained in psychology. Maybe this was one of the reasons they got along so well, even to the point that they had no problem occasionally arguing about differences in their points of view on matters.

One afternoon, Adam was complaining about the difficulties of getting his substance abuse clients to follow his admonitions to avoid circumstances that might encourage problematic activities. Julie couldn't resist pointing out what to her seemed obvious: "But why do you think they would follow your recommendations? There must be lots of reinforcers associated with their friends and the things they're used to doing together."

"Yes, but they've got to learn some self-control," he responded. "If they can't resist the temptations that get them into trouble, they'll never stop using."

Julie persisted. "But what would make them change their lifestyle? What are you depending on to make your therapy work? Just laying out some rules and making sure they understand their rationale isn't really going to do it, in most cases anyway, I'm guessing."

"I'm trying to teach them some self-control. If they can't learn to manage their own behavior, there isn't much I can do," Adam replied. "They're going to have to learn to listen to their inner voice that tells them what they've learned in therapy."

Julie just couldn't let this one go. "Inner voice? It sounds like you're thinking there is a person inside who is telling them what to do and not do. Talk about mentalism!"

"Of course there is, at least metaphorically," he said with some confidence. "You surely don't believe there is no inner self. Our private self is at the heart of who we are and

what we do. We talk with ourselves all the time, and behavior analysts are no exception. I know about reinforcement and all, but where do you think our behavior comes from? Not just from reinforcement. It comes from who we are inside."

"And the evidence for this?" Julie asked. "Don't you think we're just making up this inner person and giving it all this power? I agree we talk with ourselves, but is that anything different than talking to others? The fact that we talk 'to ourselves' doesn't mean there is a separate person who is listening and then telling us what to do" she said using air quotes.

Adam didn't have a rejoinder for this; he seemed amazed that Julie believed there was no such thing as a self. "Boy, that's really a minority point of view," he said. "I mean, there's a huge literature based on the concept of a self. How can you ignore all of that?"

"It's not too hard, actually," she said breezily. "Everybody used to think the world was flat, too."

LEARNING TO TALK ABOUT OURSELVES

Our Verbal Community

When we refer to ourselves in the first person ("I'd like to go hiking this weekend."), we are saying something about who we are. Such phrasing implies a "self" as a kind of person within us that we can report about. We may even describe conversations we have with our self, as if we can talk with this inner person (see Box 3.3). We often talk as if our private self is the source of our preferences, opinions, feelings, and thoughts, almost in the sense that they are what they are, and we cannot do anything but report on them. In other words, this inner person or homunculus is seen as a source of private causes of our behavior. Although we may often be able to point to obvious external influences, in their absence we have no hesitation in deferring to a private self as the source of our actions. So, when we say, "I'd like to go hiking this weekend," the "I" implies a causal entity that seemingly explains our desire for going hiking this weekend.

Using the interpretive approach described at the end of the last chapter, we can examine the sources of control over this sort of verbal behavior. First, however, we should agree that there is no direct evidence of the physical existence of a self or inner entity that directs our actions. Although our everyday dialect implies such a motive force, this kind of talk is simply part of our verbal repertoire, learned as we were growing up. Retreating to the position that this causal source is not physical but must be assigned to a mental universe does not legitimize the colloquial argument, given the many problems associated with mentalism.

We learn to make first person references as we are learning to talk about our public behavior. We describe our overt behavior in the same way we describe the behavior of others. The only difference is that we describe our behavior as the action of the first person singular pronoun "I," as in, "I went to the zoo today." A child learns this style of self-description or grammar just as he or she learns other verbal behavior. Endless modeling, prompting, correcting, and reinforcing underlies all acquisition of our verbal repertoire, though the full story is much more complicated. As Chapter 2 emphasizes, however, it is fundamentally quite simple—our verbal repertoire is entirely learned.

We learn to describe what seems to be our private behavior from these same social contingencies, even though, as the previous chapter pointed out, the verbal community suffers the notable disadvantage of lacking access to our private events. The resulting vocabulary implies a private world in which experiences are processed and reactions directed. Phrases such as "Tell me what you are thinking," "What were you thinking?," "Have you decided yet?," and "How do you feel about this?" encourage the view that "you" is an inner person—a self—that can be consulted and that is ultimately responsible for our actions.

It is easy to see parents teaching their children to talk this way. They not only model and teach proper use of pronouns (I versus he, she, or you) but a self-descriptive repertoire that references both public and private experiences. When parents ask, "What did you eat for breakfast this morning?," they are teaching a child to observe and describe his or her behavior as a public event, no different than other public events. Such exercises may seem the same as asking, "What would you like to do after lunch?," except that there is not yet any public behavior to be observed in this instance. If the child has adequate verbal skills, such a question may prompt thinking about possible activities. The kind of answer that will be reinforced will be similar to a report about breakfast—a description of events. However, in describing after-lunch events that have not yet occurred, the child learns to talk about his or her covert verbal behavior in a manner that suggests that it is guided not by public events but by a mental process. To others, saying "I ate cereal for breakfast" seems to be a simple description of a public fact. In contrast, in the absence of any evidence others can observe, "I want to go to the park" seems to be a similar report, but of private mental activity instead of public behavior. The eventual self-descriptive repertoire we learn implies that a world of private causes lies inside our mind that is similar to the public world that we share with others.

Who Do You Think You Are?

Most people would consider this an easy question. Who does not feel they know themselves pretty well? After all, we are around ourselves all the time and have the advantage of what seems to be an inside view of our experiences. True, our perspective is a bit biased. We "see" our behavior through our own eyes, so to speak, and others might find our answer to the question self-serving. However, even your friends would probably admit that no one can know you as well as you do.

Nevertheless, what you have read so far suggests that the answer to the question, "Who do you think you are?" lies in the contingencies established by our verbal community. We are who our verbal community tells us we are. How could it be otherwise? Our self-descriptive repertoire is fully acquired from our verbal community. It is this verbal community (more correctly, a number of different verbal communities throughout our lives) that teaches us to observe and describe our own behavior, both public and private. What we see of ourselves, what is important to us, what we are aware of, all come from the verbal contingencies maintained by these communities. The proper answer to the question, "Who do you think you are?" is "Who I think I am is no more than what my verbal communities have taught me to respond to about myself."

If we did not participate in a verbal community, or were not able to learn well from such experiences, we would not learn how to talk or think and would have no sense or awareness of ourselves. We would otherwise behave as our learning history directed us but would lack what we call a "personal perspective" toward our experiences. We would behave but would not be aware of our behavior, as hard as this is to imagine. We can see this result in babies, who have not yet learned the verbal repertoire required to benefit from such social interchanges, and in individuals with severe or profound intellectual disabilities, who have great difficulty learning a useful verbal repertoire.

In other words, our verbal community not only determines our self-perceptions but, in the process, creates the very notion that there is a self. We would not learn to

---

BOX 4.1

The Sum of Who We Are

In common parlance, personality refers to the sum total of who we are. We say that each person has a personality that others may characterize based on their experiences with the person. We may modify the term with trait-like adjectives, such as when we say someone has a happy or moody or aggressive personality. We may take this further by suggesting that people have different or multiple personalities depending on the circumstances, which allows us to adapt our characterizations to different samples of behavior without fear of contradicting ourselves. The often unspoken implication is that someone's personality underlies what they do. We may sometimes make the causal relation explicit, as when we say that a friend offers to help us move to a new apartment because he has a really helpful personality, but that does no more than lend causal status to the very behavior we are trying to explain. What we are really saying is that he is helpful because he is helpful. More often, the causal role of personality is no more than vague and assumed.

In effect, the everyday notion of personality is more or less synonymous with the idea of a self. As such, it enshrines mentalism as the core concept underlying our behavior. The causes of behavior are assumed to somehow lie inside each of us (in our personality), playing an unavoidably causal role in the behavior we display. Whatever we label this supposedly causal force, it interferes with understanding the contribution of physical variables that can be understood scientifically and used to modulate behavior in practical ways.

observe our own behavior unless social contingencies taught us to respond to it. It is only because others find it useful for us to respond discriminatively to our behavior, both public and private, that they reinforce our behavior of observing and describing it. Such contingencies would not exist without the participation of others.

This means that we only learn to observe what is important to our verbal community. It teaches us whether and how to respond to certain bodily sensations, for example. We learn to respond to what we call pain sensations with an elaborate vocabulary. However, there are considerable variations in this descriptive repertoire across cultures (Zborowski, 1969). For example, what is happening with a woman's body in childbirth is the same the world over, but women respond to the experience differently from one culture to another. The fact that we learn operant responses to pain sensations means that the extent to which we are aware of them is a function of our verbal community, which teaches us to attend to such sensations in certain ways.

What we learn to observe about our own behavior creates a perspective that is uniquely our own. Our personal perspective is merely our behavior of observing our own behavior. It is the constancy and uniformity of seeing from your own perspective that makes it seem so obvious that there really is a "you" inside that does the seeing and that is also available to act as a mental cause for your behavior. In fact, you cannot really take another person's perspective. You cannot help but take your perspective when seeing from their perspective. You cannot step outside of yourself and look back to see yourself from a different perspective because you cannot escape your own perspective. Although we cannot experience our perspective as a thing, we tend to give it noun-like qualities and assume the implied self plays a guiding role in our behavior (Hayes, 1984).

Perception, Awareness, Attention, and Consciousness

As most commonly expressed, when we perceive something, we are aware of it in some way. More behaviorally, if we are aware of or attending to an event, it means that we are responding to it in some way, even if our response is merely observational. To appreciate what this means, consider that we often respond to events without attending to them. For example, we have all had the experience of realizing that we have been driving our car for a few moments without being aware of our actions. We know we were engaging in minimally necessary driving behavior during this hopefully brief period, but we might admit we were not aware of our driving behavior while it was occurring, scary as the thought may be. Even when we are paying attention to our driving, we are not usually aware of each of the many different responses involved in this complex activity from one moment to the next. For instance, we vary the position of the throttle or steering wheel almost continuously without realizing it in reacting to traffic and road conditions.

When we talk about being aware of something, we mean that we can offer some kind of verbal description of it. A young child just learning to talk may say "Cat!" when he sees a cat in the yard. This is a minimal description, but it will probably be effective in generating social reinforcement from a parent. With improved verbal skills, the child may say "There is a cat" or "Look at the cat." Any such statements would prompt observers to agree that the child is aware of the cat. Merely looking in the direction of the cat would not be sufficient evidence of awareness, however. As exemplified by the driving example, we often look without "seeing." Events may impinge on our sensory systems, and we may respond to these events, but we do not say that we are aware of them unless we can talk about them in some way, even if only to ourselves.

Although this requirement is consistent with how we talk about awareness, there is certainly some ambiguity in this implicit definition. It may fail to include instances in which someone is indeed aware of events but does not respond publicly to their awareness, perhaps because there is no demand for it. In the absence of such responses, however, observers might not be clear whether the individual is aware of the events in question. Consider a worker using a piece of equipment in a manufacturing facility. Working alone, there is no social occasion for talking about what she is doing and, therefore, no evidence about whether she is focusing on the task. Absent such evidence, whether the worker is aware of what she is doing cannot be determined based solely on her effective use of the equipment. She may at times be as unaware of what she is doing as the person who is unaware of his driving while daydreaming or talking on a cell phone. This possibility explains why we tend to require some form of verbal verification to conclude that a person is attending to or aware of events.

In fact, our self-knowledge is often deficient. We are often unaware of what we have done or are doing and cannot usually describe the variables influencing our behavior. These limitations partly come from competing demands on our attention. We do not always have the opportunity to step back and observe our own behavior, especially in the moment, because the environment usually requires ongoing participation in a situation. However, deficient self-knowledge also arises from a weak learning history. As already discussed, our self-knowledge is inherently inadequate because of the difficulties faced by our verbal community in teaching us a self-descriptive repertoire without having adequate access to our private events. It also misdirects our observations. Instead of learning to observe our behavior in the context of past and current contingencies, our verbal community teaches us to focus on the role of private events and describe the apparent outcome in mental terms. So we say that we "had an idea" about something, usually without being able to articulate the variables that might have influenced our behavior.

If we are aware of something, we may also say that we are conscious of it. In other words, we tend to talk about awareness and consciousness in the same way.

We say we are conscious of events or our own behavior when we can talk about them, even if only to ourselves. As a way of talking about the nature of environmental stimuli controlling our behavior from one moment to another, the notion of consciousness or awareness may seem vague but at least conversationally convenient. However, these concepts become harmful to our understanding of behavior when they imply an inner person that mediates interchanges between the external world and an inner world. Abandoning the idea that there is a mind overseen by such a homunculus eliminates the customary meaning of concepts such as perception, awareness, or consciousness. We are instead left with concrete questions about the sources of environmental control over our behavior, a topic fully within the realm of a physical science.

THE BEHAVIOR OF SENSING

The Role of Reinforcement History

One of the things that encourages us to talk about a personal mental world governed by a "self" is the fact that the sensations that tell us about our interface with the environment are private. It is, therefore, not surprising that we learn to talk about these sensations as mental events that are experienced or processed by this self. In fact, seeing, hearing, tasting, smelling, and touching involve both physiological and behavioral components. To appreciate the distinction, consider that at any moment our eyes, like a camera, capture every feature or aspect of a scene that light waves reveal. However, we "see" only certain things in a scene. Of all the things a camera lens would reveal, we attend to or are aware of only what our learning history has made important to us. For example, have you ever taken a photo in which you failed to notice your own shadow intruding in the picture? You "saw" only the features of interest in the camera image when you pressed the shutter button, even though the shadow was unquestionably part of the image striking your eyes. Professional photographers learn a special skill of seeing features in a scene that amateurs often miss.

This learning history saves us from seeing, hearing, or otherwise noticing all of the stimuli impinging on our sensory systems that are not relevant to our immediate behavioral needs. Another way of saying this is that our sensory behavior comes under control of environmental stimuli that our learning history dictates. When we see something, we are engaging in seeing as a behavior that has a rich respondent and operant history. This history creates many interesting effects.

For example, we often see or hear events that are obviously not present. Given a respondent conditioning history, it should not be surprising that a conditioned stimulus can evoke the response of seeing or hearing something even when it is not present. If you live within earshot of train tracks and are accustomed to hearing a train go by around dinnertime, you may be more likely to "hear" the sounds

BOX 4.2

If a Tree Falls in the Forest...

An old and yet still contemporary notion underlying our perceptions of the world is that what we sense is turned into internal copies or representations in our brain and that it is those internal copies that play a role in generating our response to the sensory stimuli. Skinner (1964; 1974) called this idea copy theory—the idea that what we see, in the case of our visual sense, are only copies of the world. This view emphasizes the role of mental transformations of what we sense, which supposedly helps explain discrepancies between what we sense and how we respond. Contemporary psychology is hopelessly mired in this mentalistic morass. There are huge research literatures focusing on the mental processes that are said to be at work storing, retrieving, and otherwise processing "information." Recent advances in techniques for imaging brain activity have only exacerbated this focus by suggesting that these brain images represent such mental processes (Uttal, 2000).

In contrast, behavior analysts find no benefit in inventing internal copies and focusing on related mental storage and processing operations. When we see a car, for instance, proposing that images of the car travel from the eyes to the occipital cortex only presents the new problem of how the brain "sees" the images of the car as such. It is important that researchers with different specializations study the relations among environmental stimuli, the electrical and biochemical activity of the brain, and responding, but taking a mentalistic approach to this challenge makes it difficult to accommodate the role of learning, which provides well-established explanations of how we respond to physical stimuli.

In other words, as Baum (2005) suggests, the behavior analyst's answer to the question of whether a tree falling in a forest makes a sound if no one is there to hear it is "No." A falling tree creates what are informally called sound waves, but these are more properly termed pressure oscillations, not sounds. What we call sound requires not just an organism but one engaged in the behavior of hearing. Labeling a particular sound is no more than tacting our hearing behavior. To argue that a sound exists independently of a listener implies that sounds are internal copies of originating physical stimuli (pressure oscillations within a certain range of frequencies).

of a train one evening at that time when it is instead the sound of a passing truck. The same thing is going on when we "hear" the sound of the surf when holding a conch shell to our ear long after our beach vacation is over. Previous pairings of train sounds at dinnertime or the sound of the ocean when holding a conch shell at the beach evoke a conditioned hearing response, although there is more to this explanation.

Such learning effects can be found in many daily experiences. Our ability to hear a tune "in our heads" is no more than a learned hearing response. The tune need not be present for us to engage in the same hearing behavior we emit when our auditory apparatus is involved. We similarly acquire the history that allows us to "see" scenes or events that are not present or "taste" foods we are not eating. We engage in seeing behavior when we picture a loved one who is absent. We engage in tasting behavior when we imagine the taste of a favorite food. The extent of this repertoire from one person to another depends on not only our experience with different stimuli but how well our verbal community has taught us to respond to our private events.

The behavior of seeing, hearing, or tasting things occurs on a continuum of stimulus control. At one extreme, the actual stimuli are fully present, and at the other they are not present at all. Between these extremes, the actual stimuli may be more or less clear. Conditioned responding becomes more likely when actual stimuli are weaker. We report these differences when, for example, we say "I see Kelly" as opposed to saying "I think I see Kelly" or "She reminds me of Kelly" or "Is that Kelly?"

Not surprisingly, there are many aspects of our sensory learning histories that we all share, which leads to common ways of experiencing the environment. What are calledthe laws of perception are no more than ways of responding to stimuli that are commonly observed within a culture. For example, we usually see circles

---

BOX 4.3

Perchance to Dream

Dreaming is a fascinating phenomenon, but it is unavoidably behavior. When we dream, we are engaging in some of the same behavior we emit when awake. Given the nature of sleep, dreaming tends to primarily involve the behavior of seeing. What is missing, of course, is the things we "see." As this chapter details, viewing seeing and other ways of sensing as having a substantial behavioral component should make this phenomenon much easier to understand. We have already noted that the impact of physical stimuli is joined by learned behavior to produce what we casually call seeing, hearing, and so forth. These skills are emitted under varying degrees of stimulus control, however, which allows for the possibility of engaging in seeing (hearing, etc.) behavior even when the visual stimuli are weak or even nonexistent.

In the case of dreaming, though we may still not fully understand what is going on physiologically, seeing in our dreams is not apparently different from seeing under other circumstances in which the things seen are weak or not present at all, including those times when we say we are seeing a visual image or when we are daydreaming. Absent the level of stimulus control otherwise available when we are awake, it is not surprising that what we see in our dreams is disjointed or even nonsensical. The critical role of stimulus control is easily observed when we are lying in bed dozing during those last few minutes before we must get up. Whatever we are seeing in our dreams immediately disappears when we open our eyes. Our seeing behavior is instantly under the control of whatever visual stimuli are present.

as complete, even if we are briefly shown a circle containing a small gap. When we see the silhouette of two heads facing each other, their outlines forming a vase between them, we may see the silhouettes or the vase, but often not both. There are countless sensory illusions that involve common reactions across observers based on their common learning histories. Although some illusions may depend on certain features of our sensory apparatus, it is not the brain that distorts our senses but our learning history that leads us to respond in ways that do not entirely match physical events.

BOX 4.4

It Depends on Where You Live

If sensory illusions largely result from how our learning history affects our reaction to particular stimuli, we might expect that differences in these histories across cultures would yield systematic cultural variations. This prediction is indeed borne out by many studies, which often focus on optical illusions. You have probably seen the Muller-Lyre illusion, for example. It is composed of two horizontal lines of equal length, one of which has a pair of short 45 lines at each end projecting outward and the other with the same lines projecting inward. The possible illusion is that the upper horizontal line may appear longer than the lower one.

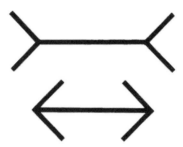

Research has consistently shown that individuals in Western countries responded significantly differently than individuals in non-Western countries. Participants living in the United States and Europe gave more responses supporting the illusion than participants living elsewhere. In reviewing this literature, one research team proposed a "carpentered world" hypothesis. This proposal acknowledges the influence of an extensive history with straight horizontal lines, which may be less prevalent in non-European countries (Segall, Campbell, & Herskovits, 1966). Such cultural variations in responses to optical illusions are consistent with the role of learning history on sensory responding.

Seeing That You Are Seeing

One of the things that encourages the notion of an inner person or self who is doing this sensing is our learned ability to respond to our own behavior of sensing the world around us. Consider the behavior of seeing. As with all other visual creatures, we see merely as a consequence of having a working visual system. Unlike other species, however, humans can learn to "see"—to be aware—that they are seeing. This is an odd way of describing what is going on, of course, because there is only one kind of seeing going on, not two. Our visual system is doing the actual seeing, but when we say that we see something (that is, saying that we see that we are seeing), we are actually saying we are aware that we are engaged in the act of seeing.

What we are doing when we say "I see the red book on the table" is responding to our discriminated visual behavior, that is, to the fact that we are engaged in the behavior of not merely seeing but seeing that particular thing. Remember, of all the stimuli impinging on our eyes at that moment, only some are exerting control because of our learning history. Because of a particular learning history, of all that our eyes capture we respond to only a small portion of those visual stimuli, such as the red book lying on the table. Seeing the book, and not all of the other features of the room, is a result of discrimination training (as well as more immediate environmental variables such as motivating operations) that results in differential responding we might call "seeing the red book," as opposed to seeing other things within our field of view. We learn to respond to particular features of our environment based on differential consequences for seeing them. For example, as children riding in a car, we do not encounter contingencies for attending to the proximity of other cars and are generally unaware of such stimuli. However, when we learn to drive, we acquire considerable skill in attending and responding to these stimuli.

So far, this description would work for any visual species. Your dog also learns to respond visually to particular stimuli more than others. Although its visual system is stimulated by all features in its visual field at any moment, a dog sees a squirrel not only because of biological variables having to do with being a dog but because of a history of reinforcement associated with chasing squirrels. However, it may fail to "see" flowers on a shrub or a bumblebee, even though they are just as available as visual stimuli as is the squirrel. Your dog has learned the differential visual response we might label "seeing squirrels."

What is uniquely human is that we learn to respond to our own discriminative visual behavior of seeing particular things or events. That is, we learn to be aware that we are seeing (or otherwise sensing). At first, an infant merely responds to the visible world in the same way that other species do. However, it soon learns to respond visually to some stimuli more than others, particularly under certain conditions. It may be more likely to see a bottle than other objects, for instance. As the child begins to acquire a modest verbal repertoire, she first learns to respond to

---

BOX 4.5

Seeeing Everything but Nothing

What if you had lost your eyesight as a baby? Naturally, you would not have acquired a lifetime of visual experiences, and visual stimuli would not play a role in your behavior. Now assume that a medical breakthrough allowed your sight to be restored and that your visual system was suddenly fully functional. What would you see?

Lacking any learning associated with visual stimuli, you would see everything but nothing. You would have sight, but you would not have learned seeing as a behavior. You would see everything, like a camera, but you would at first not respond to what you might want to see. That is, you would not recognize what you were seeing because this kind of visual behavior would not have been learned. You would know how books feel from your experience of handling them, but you would at first find it difficult to identify a book just by looking at it. You would also see more than you needed or wanted at any moment because you would lack the learning history that would otherwise bring your seeing behavior more under control of some stimuli rather than others. Upon walking into a room, you would not immediately focus on things pertinent to your being there (a book on a table, for instance) to the exclusion of irrelevant stimuli (all of the other objects in the room). Over time, you would learn to see in the way that sighted individuals do, but it would require acquiring the necessary learning history.

This exercise may be more meaningful in the case of hearing. Thanks to cochlear implant technology, it is now possible for individuals who have been profoundly deaf since birth to receive electrical signals that they can learn to respond to as sounds, though the signals do not faithfully mimic the sensations available to hearing individuals. Such individuals must learn to respond to these signals in the way that hearing individuals have learned to respond to auditory stimuli. The point is that seeing and hearing are kinds of behavior that must be learned.

---

a bird by saying "Bird!" With more parental training ("Look! There is a bird. Do you see the bird?"), instead of merely seeing the bird, or even responding to the bird verbally, she eventually learns to verbally respond to the behavior of seeing a bird by saying, "I see the bird." In other words, the child learns to respond verbally to her discriminative sensing behavior. Of course, this self-descriptive repertoire gradually grows much more complex.

As already discussed, this ability to respond to our own discriminative behavior depends entirely on the existence of a verbal community. It is in the interest of this community that its members learn to describe their private events, so special contingencies have evolved to teach this repertoire. For example, it can be valuable for others to learn that you smell smoke or hear a child crying in another room. Members of other species lack access to a verbal community, so they merely see, hear, and otherwise sense stimuli based on learning histories but are not able to respond to the fact that they are doing so. For example, a dog sees a squirrel but would not encounter contingencies that teach it to respond to the fact that it is engaged in the behavior of seeing a squirrel. Such behavior would be different from merely responding to the squirrel as a visual stimulus by barking or chasing it. In the canine version of awareness, a dog would have to learn some distinctive means of responding to the fact that it is seeing a squirrel, in effect, some way of saying, "I am aware that I am seeing a squirrel."

"Seeing" that you are seeing is part of what we call awareness, and dogs and other animals cannot generally be aware in this way. Although it is obvious that the behavior of seeing squirrels prompts other actions, such as chasing them, to argue that they are therefore aware that they are seeing the squirrel is anthropomorphizing. The fact that a dog barks at a squirrel provides no evidence that it is engaging in the same behavior a child does when it says "I see a bird." The following exercise shows there is good reason to assume that the dog is doing no more than any other animal that simply responds to events in its environment.

In principle, it is possible for you to serve as a verbal community of sorts for your dog by arranging special contingencies that would not otherwise occur for a dog, but it is unlikely that you would provide a history sufficient to create the desired result. You would not have to teach your dog the discriminated behavior of "seeing squirrels." The natural contingencies created by its biology and reinforcement history would take care of that for most dogs. However, to teach it to respond to the fact that at a particular moment it is engaging in the behavior of seeing a squirrel, you would have to provide many trials in which you were pretty clear that this behavior was occurring. As in teaching a child to report what it sees, on each occasion you would then need to prompt and reinforce a self-descriptive response of some sort comparable to a child saying "I see a bird." For a dog this would have to be a behavior within its capabilities that would not otherwise occur naturally. It would be important that this behavior come solely under control of the act of seeing squirrels. This means it should not be an existing behavior already under other sources of control, including those that involve responding to the squirrel itself, for instance by barking or chasing. It must also be a behavior that could not be learned without your explicit training trials. It might not be too hard to arrange these conditions in a laboratory, but they would surely not come together very often under everyday conditions, and they would never occur without your role in arranging reinforcement contingencies. Even if successful, this accomplishment would be only the very beginning of teaching your dog a self-descriptive repertoire comparable to that learned by most humans.

In sum, "seeing" that we are seeing is an example of being aware of our own behavior. Other species merely respond to the world around them, but because of our verbal community, we learn to respond to the fact that we are engaged in

BOX 4.6

This May Hurt a Little Bit

When a doctor gives you this warning, you know you are not going to like what comes next. But what does it mean to be in pain? Surely our answers would be almost the same, and yet most of us have had the experience of suffering some physical trauma but not feeling any pain at the time. We find a bruise or scratch but realize we did not notice the sensation of pain when it happened. In more remarkable instances, people can experience major trauma from a car wreck or on the battlefield but not behave as if they are in pain.

So what is pain then? If it is merely our body reacting to some insult, then why do we respond so inconsistently from one circumstance to another? Rachlin (1985) has argued from a molar perspective (see Box 3.1) that pain is no more than engaging in what might be called pain behavior. From this perspective, being in pain is no more or less than showing pain, whether that involves screaming, limping, complaining, grimacing, and so forth. As with the example of Tim loving football in Box 3.1, Rachlin argues that being in pain is a matter of how often we engage in pain behavior. We would agree that someone is suffering from arthritis pain if we observe pain behavior often and across many situations. If we only hear them complain of being in pain under certain circumstances, such as when asked to help out or when sympathetic friends are around, we might be a bit suspicious about pain complaints. Of course, it might be argued that one can be in pain but not show it, but even privately acknowledging being in pain is itself pain behavior. In other words, being in pain involves showing it in some way, whether to others or just to oneself. If there is no such pain behavior, Rachlin argues that there is no pain. Feeling pain is itself pain behavior.

Rachlin's position is that some of our terms for seemingly mental events (being in love, for example) are really just labels for activities that he proposes should be viewed as molar in character. Being in love or in pain (they only sometimes seem to be the same thing) involves engaging in loving or pain behavior, whether public or private. It is unnecessary and distracting to describe that behavior as "showing" or "revealing" a mental activity or event.

---

what might be called sensory responding. It takes a special kind of contingency to teach this skill, a contingency that only arises in a verbal community to which it is important that its members are able to respond in this way to their own behavior. The contingencies are special in that they require social reinforcement contingent on private responses to which the verbal community has no direct access. Although the resulting self-descriptive repertoire is not without its shortcomings, it allows us to describe what we are experiencing to others, as well as to ourselves.

MANAGING OUR BEHAVIOR

Self-Control

Our ability to describe our private behavior implies that we are also able to control it. Aside from the implicit mentalism, the notion of self-control seems obvious, as it does to Adam in the vignette at the beginning of the chapter. We seem to control our own behavior much as we control the behavior of others. We manipulate the variables that are apparently functionally related to the behavior of interest. Skinner (1953) cataloged some familiar techniques of self-control. For example, we often control our behavior by using various forms of *physical restraint* that make it difficult or impossible to engage in problematic behavior. We put our hands in our pockets to resist biting our fingernails. We wear a sling in order to avoid using an injured arm. We leave a situation so that we will not encounter temptation or behave in a way we might regret. We put money into a piggy bank or a savings account so we will be less likely to spend it.

We may also *change the stimuli* that might otherwise occasion undesired behavior. We put on sunglasses when we go outside on a sunny day so we will not squint. We put freshly baked cookies in a jar out of sight in a cabinet rather than leave them on the counter so we will be less likely to nibble. We shut our eyes at the movies when unpleasant scenes appear so we will not be scared. We put a bookmark in a book we are reading so we will later turn to where we left off. We use a magnifying glass when removing a splinter so we can grasp it successfully. We wear a hearing aid so we can hear more clearly. We make a video when we practice a speech in order to improve our delivery.

We sometimes *manipulate deprivation conditions* to make our behavior more or less likely. We prepare for a big dinner by skipping lunch so we can eat more later. In contrast, we order a big salad with our meal at a restaurant so we will be less likely to order dessert at the end of the meal. We may start a party drinking non-alcoholic beverages so we will be less tempted to consume too much alcohol as the evening wears on. We may eat less at a meal so we will be ready for a bout of physical exercise that is planned afterward.

We may find ourselves *manipulating emotional variables* to manage our behavior. We might remove stimuli that evoke emotional reactions by leaving a situation, such as when we walk away from someone with whom we are having a heated argument. We may bite our tongue so that we do not laugh at an inappropriate moment. We prepare to confront someone who has been bothering us by reviewing the ways they have been rude or unkind to us so as to evoke previous emotional feelings. We lessen our emotional responses to a situation that angers us by delaying a response. We get in the right mood for a concert by listening to the kind of music we will be hearing.

BOX 4.7

A Reminder About MOs

This book is about the philosophy of the science of behavior, not the scientific discoveries themselves, so its themes touch on the mechanisms and processes of behavior only in passing. Nevertheless, talking about behavior without stepping in mentalism's messes requires a thorough understanding of all that research has revealed about how behavior actually works. The contributions of reinforcement contingencies emerge at every turn in these chapters, but it is no less important to emphasize the significant role played by motivating operations (MOs).

A discussion of how we talk about self-control is a good place to remind ourselves of the important role of motivating operations. Many of the examples in this section involve manipulating the environment in ways that increase or decrease the reinforcing effectiveness of some stimulus, object, or event and that similarly change the frequency of behavior that has been reinforced by such stimuli, objects, or events. Of course, these are, in part, the defining features of motivating operations (Michael, 1982, 1993, and 2000). So, we resist taking a nap in the afternoon so that we are more sleep deprived at night and will more easily go to sleep, or we eat lots of low calorie pretzels while waiting in the bar for a table at a restaurant so that we will not order as much food later. These manipulations impact behavior by altering the efficacy of reinforcers or punishers and by changing the likelihood of behavior associated with those consequences.

Sometimes we use *aversive stimulation* to control our behavior. We put the alarm clock on the other side of the room to ensure that we will have to get out of bed to shut off the aversive sound. We scold ourselves for our own bad behavior, saying things that we might find punishing if others said them to us. We make our new year's resolutions public so that breaking them will have aversive social consequences.

We *use drugs or other substances* to modulate the effects of other variables. We take drugs to lessen pain or discomfort or to help us go to sleep at night. We drink caffeinated beverages to make us more energetic. We may consume alcohol for its benefits in lubricating social interchanges, and some may use illegal drugs because they may enhance enjoyment of other activities.

There are many other examples of what is usually described as self-control, but we cannot ignore the reference to the self as the motive origin of such behavior. We have already considered the mentalism implicit in the notion of a self as an internal source of control over our interface with the world. It simply does no good to explain our behavior in such terms. An explanation of our behavior that includes a self in a causal chain of events is only misleading and frustrates a search for the real explanatory variables.

In considering what might seem to be instances of self-control, it is important to identify not just the behavior being controlled but the behavior required to engineer that outcome. What is casually referred to as self-control is largely a matter of engaging in the same behavior we have learned to use in influencing the behavior of others. By clearly identifying the controlling behavior, we can better appreciate that it originates not from an internal self but from a reinforcement history.

Self-Reinforcement

Many of the examples of what we colloquially call self-control suggest a role for self-reinforcement. The apparent explanation for those actions that result in some beneficial outcome is that the individual is arranging the environment for the purpose of reinforcing his or her own behavior. One of the problems with this explanation is addressed in the next chapter, which considers the awkwardness of explaining behavior in terms of its purpose. However, the idea that we can reinforce our own behavior in the same manner as we reinforce the actions of others is a more complicated problem.

Before proceeding, it is important to remind ourselves that reinforcement as a process has its effects on response classes, not the individual. That is, the effects of reinforcement may be found in the response classes of the organism, not the organism in some whole sense. This is partly a matter of careful technical language, but it is rooted in scientifically established fact. Without this clarification, all instances of reinforcement, including those arranged by other people, could be said to involve self-reinforcement. The usual connotation of self-reinforcement is that you are managing particular behaviors in your own repertoire. If self-reinforcement meant merely doing something for yourself in a general sense, then anything you do that produces reinforcement could be seen as self-reinforcement, even if others had arranged the reinforcement contingency (Catania, 1975). This expansive usage would make the phrase meaningless.

Situations that could be described as involving self-reinforcement necessarily include two behaviors. There is the behavior that is reinforced, as well as the individual's behavior of reinforcing that first behavior. Let us consider the example of Matt, who is studying for a test one evening. He decides that he will allow himself to have a beer if he studies for two hours straight. The beer, which is chilling away in the refrigerator, is otherwise available throughout the study session, but Matt plans to drink it only if he manages two hours of concentrated test preparation. Many would see the beer as a reinforcer for studying, and because Matt is the one setting up the contingency, it would seem to be an instance of self-reinforcement, assuming it all works out and that drinking beer makes the likelihood of studying under such conditions in the future more likely as a result of the contingency. In this example, there is the behavior of studying, which Matt hopes will be affected by the beer contingency, as well as the behavior involved in reinforcing the behavior of studying (drinking the beer only after the requisite period of studying).

A thorough analysis of the technical details of what is going on in this example is a bit complicated and might be best saved for a careful reading of a paper by Catania (1975) titled "The myth of self-reinforcement." The key is that the notion of self-reinforcement depends on our ability to discriminate our own behavior. In the example, Matt must be able to discriminate studying for two solid hours from any lesser achievement. His ability to do so therefore means that he would allow himself to drink the readily available beer only if meeting the criterion for reinforcement was already important. If the target behavior (studying) was sufficiently important, the behavior of studying would itself acquire conditioned reinforcing properties. Merely accumulating study time would likely be reinforcing by itself.

What, then, is gained by describing the sequence of events "study, then beer" as self-reinforcement? Just because beer might be a good reinforcer for Matt and because it follows a period of studying, even one that was set out in advance as a criterion for drinking the beer, it does not follow that the sequence constitutes a reinforcement contingency, whether it was arranged by Matt himself or even by his roommate. (His roommate might arrange such a contingency and studying under these conditions might increase, but it is only a reinforcement contingency if the increase was due to the contingency, as opposed to other variables.) The question is not whether self-reinforcement operations can be found in this situation but whether there is a self-reinforcement process involved.

In response to the question, "Does self-reinforcement reinforce?," Catania (1975, p. 197) proposes that there is nothing more than ordinary reinforcement going on and not a special variation that should be called self-reinforcement. It remains important to understand the variables underlying what is casually labeled self-reinforcement, of course. After all, it is widely used under practical conditions, such as when school children are prompted to reward themselves for good performance. However, Catania argues that misnaming it, and thereby implying a mental component, distracts us from the proper scientific agenda.

BOX 4.8

When Reinforcement is Automatic

Our discussion of whether we should conceptualize a special variety of reinforcement called self-reinforcement leads to the conclusion that it is conceptually misleading and therefore not a good idea. This conclusion might in turn seem to raise the question of whether it is useful to describe reinforcement in order to have its effects automatically. After all, the notion of self-reinforcement implies that the effects of reinforcement might often occur without any special arrangements, particularly those involving other people. Does the idea of automatic reinforcement also raise conceptual issues?

In a way, it does, though this does not mean they are problematic. Vaughan & Michael (1982) noted that Skinner used the reference frequently in his writings, though never quite giving it formal technical status. His usages were more ordinary, in the sense of "reinforcement that is not mediated by the deliberate action of another person" (Vaughan & Michael, 1982, p. 219). At the least, this proposal avoids the need to claim that complex human behavior must only be explained by reinforcement that involves explicit environmental arrangements involving others.

A significant role for automatic reinforcement might seem obvious, but it involves a slippery slope. The risk lies in the all too convenient temptation to invent automatic reinforcement contingencies when more obvious arrangements are not evident. In everyday professional practice, it is simply not feasible to gather the evidence necessary to identify automatic reinforcement contingencies, so we may suppose they are there and operating as needed to explain behavior. Our interpretations may well be correct, but we will never know for sure. Of course, practitioners are often in this same interpretive position in speculating about the role of more obvious, arranged contingencies, but those speculations are more easily tested, if needs be.

Vaughan & Michael (1982) propose five circumstances that seem to involve automatic reinforcement, including its role in punishment. Some involve merely the behavior of perceiving certain events, such as seeing pictures of family members or hearing a certain type of music. However, they report that the most common examples in Skinner's writing involve some action by the individual that changes the environment in a way that appears to be reinforcing, as when a musician plays a tune she has recently heard.

Many such examples might seem to be obvious instances of reinforcement contingencies that occur without prearrangement, but the limits of the term "automatic" are not so easily defined. For instance, although some automatically reinforcing stimuli might be unlearned, it is hard to imagine that most are not the result of a learning history. This learning history very often involves others, who in some sense are therefore involved in the development of the conditioned reinforcers that play a role in automatic reinforcement contingencies. Telling a joke that makes others laugh is usually automatically reinforcing, given a history that has established laughter as a conditioned reinforcer for the speaker. The greater challenge is in evaluating whether the listener's laughing is contrived, but this is a worrisome problem only at a methodological level. The notion of automatic reinforcement not only raises no conceptual problems, it is a critical extension of reinforcement to the subtler aspects of behavior—those circumstances in which the cooperation of others is not necessary.

CHAPTER SUMMARY

1. In everyday parlance, we talk about our "self" as an inner entity that is the source of our preferences, opinions, feelings, and thoughts. There is no direct evidence of this "self," which is given a causal, mentalistic role in our behavior. We learn to talk about our public and private behavior from our verbal community.

2. We learn to see our own behavior as we are taught by our verbal community. Our self-descriptive behavior is entirely learned in this way. Absent this influence, we would not learn this aspect of our repertoire and would not be aware of our own behavior. We learn to respond to those aspects of our behavior, including private events, based on what is important to our verbal community.

3. We often respond in ways we are not aware of. To be aware of our behavior means we can describe it in some way. However, our self-knowledge is often deficient because it is difficult for others to teach us to respond to events they cannot see.

4. Seeing, hearing, and other kinds of sensing have both biological and behavioral components. It is less obvious that seeing, etc. are forms of responding that depend on learning history. As a result, we engage in seeing when we respond to certain stimuli in our visual field but not others. We also engage in seeing behavior even though visual stimuli may be weak or entirely absent. This argument applies to all forms of sensory behavior.

5. We learn to respond to our discriminated sensory behavior (e.g., seeing) as a result of contingencies established by our verbal community. We are labeling this behavior when we say that we "see" something.

6. Non-human species do not learn this skill and merely see based on their learning histories but are not able to respond to their doing so. It is possible to teach this performance to animals, but the result would be far short of what humans learn.

7. There are many ways in which we engage is what we colloquially call self-control, including physical restraint, changing stimuli, manipulating deprivation conditions, manipulating emotional variables, using aversive stimulation, and using drugs or other substances.

8. Attempting to explain self-control as if the self was the origin of such behavior is mentalistic and not useful. This kind of behavior, which we apply to ourselves as we do to others, originates in our learning history.

9. The process of reinforcement has effects on response classes, not the individual as a whole.

10. When talking about self-reinforcement, there are two behaviors to explain: the behavior that is supposedly reinforced and the behavior of arranging and delivering reinforcers. Because self-reinforcement depends on our ability to discriminate our own behavior, such behavior is already important and merely

engaging in it might well be reinforcing. This analysis suggests that the idea of self-reinforcement is unnecessary.

TEXT STUDY GUIDE

1. Describe the everyday view of the self. Why is this perspective mentalistic?
2. How do we learn to talk about our "self"?
3. Explain the role of the verbal community in self-perception.
4. How do behavior analysts approach perception, awareness, and consciousness?
5. Why might it be said that our self-knowledge is unavoidably deficient?
6. What does it mean to say that sensing involves both physiological and behavioral components?
7. Explain how viewing seeing and hearing as behaviors helps explain seeing or hearing events that are not present.
8. What does it mean to say, "I see ..."?
9. Explain the requirements for learning to respond to our sensory behavior. Why can non-human species not learn to do this?
10. List and give an example of different ways we often control our own behavior.
11. Why is it important to understand that the process of reinforcement has its effects on response classes, not the individual?
12. What are the two behaviors that must be explained in any self-reinforcement situation?
13. Why is it important to acknowledge that self-reinforcement depends on our ability to discriminate our own behavior?

BOX STUDY GUIDE

1. What is the problem with the everyday idea of personality?
2. What is copy theory? Why is it mentalistic?
3. Explain why behavior analysts take the position that a falling tree makes no sound if no one is there to hear it.
4. Explain dreaming in terms of stimulus control.
5. Why would sensory illusions vary from one culture to another?
6. Explain the behavioral consequences of not being able to learn seeing as behavior.
7. Explain the argument there is no pain without pain behavior.
8. Explain how motivating operations are a key aspect of self-control.

9. Define automatic reinforcement. What are the risks and challenges associated with this extension of the concept of reinforcement?

DISCUSSION TOPICS AND EXERCISES

1. Imagine a culture that did not teach its members to respond to or report pain. Although individuals would get sick, sustain injuries, and so forth, assume that the verbal community did not teach its members to describe what we call painful sensations. What kind of pain behavior would we observe in such a culture?

2. Consider the situation in which a child is asked what she wants to do tomorrow. Provide an explanation of the sources of control over her verbal behavior in a way that does not involve mentalism.

3. Consider cultural differences in what verbal communities may teach its members to respond to, such as differences in pain behavior. Are there aspects of our private events or our behavior that our verbal communities fail to teach us to be aware of?

4. A dog learns to ring a bell next to the outside door, which prompts its owner to let it outside to urinate. It might be argued that the dog has learned to be aware of its private stimulation associated with the need to urinate. Discuss why this performance is NOT an example of a dog learning a self-descriptive performance comparable to that of a child saying "I see a bird."

5. Develop a behavioral explanation of hallucinations.

SUGGESTED READINGS

Catania, A. C. (1975). The myth of self-reinforcement. *Behaviorism*, *3(2)*, 192–199.

Schlinger, H. D. (1993). Separating discriminative versus function-altering effects of verbal stimuli. *The Behavior Analyst, 16(1)*, 9–23.

Skinner, B. F. (1953). *Science and human behavior*. New York: MacMillan. (Chapter XV: Self-control; Chapter XVII: Private events in a natural science; and Chapter XVIII: The self)

Chapter 5

The Misdirection of Everyday Dialect

Julie knew she was struggling with the material in her conceptual issues class. It wasn't the textbook exactly, although she kept wanting more examples to help her figure out some of the points. Class discussions helped a lot, but there was never enough time and they didn't always go where she wanted. If anything, she was now convinced that her interests were more practical than intellectual—after all, that's why she was working on her Master's in ABA. She just wanted to earn her certification and get started with her career, not struggle with esoteric material that seemed to have little to do with autism treatment. In spite of her professor's warning that this material was important for practitioners, she wasn't convinced.

"I'm just not into this conceptual stuff," Julie confessed, as she dumped her backpack on the table in the professor's office and collapsed into a chair. "I'm kind of getting it, but it all seems so abstract, just so much verbal behavior," she said, intentionally turning the book's phrase on itself.

Dr. Francis gave her a quick smile. "You're not exactly alone. Each year, some of the students really get into the issues raised in the book, and others learn what they have to but don't take it to heart. I never can predict who is going to be in which group. I'm sometimes surprised."

"I guess I'm in the second group," Julie volunteered. "I think I get the arguments in the book, but I'm just not interested in going to the trouble of learning to talk this way. It's worse than trying to learn a foreign language."

"Definitely worse," Dr. Francis agreed. "It's a struggle to get to the point that you can avoid mentalism and use good behavioral terminology fluently. Unfortunately, you can't get there without the struggle, and it has to go on long after our course is over. Besides that, there won't be anyone around pushing you to make the effort, so most practitioners wind up being stuck with a sloppy verbal repertoire when it comes to conceptual issues. They're OK with that until they run into colleagues who know better, like at a convention, but then it's too late to join the party."

"But does it really make a difference if a practitioner doesn't get good at talking behaviorally?" Julie asked. "I mean, as long as you understand the underlying issues, does it matter if you're fluent?"

"It matters, but it's hard to say just how much it matters. You've got to be careful about giving yourself too much license, however. If you can't replace everyday language with some pretty good behavioral phrasing, I'd be worried about how well you understand the underlying issues. Being able at least to identify and understand the issues is fundamental. If you're not there, I'd say there is a pretty big price to be paid as a clinician. Our technology is more tightly interwoven with these conceptual issues than most probably suspect. Show me an ABA practitioner who isn't conversant with these issues, and I'll bet you find problems with their clinical approach."

"Now you're trying to scare me," Julie joked.

"Well, not really. All I can say is understanding conceptual issues has been very important to me in just about everything I've done in my career. It's part of what it means to be a behavior analyst."

KNOWLEDGE AND UNDERSTANDING

As a noun, knowledge seems to be a thing, something we know, display, or possess. Because others could doubt that we have certain knowledge, it is only when we act in ways said to show understanding, or behave in ways demonstrating such knowledge, that they might say we know something. Knowledge, therefore, seems to be some sort of mental aggregation that we acquire through experience and then access and display as necessary. Knowledge is one of the ways we explain our behavior. We are able to do what we do because of what we know.

This way of talking about our behavior is thoroughly mentalistic, of course. Our tendency to put the source of our behavior in our mind is consistent with the notion that the basis for our actions—what we know—must also be inside us. Rather than taking knowledge or knowing as a way of explaining behavior, behavior analysts instead consider the circumstances that generate verbal behavior involving these terms. When are we likely to say that someone knows or understands something or has certain knowledge?

Philosophers and psychologists have worried about possible forms of knowing for some time. One common distinction is between *knowing how* and *knowing about*. We tend to talk about knowing how to do something when we have a history of observing relevant behavior. If I have heard Rachael speak French on various occasions, I am more likely to say that she knows how to speak French than if I had not made such observations. Saying that Rachael speaks French is the result of a long reinforcement history for tacting events around us. Saying, "Rachael speaks French" is not fundamentally different than saying, "I saw Katie today." Furthermore, the extent of our sample of Rachael speaking French may prompt various qualifications of our description, just as we might qualify our statement about seeing Katie. We might say, "I think I saw Katie today" or "I might have seen Katie today," if stimulus control was weak, just as we might say, "I think Rachael speaks French" if our sample of her French-speaking behavior was limited.

It could be argued, however, that saying that I saw Katie today is different from saying that Rachael speaks French in that the former statement merely reports a single event, whereas the latter implies a repertoire with a past and an implied future. I might never see Katie again, but if Rachael speaks French, she has presumably done so in the past and may well do so on future occasions. I could have said only that I heard Rachael speak French, apparently reporting a single observation. Saying instead that she speaks French implies the existence of a knowledge of French that must still exist even when she is speaking English or not speaking at all.

This view raises the seemingly troublesome question about where her French-speaking knowledge is during those periods. This question is no different from asking where your walking behavior is when you are seated, however. Putting aside the biological prerequisites for any behavior, it is a meaningless question. Behavior does not reside anywhere when it is not occurring. It is the interface between organism and environment or the result of interactions between these entities. Particular instances of behavior occur as that interface changes from moment to moment. At most, we might say that the history of a particular behavior resides in the still unknown recesses of our physiological machinery, but our behavior is not stored anywhere.

Knowing *about* something is similar to knowing *how* to do something except that when we say that someone knows about something their behavior must be appropriate to relevant discriminative stimuli. If I say that I know about vintage Porsches, you might expect me to answer your questions about these sports cars, and my answers must be appropriate. My talk about vintage Porsches is appropriate if it has been reinforced, and not punished, in the past. It is my observation of my own behavior of talking about old Porsches that leads me to say that I know about them. If I cannot answer your questions, or if my answers do not result in reinforcement, I might be less likely to boast about what I know.

In sum, there is nothing mysterious about understanding or knowing. No invocation of mentalistic concepts is necessary to explain vernacular references to individuals understanding or knowing things. Put simply, these are just ways we learn to talk about behavior. The sole basis for such talk is our observations of behavior, whether ours or someone else's, under certain conditions. We say that we understand, or know about, or know how to do something when we observe certain behavior, usually under specific stimulus conditions. The explanation of the behavior we observe lies in a reinforcement history, and there is no scientific basis for supposing that there must be an intervening mental storage locker that provides the origin for the resulting behavior.

BOX 5.1

Having an Idea

We have all had the experience of having an idea. We usually characterize this common behavior in everyday terms as a mental activity that seems to occur rather suddenly and sometimes without apparent effort or preparation. Such ideas may often be seen as solutions to problems, both large and small.

Mentalism aside, we are certainly behaving when we have an idea. This behavior—what "pops into our head"—is often a bit of verbal behavior that is no different than talking covertly. It may sometimes be a sensory behavior, as when we hear a sound or see something, although actual stimulation of our sensory organs is not always involved. As Chapter 4 explained, the behavior of seeing, hearing, and so forth does not always require sensory stimulation.

The obvious question is where the behavior of "having an idea" comes from. The connotation is that this behavior appears lacking any obvious origin, that it comes simply out of the blue. This is not a surprising conclusion when the immediate causes for behavior are unclear. We conclude that the event was spontaneous, as if that passes for an explanation. In addition to the fact that we are not very good at identifying the relevant environmental conditions, however, we are usually not watching for them anyway. We are engaged in the moment, not thoughtfully observing. Furthermore, the temptation to look for causes of any behavior only in current circumstances hides the fact that causal variables usually involve historical influences that are not easily recognized. Given these challenges, it is hardly surprising that we casually attribute our ideas to mental processes.

A more parsimonious approach is to appreciate that there is no reason to view "having" an idea as different from "having" any particular behavior. Any bit of behavior is not there at one moment and there the next. That is, before it was occurring, it was not occurring. In this sense, all behavior can be said to occur suddenly. Characterizing a behavior as spontaneous may only reflect our inability to predict its occurrence. At one moment, you are studying for an exam and the next moment you are going to the door to let the cat out. The behavior of getting up and going to the door did not occur gradually; it replaced studying more or less all at once.

The reasons we engage in a behavior may or may not be evident in any one instance, but any uncertainty should not encourage inventing proximate mental causes. It may be unsatisfying or even frustrating to admit, but the reasons for any action are complex, largely historical, and usually not obvious, whether the behavior is public or private.

PURPOSE, INTENTION, AND GOALS

We often talk about our behavior in terms of its purpose, though such references are sometimes indirect. We may explain rummaging through a tool box by saying that we intend to fix a squeaky door. We say that we are going to the grocery store to get some dog food. Before leaving the house, we may say we are going upstairs to get the car keys. Upon returning from the store, we say that our dog is sitting to get food. We may explain why we are going through folders in the file cabinet by saying that we are looking for a certain document.

These and similar statements share an implication that our behavior is due to, or at least guided by, some future outcome. The purpose of getting the oil is fixing the squeaky door, which implies that the behavior of getting the oil is controlled by the future event of fixing the door. The behavior of going to the store is controlled by the not-yet-achieved outcome of buying dog food. We are going upstairs because we need to get the car keys. The dog's sitting behavior is caused by the future prospect of getting food. The behavior of looking for something is determined by the prospect of finding the thing we are looking for.

Whether we refer to purpose, incentive, intention, expectation, want, wish, or goal, this kind of explanation runs afoul of a well-accepted principle in the physical sciences—that it is not helpful to explain one event in terms of some other event that has not yet occurred. Influences on behavior can be in the past or present, but they cannot be in the future because an event must occur in order to produce a result, though everyday phrasing implies otherwise. Explanations framed in terms of final causes are called **teleological** and are especially problematic for a science of behavior. Explanations of a behavior in terms of its purpose are necessarily teleological and tend to invoke mentalism by implying that a mental process such as trying, expecting, or intending underlies the behavior and explains why it is occurring.

This kind of explanation is often given away by the preposition "to" or the prepositional phrase "in order to." So when we say that our dog is sitting "to" get food, we are making an implicit explanation of sitting in terms of the as yet unrealized outcome of getting food. This kind of statement is only a hair's breadth away from saying that the dog is trying or intending to get food by sitting. Of course, we are merely inventing trying or intending as a mental operation, guided by a colloquial dialect that puts mental processes in charge of behavior. In observing our dog's behavior, there is no evidence of anything we might call trying or intending, only the behavior of sitting. Any reference to mental processes implying purpose, even indirect, is gratuitous.

It is especially tempting to argue that our behavior is purposive in nature when we are looking for something. It seems so obvious that our looking behavior is controlled by the object of our search. When we look for something, such as our car keys, the variability in our actions from one occasion to another is notable. We do not do just one thing when looking for something. We look in different places, high and low, opening things, uncovering things, and so forth. Across different episodes of looking for your car keys, you are likely to engage in different behaviors. If you are at work, you will look in different ways than if you are at home or at a restaurant. Furthermore, looking behavior ceases when you find your keys. These characteristics of looking for something beg for explanation in terms of purpose. We may even look for something that we have never before searched for, such as a certain product at the grocery store that a friend recommended.

At this point, you should be able to supply an explanation of the behavior of looking for something that avoids mentalism and is consistent with the science of behavior. Given a motivating operation in the form of needing something we do not have, when we look for something we simply engage in a response class that has previously produced reinforcers. True, the details of our looking behavior vary from one episode to another, but the concept of response classes accommodates this variability. If you enjoy running and sometimes enter 10K races, for example, you do not engage in exactly the same running behavior each time. Each footfall along the route is unique, and you must accommodate other runners nearby. Furthermore, your pace varies throughout each race depending on the weather and the route's topography, and you are likely to follow a different route in each race. So, the fact that looking behavior seems uniquely guided by the particular thing we are searching for and its circumstances may be explained in terms of our history of looking for different kinds of things under different circumstances and the general nature of operant response classes. Even though looking for something seems to be directed toward the future, it is actually controlled by our past.

Talking about purpose as a cause of behavior is only one kind of reference to purpose. A second way we talk about purpose is as a self-report of our private experience (Baum, 2005). These references are often to our intentions. For instance, we might explain something we did for our friend Brittany by reporting that we were *trying* to make her feel better. Of course, this statement of intentions is purposive in nature. We are saying that our behavior can be explained in terms of its purpose of making Brittany feel better, which can only follow our actions.

Other self-reports may be in terms of our feelings (Baum, 2005). We often attempt to explain our actions by saying we did it because we felt like it. We also refer to feelings as causes of current or future behavior. We may say that we feel like taking a nap or having pizza tonight. Such apparent self-reports in terms of private feelings are purposive in nature because they implicitly refer to the future. What does it mean to say that you feel like eating pizza tonight? Because tonight is not yet here, what accounts for the reported feeling now?

One possibility is that we are sensing actual bodily reactions to environmental circumstances, as Chapter 3 discussed. However, our references to feelings are more often only a matter of vernacular vocabulary. That is, when we say that we feel like pizza tonight, we may only be responding to the fact that we heard a friend talking about pizza or that we just saw a pizza advertisement on TV. There may be no genuine physical feeling or sensation involved. Given our vocabulary, public and possibly private stimuli increase the likelihood of making intentional

BOX 5.2

Planning on Going Somewhere?

Explaining behavior in terms of future outcomes is especially tempting in the case of "planning" to do something. After all, whether the planning efforts are straightforward or complex, it would seem as if they are influenced by the intended but not yet achieved outcome, doing whatever was previously planned. For example, going to a concert with friends usually requires some planning. The behavior involved might include talking with your friends to see who wants to go, buying tickets, deciding how to get there, and so forth. All of this planning is "for the purpose" of actually attending the concert.

Describing and explaining such planning behavior without purposive implications begins with acknowledging that all of the associated behavior already has a reinforcement history that must not be ignored in explaining why it occurs. You have talked with friends before, bought tickets before, and negotiated transportation before, and such behavior produced consequences that loom large in its explanation. Furthermore, these behaviors have involved many variations from occasion to occasion and provide a ready repertoire that different circumstances may require.

This much is straightforward, but what pulls these behaviors together in a coordinated way in relation to this particular concert? The answer lies in the concept of motivating operations (see Box 4.7). When a friend calls you all excited about an upcoming concert or you see an advertisement about it, such stimuli function as motivating operations (technically, transitive conditioned motivating operations, although this example might justify some discussion). Your friend's phone call or a television spot establish the concert as a conditioned reinforcer and evoke behavior that has been followed by that reinforcer in the past, behavior we might call "planning" to go to the concert. The complexity of this example allows for other possible influences, of course, such as the fact that talking with your friends about getting tickets and who is going to drive probably involves additional sources of reinforcement. In any event, approaching planning as influenced only by past and present environmental factors allows us to directly study how motivating operations work, an option not available with the mentalistic notion of purpose.

statements in terms of wanting, desiring, wishing, longing for, craving, hoping for, and feeling like. These kinds of statements may only be a way of describing a certain thing or experience as reinforcing or efforts to obtain it that we have previously engaged in. In this sense, intentional statements make a kind of prediction (Baum, 2005).

A third way of talking about the purpose of some action may only involve describing its function (Baum, 2005). This sort of reference is not a problem for a science of behavior because it merely points to behavioral outcomes. If we say that the purpose of our dog sitting is getting food, we might only be describing the function of sitting as producing food. In this sense, all activities could be described in terms of their purposes as functions. Even reference to food as a goal in this scenario may only be a way of specifying that food has in the past often been a reinforcer for sitting. Mentalistic phrases such as saying that our dog is trying to get food by sitting could be seen as saying that it is engaging in behavior that has produced food in the past. In other words, talking about purpose as the function of behavior is a way of identifying the relation between a behavior and its historical consequences. This kind of reference is not necessarily teleological, though it may often be uncomfortably close.

PROBLEM SOLVING

When we talk about problem solving, we describe situations in which the individual has no behavior immediately available that can resolve a condition of deprivation or aversive stimulation (Skinner, 1953, 1969). It may at first seem awkward to describe problem solving this way, but it fits the circumstances that lead us to use this label. We might agree that we face a problem when we have not eaten all day (a condition of deprivation) but have no obvious way to get food. Most people would also call it a problem when we are trying to study but are distracted by a noisy party next door (an aversive condition).

Many circumstances presenting similar conditions of deprivation or aversiveness are not so obvious as these examples, however, and we might not always frame them as problems. For example, if you are at the library and forgot your earphones and cannot listen to your music, this deprivation constitutes a problem no different than not having eaten all day, given that there is nothing you can immediately do to change your environment and reduce that deprivation. Aversive conditions are not always so obvious. If a classroom lecture is less than riveting and you wonder how many panels there are in the ceiling, the lack of an answer constitutes a mildly aversive state of affairs, just as it would if someone asked you that question.

Although this last example seems a pretty trivial aversive condition, the test of its aversiveness is whether behavior that terminates the condition will function as a reinforcer. If you go to the trouble of counting the ceiling panels and having an answer removes that distraction (you no longer wonder about ceiling tiles and turn your attention to other things, maybe even the lecture), this contingency satisfies the definition of an aversive condition that has long been useful in the operant literature.

In this example, counting ceiling panels is behavior that leads to a solution of the problem. Problem-solving behavior is behavior that alters the situation so behavior that solves the problem can be emitted. If you have not eaten all day and have no immediate access to food, the behavior you engage in that makes food available is problem-solving behavior. Of course, once the problem has been solved (you have determined how many panels are in the ceiling or you now can eat), the problem no longer exists because the key feature of deprivation or aversiveness is no longer present.

Skinner defined a problem-solving solution as a "response [that] alters the situation so that the problem disappears" (1953, p. 252). However, he noted that simply emitting a solution is not necessarily what we usually call "solving a problem." A solution that someone else offers or that accidentally occurs does not involve problem solving. It might also be misleading to call trial-and-error behavior problem solving. We know problem situations typically generate variability in responding based on a history in which at least some of these variations have occasionally produced reinforcement. For example, if your apartment key does not work on the first try, you are likely to insert or twist it in a slightly different way on a second or third attempt because these alternative topographies have probably been reinforced in the past. Although this trial-and-error behavior may solve the problem in some sense, it may be functionally different than the behavior we customarily call problem solving, which has the connotation of behavior that does not depend on other people or mere persistence. So, if the problem is that you cannot open the door and get into your apartment, problem-solving behavior might involve borrowing a ladder from a neighbor and climbing in through a window. Of course, although this would solve the immediate problem, more work lies ahead in getting the door lock to work.

It is hard not to notice the temptation to explain problem-solving behavior in teleological terms. The seemingly obvious goal directedness of such behavior makes it difficult to talk in terms of a reinforcement history of manipulating the environment, but we all have such a history. Throughout our childhood, we face problem situations and learn, often with the guidance of others, how to behave in ways that make possible the behavior that will solve the problem. Skinner (1953) discussed a number of techniques we learn, including arranging or rearranging stimuli (as in many word games) or listing and reviewing possible solutions. Although we often solve the presenting problem in each instance, we also develop a general skill of solving problems. As adults, we often hone that skill in our careers. A carpenter gets quite good at solving problems encountered in building a house, just as a scientist is trained to approach experimental challenges in particular ways that increase the likelihood of finding solutions.

RULES, ADVICE, AND INSTRUCTIONS

We often explain things we do by pointing to certain rules that apparently led to those actions. A rule is a bit of verbal behavior, although there is no particular grammatical form required to earn this label. Some rules are clearly demands or orders, such as "Eat your vegetables," or "No smoking," but others are gentler, such as "You should think about how you sound when you talk that way." The latter phrasing might be called advice, which shares the same characteristics as rules.

BOX 5.3

Memory versus Remembering

The concept of memory has long been a popular topic in psychological research. A vast literature attempts to investigate what it is and how it works, and many terms (often borrowed from computer lingo) refer to cognitive or neurological processes when we remember or forget. And yet, behavior analysts tend to pay this concept and its literature relatively little attention (although see, for example, White, 2001; White 2002; and Wright, Katz, & Ma, 2012). Neither basic nor applied behavioral research attempt to describe memory processes or assign memory any explicit explanatory value.

Is this inattention merely due to the fact that conventional references to memory are usually accompanied by all of the challenges of mentalism? This is certainly a justifiable concern. Although the physiological basis for behavior associated with remembering or forgetting has received considerable attention in recent years, this research has significant practical and conceptual problems relating observable behavior to what is going on in the brain. Mentalism is rampant in this research literature, no matter the sophistication of neuroimaging techniques that reveal certain changes in brain activity under various experimental conditions. Behavior analysts understandably shy away from these problems (Faux, 2002; Uttal, 2011). As with other mental concepts, it is too easy to invent cognitive structures and processes as needed and too difficult to falsify them.

Instead, behavior analysts have what they consider more profitable ways of talking about what is, after all, a form of behaving that we label remembering and forgetting, regardless of the physiological mechanisms that enable it. By studying these phenomena as behavior, we can bring to bear all that has been learned about the factors that influence all kinds of behavior. We can study the environmental variables that influence remembering and forgetting, for instance, which may lead to practical procedures for addressing problems with these behaviors in daily living. This is not to say that the physiological basis of remembering and forgetting is unimportant or does not need to be pursued but that it is no more important here than for other kinds of behavior. These biological phenomena do not define the behavior but merely help explain how the brain contributes to its explanation. Furthermore, however much may be learned about brain activity associated with this behavior, the relations established through research focused on learning processes relating behavior and environment stand on their own (see Box 10.1). As well, this literature should set the agenda for understanding the role of the brain underlying the behavior we call remembering.

Instructions, such as "Take the first right past the bank," also share these features. Although rules, advice, and instructions are often oral verbal behavior, textual and gestural behavior also qualifies. This means that in addition to posted signs, we can even include diagrams, maps, and similar displays, as well as gestures.

Regardless of any distinctions in common parlance, rules, advice, and instructions are often verbal discriminative stimuli and are presented under control of some relation between a behavior and its consequences (Baum, 2005; Cerutti, 1989; Skinner, 1953, 1969). The speaker's experience with this reinforcement relation (the availability of an umbrella and the likelihood of getting wet) provides the context for giving the rule. Even when the speaker has no direct experience with the reinforcement relation and is merely repeating a rule given by someone else, the rule suggests some reinforcement relation that underlies its origin. Sometimes rules specify the consequences for adhering to them ("If you hold the bat this way, the ball will go further") and may therefore be called contingency specifying stimuli. Others describe the consequence for failing to follow them ("If you don't put on a coat, you'll catch a cold"). (See Box 5.4.)

Behavior complying with the rule is likely to benefit from the speaker's experience with the reinforcement relation. Compliance with the rule may bring the listener's behavior into contact with the reinforcement relation, thereby making his or her behavior more effective. Holding a baseball bat in a particular manner may, indeed, result in hitting balls farther than before, presumably a reinforcing outcome. Reinforcers may also be socially mediated, especially in childhood when adults are trying to teach rule following. Speakers often offer social reinforcers, or even arrange other kinds of reinforcers, for complying with a rule. Whether their source stems from the natural outcomes of compliance or is social in nature, such reinforcement is usually intermittent, which means we often comply with rules when there is no obvious reinforcement for doing so.

Complying with a rule may save the listener from having to go through the same learning experiences as the speaker or others who articulated the rule. This can be especially important when those learning experiences involve situations that come with a high price. Telling a child to look both ways before crossing the street is obviously preferable to allowing the child to encounter the natural consequences of crossing without looking. Giving a new employee instructions about how to use a piece of equipment may save unnecessary wear and tear on the equipment, reduce the risk of injury, or increase the odds that products will meet standards.

When rules are effective in managing the behavior of listeners, they are efficient for the speaker, who need only emit some verbal behavior instead of going to the trouble of bringing the listener's behavior into contact with controlling consequences. Putting rules into textual form such as a sign ("No smoking") that will be seen by many individuals makes this approach to controlling behavior even more efficient, even though the rule may not produce compliance by all who contact it. Of course, the likelihood of listeners complying with the rule depends on their reinforcement history for following rules and many factors specific to each instance of a rule and the circumstances under which it is encountered. The fact that we have all heard a parent say "If I've told you once, I've told you a thousand times..." suggests that rules may often fail to control the listener's behavior.

BOX 5.4

Rules as Function-Altering Stimuli

The argument that verbal behavior in the form of rules often controls behavior as discriminative stimuli is relatively straightforward, but it provides an incomplete, if not misleading, picture of how a speaker's verbal behavior may control the behavior of others. Some verbal stimuli have effects on the behavior of listeners even though they are not discriminative stimuli. That is, they do not evoke behavior because they have acquired discriminative stimulus functions. Instead, verbal stimuli may control behavior by altering the functions of other events and are therefore called function-altering stimuli (Cerruti, 1989; Schlinger, 1993; Schlinger & Blakely, 1987). Verbal stimuli can alter the functions of other events much as operant and respondent conditioning processes do. For example, if your roommate instructs you to watch out the window for her date to arrive and to give her a heads-up, it may be that her date's arrival serves to evoke your warning not because of direct history of differential reinforcement but because of your friend's instruction.

Distinguishing between the discriminative and function-altering effects of verbal stimuli is not easy. Evidence of a discriminative training history would help, but we can usually only speculate about the possibility that a particular verbal stimulus has acquired discriminative stimulus functions. Identifying function-altering effects is challenging as well. One approach is to consider whether a sample of verbal behavior involves contingency-specifying stimuli (Schlinger & Blakely, 1987). Contingency-specifying stimuli specify the events to be related by naming two or three events, such as a stimulus, a response, or a consequence. However, contingency-specifying stimuli may evoke responding both with and in the absence of discrimination training. Schlinger (1993) argues that rules may be best interpreted as function-altering stimuli when their contingency-specifying stimuli cannot be explained in terms of discriminative stimuli. For example, a teacher might tell students that each time she puts a check mark on the board they earn an extra minute of recess. The check marks are presumably endowed with reinforcing properties as a result of the contingency-specifying elements in the teacher's rule prior to any contact with promised consequences.

If you are not already familiar with the concept of function-altering stimuli, it will take far more than the preceding paragraphs to incorporate this interpretation of rules, advice, and instructions into your repertoire. However, conceptual arguments and proposed advances concerning the way we talk about behavior are an important feature of the field's growing maturity and yet another reason for you to make conceptual matters a key component of your continuing education as a practitioner.

When rules are effective, the resulting behavior is said to be *rule following* or *rule governed*. This description should be applied cautiously, however, because the fact that the listener's behavior is consistent with a rule does not necessarily mean it occurred because of the rule. For example, just because you write a term paper that is consistent with the rules of grammar does not mean you were following those rules. Your writing is the result of a history that includes consequences for complying, or failing to comply, with grammatical rules, but you are unlikely to consult those rules, or even remember them, when you write. Such behavior is merely more or less consistent with the rules of grammar. On the other hand, when you recite the "i before e" rule in trying to remember how to spell "receive," the resulting spelling might be properly described as rule governed.

One way behavior can come to be consistent with a rule, though not controlled by it, is through a history of consequences for the behavior. Even when a behavior is initially controlled by a rule, the behavior still produces consequences that make it more or less likely under similar conditions in the future. Every moment of our behavior encounters such differential reinforcement, which gradually shapes our responding toward greater effectiveness. The resulting behavior is called *contingency shaped*. Although we often think of shaping as a particular procedure practitioners often use to create a response class with particular characteristics, natural or unplanned contingencies often involve the same gradually adjusting features and yield the same specificity.

Unplanned contingencies may sometimes take longer to produce an ideal performance than might carefully arranged contingencies because they may not yield consistent outcomes on every trial. For example, holding a baseball bat in a particular way may lead to a hit or a strike, depending on the pitch and the batter's swing. Without coaching, it might take many trials for the most effective way of holding a bat to emerge. On the other hand, unplanned contingencies may sometimes be difficult to beat, even by a skilled trainer. When the environment provides consistent consequences for responding, it may not take long for responding to reach an ideal form. When learning to drive a car, for example, new drivers must learn how to modulate the throttle to produce the desired effects on acceleration or deceleration. Because the throttle linkage reacts to behavioral inputs in a very consistent manner, drivers usually learn how to operate the throttle quickly and without detailed instruction.

The more fully and accurately a rule specifies behavior that will produce reinforcing consequences, the more likely it is that the rule will be effective. Put the other way, if a rule asks for behavior that is unlikely to be reinforced, it is less likely to be effective. Other ways of responding that do produce reinforcement are likely to develop instead. This means a rule's effectiveness depends largely on the extent to which it produces behavior that will be supported by its consequences. To the degree that there is any slippage between the behavior specified by the rule and that supported by environmental contingencies, the contingencies will eventually win every time. Behavior that may have initially been rule governed will gradually change in ways that are more likely to be reinforced.

Discrepancies between the behavior required by the rule and the behavior supported by consequences therefore underlie the ineffectiveness of rules. Consider a new employee who receives training on how to use a piece of equipment. She may participate in a training class, be asked to learn an instruction manual, and be monitored by a supervisor, all with the goal of insuring that she uses the equipment in a particular way. She may initially perform as trained, but as she gains experience using the equipment, she may find it easier, quicker, or more effective to use the equipment somewhat differently than she was trained. The company's instructions may have originated because of concerns about safety, product quality, or minimizing wear and tear on the equipment, but her experience with contingencies may shape her behavior in ways contrary to her training. Her co-workers may even aid this transition by giving her guidance (rules) based on their own experiences. As long as the company's training asks for behavior that is not entirely supported by on-the-job contingencies, employees will eventually learn to ignore the rules. The challenge for the company is to figure out how to arrange the job so that the contingencies encountered by employees support the behavior described by the rules or to consider whether the rules should be changed to accommodate the natural contingencies.

BOX 5.5

But There's More

There is a substantial literature concerning rules as an influence on behavior (for example, see Hayes, 1989). Although some of the issues addressed in this literature are conceptual in nature, there are important experimental themes that have been pursed as well, and their results have implications for practical efforts to manage behavior.

For example, one aspect of verbal behavior that has been investigated concerns the impact of rules or instructions on the sensitivity of the listener's behavior to contingencies. This line of research has revealed that behavior that results from instructions may often be less sensitive to contingencies than behavior that has been shaped (Catania, Mathews, & Shimoff, 1982). This research has implications for how practitioners go about establishing behavioral performances. Although it is certainly less effortful to instruct rather than to shape a performance, a side effect of this approach may be to limit how well the resulting behavior adapts to the subtleties of the natural contingencies associated with the behavior (see Catania, 2007, chapter 15). This distinction is particularly evident when trying to teach complex physical movements, such as those required in sports. Teaching a young child to hit a pitched ball with a bat can certainly proceed with extensive instructions, but might they delay progress in shaping the skill via the natural contingencies associated with swinging at pitched balls?

In other words, in the long run compliance with rules depends on how accurately the rules describe behavior that is supported by the contingencies. Supplementary consequences may be effective in generating good compliance with rules for a while, but eventually the effects of exposure to the natural consequences for such behavior, and for alternative ways of behaving, are likely to be sufficient to shift responding so it is consistent with those natural contingencies. Furthermore, efforts to augment control by rules by arranging supplementary contingencies must continue as long as the natural contingencies tend to push behavior in other directions. This is often more trouble than redesigning the rules or the environment so that there is a good match between rules and contingencies.

CHAPTER SUMMARY

1. Viewing knowledge as a thing, something we possess and display, is mentalistic. Behavior analysts instead consider the circumstances that generate this kind of verbal behavior.

2. Discussions of knowledge often distinguish between knowing how versus knowing about. The former involves a history of observing relevant behavior, whereas for the latter the behavior must be appropriate to relevant discriminative stimuli. In both cases, such tacts are simply based on our observations of behavior, and there is no reason to invoke mentalistic concepts or processes.

3. Explanation of behavior in terms of its purpose or intentions or goals is called teleological. This approach violates a fundamental position in science that something cannot be explained in terms of future events. Teleological explanations are mentalistic by implying mental processes such as trying, wanting, expecting, or intending.

4. Other references to purpose as a cause of behavior may involve intentions or feelings, which usually depend not on actual sensations but merely everyday vocabulary.

5. Still another kind of reference to purpose may involve describing its function. This only points to behavioral outcomes and may only be a sloppy way of talking about the relation between a behavior and its consequences.

6. Vernacular references to problem solving describe situations in which the individual has no behavior immediately available that can resolve a condition of deprivation or aversive stimulation.

7. This definition includes problems that may be quite subtle, but the test of whether a certain state of affairs is a problem lies in whether its solution (behavior that reduces the deprivation or removes the aversive condition) is reinforcing.

8. By itself, emitting a solution is not necessarily usefully described as problem solving. If someone else offers a solution or if we simply stumble onto it, this

label might be misleading. Problem solving involves behavior that changes the environment so that the behavior that removes the problem can be emitted.

9. What are often called rules, advice, or instructions involve verbal discriminative stimuli that are presented under control of some relation between a behavior and its consequences. The speaker's experience with this reinforcement relation provides the context for giving a rule, which may specify consequences for following or failing to follow the rule.

10. Following the rule may benefit the listener by bringing their behavior into contact with the reinforcement relation with which the speaker has some experience. When effective, rules are an efficient way for the speaker to manage a listener's behavior.

11. Rule following or rule-governed behavior means that the listener's behavior is under control of the rule, not merely consistent with it. Behavior may be consistent with a rule as a result of other factors, such as a history of consequences for the behavior. In this case, the behavior is called contingency shaped or implicitly shaped.

12. Rule-governed behavior produces consequences that may gradually override the effects of the rule, which is often the reason rules fail to be effective. This suggests that rules must specify behavior that is closely supported by the natural consequences for the behavior if they are to be useful.

TEXT STUDY GUIDE

1. How is the concept of knowledge and understanding mentalistic?

2. What is the behavioral distinction between knowing how and knowing about?

3. Where is a behavior when it is not being emitted?

4. Why are teleological explanations considered problematic in science and carefully avoided?

5. How should we go about describing or explaining behavior that seems purposive?

6. In addition to talking about purpose as a cause of behavior, the text describes two other ways we invoke purpose as an explanation. Describe these two other ways.

7. How does Skinner define problem solving? In his terms, what is a problem? How must it be resolved in order to describe behavior as problem solving?

8. Why should we not consider trial-and-error behavior problem solving?

9. How do behavior analysts define rules, advice, or instructions?

10. What is the basis for rules in terms of the speaker's verbal behavior? What makes the rule effective for the listener?

11. Distinguish between rule-governed versus contingency-shaped behavior.

12. What is required for rules to be effective in the long run?

BOX STUDY GUIDE

1. What is a behaviorally useful way to talk about having an idea? How does the notion of "having" an idea imply mentalism?

2. Why might it be said that having an idea is similar to "having" other behavior?

3. How might motivating operations be involved in the explanation of planning to do something?

4. What is the difference between talking about memory versus the behavior of remembering?

5. What are function-altering stimuli?

6. Give an example of verbal behavior that involves contingency-specifying stimuli.

DISCUSSION TOPICS AND EXERCISES

1. Consider everyday examples of how we explain behavior in terms of purpose. Reframe those examples in behavioral terms without reference to future events.

2. Consider examples of problem solving that do not involve other people or mere persistence.

3. Consider everyday examples of rules that seem to be ineffective. Discuss why they might be ineffective and how they might be improved to increase their effectiveness. How could you adjust the rules or the contingencies so that the rule was effective in prompting the desired behavior?

4. Discuss when it might be appropriate to attempt to manage behavior with rules as opposed to arranging contingencies.

SUGGESTED READINGS

Branch, M. N. (1977). On the role of memory in the analysis of behavior. *Journal of the Experimental Analysis of Behavior, 29(2)*, 171–179.

Skinner, B. F. (1953). *About behaviorism.* New York: Alfred A. Knopf. (Chapter 4: Operant Behavior)

Chapter 6

Is There Something Special About Reasoning?[1]

Bridget had been working with Alan for more than two years, and he had made enormous progress. Alan had been diagnosed as autistic when he was three years old. When she first met him shortly thereafter, he was a mess. Self-stimulatory behavior and tantrums were routine occurrences, and his social repertoire was limited in the usual ways. He did talk some, but he had a long way to go before his verbal repertoire would be appropriate for his age. His parents handled things as well as could be expected, but they were at their wits' end.

As a BCBA, this was the kind of challenge Bridget had trained for. She had done the necessary assessment, designed an intervention plan, kept it current, trained the Board Certified assistant Behavior Analyst working with her, and monitored every step of the way. With a good bit of training, Alan's parents had played a key role as well, and she couldn't have asked more of them.

Fortunately, it was all paying off. Alan had shown relatively rapid progress. His more challenging behavior wasn't much of a problem anymore. That had been the easy part. His social skills were at least much improved, though you could still see ways he didn't fully fit in with other children. Best of all, however, he had made impressive improvements in his ability to express himself and hold conversations. In fact, they were now working on more advanced aspects of his verbal skills.

Alan had reached the point that he carried out meaningful conversations about past and present events and was making good progress with rudimentary reasoning skills, such as sequencing objects of pictures in different ways, arranging pictures of activities in appropriate order, finding differences and similarities in sets, and answering questions about events in pictures. Bridget felt he was ready to develop his ability to build on these observations to solve problems and reason in more advanced ways with himself or others about situations and events. The question was how to accomplish this objective. She knew

---

[1]This chapter is based on Terrell & Johnston (1989), as well as Skinner (1957).

she could develop appropriate teaching procedures if she could figure out the component skills. They weren't obvious. What exactly do you teach someone if you want to improve their ability to reason about events and circumstances in their lives and figure out how to solve problems, both large and small?

WHAT IS REASONING?

More Than Verbal Behavior?

It seems obvious that humans "think things through," "put two and two together," "consider the evidence," "draw conclusions," and in various ways engage in what we call reasoning. Of course, whatever the characteristics of the behavior we are describing, our label for it—reasoning—is just a word, a verbal response. Because this word is a noun does not mean reasoning is a distinct physical thing, process, or phenomenon apart from operant behavior. In the words of Chapter 2, "it's just verbal behavior."

This assessment should not be taken as demeaning, merely an objective evaluation in light of available science. We may still be impressed with elaborate and persuasive arguments, calling the best of them brilliant. Our ability to reason, whether in small private moments or carefully displayed in public venues, seems the zenith of human intellect. However, these assessments are themselves verbal behavior and should not encourage us to assign reasoning any special qualities or status, even as we acknowledge it is no more than behavior.

Although what we casually refer to as reasoning is "just" verbal behavior, is there a basis for distinguishing it from other aspects of verbal behavior? Is it a special kind of verbal behavior, or are we only tempted to ask this question because our vernacular dialect has a word—reasoning—that seems to demand explanation? After all, just because we have what is admittedly a rudimentary label for some features of behavior does not necessarily mean there is an important behavioral phenomenon to be studied. Can we even define reasoning in a useful way, and how might an understanding of reasoning based on the science of behavior analysis be useful? To answer these questions, let us consider the factors that prompt us to describe verbal behavior as involving reasoning.

The Proposition

Although the verbal behavior generally called reasoning might seem different from other forms of verbal behavior—at the least, much more complex—it involves the same verbal response classes Skinner introduced in his seminal book, *Verbal behavior* (1957). By way of explanation, consider the proposition, the basic component of reasoning. In everyday terms, a proposition is what we know, believe, think, judge, or assume. When we say that the sky is blue or that a certain political position will be best for the country, we are offering a proposition.

When we make statements about what we know, we are emitting verbal behavior Skinner called *tacts*—verbal responses that are consistently reinforced in the presence of a particular object or event or a property of an object or event. You are probably emitting a tact when you say, "car," if this response is consistently reinforced in the presence of cars. If a car is the sole source of control over the response, it is called a pure tact. If some property of the object or event (its color, for example) controls the response, it is called an abstract tact. If you say "black" in describing a black car, it is called an abstract tact. In other words, an object may prompt different verbal responses, which may be pure or abstract tacts.

A proposition takes tacts one step further by connecting different forms of tacts with an additional verbal response, the **assertive autoclitic**, "is." When you say "The car *is* black," you declare a particular state of affairs and encourage the listener to agree. The statement "The car is black" asserts a relation between the pure and abstract tacts "car" and "black." Propositions are evoked by the relations between an object (car) and one of its properties (blackness).

Tacts relate verbal behavior to non-verbal features in the environment. However, much of our environment consists of the verbal behavior of others. Verbal behavior that is related to other verbal behavior is called *intraverbal*. The subjects and predicates of propositions may therefore be related to the verbal environment as intraverbals rather than as tacts. When you say "Sentences have a subject and a verb," you are tacting the relation between intraverbals and their stimulating circumstances.

Propositions also may include what is called a **quantifying autoclitic**. Under certain conditions, the tact, "car," might be "the car," "a car," "some cars," "all cars," or "no cars." Skinner proposed that these autoclitic features do not modify the subject of the proposition but instead modify the reaction of the listener to the proposition itself. If you say, "All cars have wheels," you encourage the listener to agree that not merely some, but all cars are so equipped.

In sum, propositions are a complex unit of verbal behavior made up of basic verbal response classes, including tacts or intraverbals, modified by certain autoclitics. Propositions function as tacts because they are controlled by the objects of simple tacts or intraverbals. However, they also tact the relations between verbal behavior and its environmental control. When we say "The car is black," we tact not only the relation between "car" and "black" but our tendency to assign blackness to the car. Similarly, when you pay a girlfriend a compliment by saying "Your dress is pretty," you are tacting the relation between dress and pretty, as well as your willingness to evaluate the dress in that way.

Propositions involve the speaker's behavior, and it is important to consider its consequences, not just for the speaker but for listeners. In general, if the speaker's verbal behavior produces reinforcing outcomes, we may consider it effective. If the outcomes reduce the likelihood of reinforcement, it may be considered ineffective. The speaker's behavior of emitting a proposition is likely to be reinforced when a listener accepts or believes it. In this context, Skinner defined believing what someone tells us as "... a function of, or identical with, our tendency to act upon the verbal stimuli which he provides" (1957, p. 160). This means that a proposition may be effective (accepted or believed by a listener) or ineffective (rejected or ignored by a listener) regardless of whether it is true. With reference to the example of complimenting a girlfriend's dress, if her reaction is to smile and thank you, it may not matter if you are the only one who believes the dress is pretty.

The listener's behavior with reference to the proposition may also be effective or ineffective regardless of the truth of the proposition. If a proposition helps a listener respond effectively in the described situation, it may be considered true, whatever other criteria might apply to its accuracy. Continuing our example, although no one else may believe the dress is pretty, if your girlfriend finds it reinforcing to wear the dress as a result of your compliment, the proposition is effective for her. Of course, a reinforcing outcome for her will be more likely if others also compliment her wearing the dress. As Skinner pointed out for tacts in general, "behavior in the form of the tact works for the benefit of the listener by extending his contact with the environment, and such behavior is set up in the verbal community for this reason" (1957, p. 85).

Verbal behavior in the form of a proposition can therefore be defined as effective in two ways. If the listener acts on (accepts or believes) the proposition as a verbal stimulus, it is effective for the speaker. If acting on it produces reinforcing outcomes for the listener, the proposition is effective again. In both instances, the proposition need not be true by other criteria.

Premises and Conclusions

Because the outcome of listeners accepting our propositions is reinforcing, we learn to emit propositions in ways that increase the likelihood of that result. For example, a speaker may improve the chances of a listener accepting a proposition by first offering other propositions that may be more readily accepted. Logicians call these more believable propositions premises, and the proposition whose acceptability is thereby enhanced is called the conclusion. In other words, certain premises may be much more likely to be accepted by the listener than others, and proposing them in a certain sequence may increase the likelihood that the listener agrees with the concluding premise. Some people may become quite skilled in offering propositions in ways that often convince others to agree with their conclusion.

Consider a prosecutor who wishes the jury to agree with the proposition that a defendant is guilty of a crime, an outcome that will be reinforcing to the prosecutor. In order to improve the chances that this proposition will be accepted, the prosecutor may assert other propositions that members of the jury will find credible. These other assertions may include evidence supporting the guilt of the defendant, such as his presence at the scene of the crime, forensic evidence of the defendant's involvement, the testimony of eyewitnesses, and so forth. If these evidentiary propositions are accepted, the members of the jury may vote to convict the defendant as guilty.

We reason with others when we emit verbal behavior that alters the likelihood of the listener accepting certain propositions. (We also reason with ourselves in the same way when we take the roles of both speaker and listener.) Premises may be spoken or written and occur in different sequences. This verbal behavior may then prompt the emission of new propositions, such as conclusions. As we will see below, logicians may categorize such verbal behavior in different ways depending on how premises are arranged, but from a behavior analytic point of view, all variations involve the same features.

It may be tempting to think about reasoning in relatively formal ways, such as when scientists draw conclusions about the results of their experiments. A series of premises may be stated concerning features of certain assumptions and facts known beforehand, an experiment's methods, the nature of the data under different conditions, and ways of looking at the data, followed by a conclusion about what the study reveals, possibly in relation to a particular theory. Some of this reasoning is often laid out in advance by a researcher when designing a study and then formally proposed to colleagues in a published report.

Most of the time, however, we are not very particular about criteria for labeling verbal behavior as reasoning. If we are sitting in the living room, hear a noise in the kitchen, and assume (conclude) it is our roommate, we are unlikely to lay out a formal sequence of premises (including the fact that we saw our roommate go into the kitchen) as prompts for accepting that conclusion. However, you might acknowledge that the fact that you saw your roommate go into the kitchen is the reason for your conclusion, and if pressed you might be able to build a systematic sequence of premises.

These variations in what we might call reasoning suggest that it would be difficult to come up with a definition of reasoning that allows examples to be unambiguously classified as falling in or outside of its boundaries. This challenge should not be surprising, however. "Reasoning" is a colloquial notion that evolved in our language without the benefit of a scientific understanding of its foundation in operant behavior. As with other vernacular terms, its highly varied usage in everyday talk does not consistently identify discrete response classes or patterns of behavior. Reasoning is merely verbal behavior that influences the probability that listeners will accept certain propositions.

Logicality and Rules

We tact regularities or patterns around us the same way we tact single events, and these patterns often involve our behavior. Sometimes tacts of behavioral patterns or regularities result in statements called rules. For instance, the rules of grammar are tacts of certain regularities in our verbal behavior. As we discussed in the previous chapter, rules often originate as descriptions of consistent patterns of events, and as such they may serve as a means of controlling human behavior. A rule may describe a contingency of some sort, and, under the right conditions, it may prompt us to behave in a way that is consistent with that contingency. However, behavior that is initially governed by a rule also produces consequences, which accumulate their own effects on how we behave. Just because our behavior is consistent with a rule does not mean it is controlled by the rule; it may instead be under control of the history of consequences it has produced. Thus, when we are first learning the rules of grammar, they may help control the way we talk. Eventually, the organization of our everyday speech is substantially influenced by its social consequences, though it may still be consistent with at least a few rules of grammar.

One kind of verbal pattern that has been extensively cataloged concerns regularities in the manner that speakers emit premises that influence the likelihood that listeners will emit or accept a conclusion. Some arrangements of premises are more effective than others in augmenting the probability that conclusions will be accepted. These consistencies are the result of reinforcement practices in verbal communities that include scientists, logicians, and others. These arrangements or patterns are called the rules of logicality, which tact regularities in how propositions are stated. When propositions correspond to these rules, the probability of reinforcement in the form of listeners accepting or emitting the conclusion is maximized.

Deductive Reasoning

Perhaps the best known set of rules of logic are the rules of deductive inference. Many students have been exposed to these rules in a college course on logic, though it is safe to say that the result, as with the rules of grammar, usually falls short of a rule-governed repertoire. The rules of deductive inference specify various arrangements of propositions that correspond to certain conditions, along with a concluding proposition that also corresponds to those conditions. Patterns of verbal responding that match these rules may produce relatively consistent acceptance of the concluding proposition by listeners. Conjunctions, disjunctions, and implications are three examples of the rules of deductive inference.

Consider the arrangement of propositions logicians call a conjunction. A conjunction relates two propositions that would otherwise be emitted separately ("It is cold outside" and "I am writing") with the verbal response "and." Connecting the two propositions this way is a more complex propositional response than stating each separately. If a listener accepts any two simple propositions separately, it is likely that a conjunctive proposition (connecting them with the response "and") will also be accepted.

BOX 6.1

Reasoning in Circles

We say that an argument is logically circular (a type of deductive fallacy) when it seems to "prove" itself. Although circularity may appear in many forms, it involves statements to the effect that "A implies B which implies A." For example, the statement that "combustion requires the presence of oxygen because you cannot start a fire without oxygen" is circular because the argument begins with what it winds up with. We are suspicious of circular reasoning because it seems too invulnerable to disproof, and it is. If the premise is true, the conclusion must be true, but there is no test in the argument by which the conclusion might be false.

Behavior analysis has been accused of this kind of reasoning in its conception of reinforcement, to wit: A consequence functions as a reinforcer if it increases responding, and this increase is explained by the fact that such responding is reinforced by the consequence. There are different ways of expressing this kind of relational argument, but the apparent flaw seems to be clear. Or is it?

Tonneau (2008) considers this issue in terms of a distinction between descriptive versus explanatory statements. Some behavior analysts (Catania, 1984) have argued that behavior terms such as reinforcement are descriptive, rather than explanatory. This position holds that reinforcement only names a relation between the environment and responding, rather than attempting to explain the outcome. With this approach, no complaint about circularity is valid. On the other hand, others (Hineline, 2003) argue that reinforcement is a proper explanation, given sufficient context. After all, a great deal has been scientifically established concerning the nature of reinforcement, and what we know is part of what we reference when arguing why reinforcement explains behavior change.

In summarizing discussions of this topic, Tonneau (2008) explores the role of description and explanation in science and concludes that the concept of reinforcement is both descriptive and explanatory. He concludes: "When behavior analysts attribute the prevalence of a response to reinforcement, they describe a particular type of relation between responses, subsequent events, and further responding (A), and in the process they explain why a response persists or increases in prevalence (B). Notice that A and B are distinct (even though they overlap), as they must be if the description of A is to serve as an explanation of B" (Tonneau, 2008, p. 91).

Disjunctive propositions connect two simple propositions with the response "or," as in "Either the dog is brown, or it is not my dog." If a disjunctive proposition is accepted as a premise, and if the second premise that negates one of the disjuncts is also accepted, it is highly likely that a listener will accept a concluding proposition in the form of the other disjunct. That is, if a second premise—"The dog is black"—is accepted, the probability is high that a listener will accept the concluding proposition "It is not my dog."

An implication also connects two simple propositions by an additional verbal response. Perhaps the most common form involves "If..., then..." statements such as "If there is combustion, then oxygen must be present." If a listener accepts this proposition, and also accepts a simple proposition that is the antecedent of the implication ("There is combustion"), it is very likely that the listener will also accept the consequent of the implication ("Oxygen is present"). Note that accepting the propositions that combustion implies oxygen and that combustion is present facilitates accepting the concluding proposition that oxygen is present.

We reason deductively when we emit propositions in a way that corresponds to these rules of logic. We may not be engaging in rule-governed behavior when we do this, however. Reasoning may be considered deductive in form if it can merely be described by these rules. Although it might seem that there is something special about deductive reasoning that assures that concluding propositions must be true, this result is not guaranteed. Deductively valid reasoning can lead to acceptance of conclusions that turn out to be false. (In the disjunctive example above, the black dog may actually be yours because unbeknownst to you someone dyed your brown dog black.) In any case, what characterizes deductive inference is the high probability of listener agreement that is occasioned by verbal behavior corresponding to deductive rules.

Inductive Reasoning

Premises may be offered in an arrangement that enhances the acceptability of a concluding proposition but that does not conform to the rules of deductive inference. These patterns of verbal behavior may be called inductive reasoning. Logicians characterize reasoning as deductive only if it corresponds to the rules of deductive inference, and this leaves inductive reasoning to be defined in the absence of such formal rules. From a behavioral perspective, however, the patterns of verbal behavior we call inductive reasoning are as much rules as the more formally stated rules of deductive inference. Both are behaviorally defined by patterns or regularities in verbal responding that result in a higher probability of the listener accepting a proposition than might otherwise be the case.

One example of inductive rules is Mills's Method of Agreement (1973/1843). If there appears to be a common factor regarding a phenomenon across a number of otherwise different circumstances, that factor may be considered as the cause of the phenomenon. So, if medical researchers are searching for the cause of symptoms observed in different people living in a certain area of the country and note that they share a particular dietary practice, this practice might be further examined as a source of the symptoms. Mills's Method of Differences is another inductive rule. If a particular phenomenon occurs only when another event occurs, and never in its absence, it may be reasoned that the two events are causally related. Reasoning by analogy is another inductive tactic. For example, if two couples go out for dinner and eat the same items on the menu and three of the four get sick to their stomach later that evening, you might infer that the fourth person is likely to get sick as well.

Is there a difference? This discussion of deductive and inductive reasoning might seem to accept the traditional distinction between them as distinct forms of reasoning. However, this distinction does not work for behavior analysts because we approach all examples of reasoning as verbal behavior and not a special kind of verbal behavior at that. The traditional position that deductive and inductive reasoning are distinct lies in assumptions about reasoning as a mental activity. However, a scientific approach to operant behavior offers no empirical justification for this distinction. Our understanding of how verbal behavior works and the best way to approach its analysis suggests that any distinction between deductive and inductive reasoning is nominal rather than functional. Although inductive reasoning is traditionally distinguished from deductive reasoning by rules that have a more informal style, we have seen that inductive reasoning can also be characterized by patterns or regularities in how premises are emitted that increase the probability of listener agreement. From a behavioral perspective, both deductive and inductive reasoning involve ways of offering premises (rules) that often result in listeners accepting conclusions.

Furthermore, there are many variables that influence the listener's behavior in addition to whether premises match the requirements of certain rules. For example, a prosecutor's arguments about the guilt of the defendant might be deductively sound, but other aspects of his or her behavior can also affect the probability of a guilty verdict from the jury. Factors such as a prosecutor's interactions with witnesses, defense attorneys, and the judge may sway members of the jury more than the deductive validity of the prosecutor's syllogisms.

Deductively fallacious reasoning is also often convincing to listeners. For example, noticing that the ground is wet one morning, we comment that it must have rained last night. Logicians label the implicit syllogism as *illicit modus ponens*, a deductive fallacy. More formally, the argument is as follow: "(A) If it rained last night, then the ground will be wet this morning. (B) The ground is wet, (C) therefore it must have rained last night." This reasoning is fallacious because other factors (the automatic lawn sprinklers coming on) could explain why the ground is wet. In order to be deductively valid, the first premise would have to start off, "If *and only if*..."

Deductively fallacious reasoning is hardly uncommon. Indeed, scientists are often in the position of drawing conclusions that are consistent with the deductive fallacy termed *illicit modus ponens* were they to even wonder about such matters. Because they are asking about phenomena they do not yet completely understand, they typically do not know enough to make an "if and only if" statement. So, a researcher might reason that if a particular state of affairs is true, a certain result will be obtained. When the anticipated result is obtained, the researcher may be

BOX 6.2

Science, Logicality, and Truth

It is hard to let go of the idea that logical (deductively valid) reasoning must be true, as well as the corollary position that illogical reasoning must be false, even though there are countless examples that violate both precepts. This conviction about the necessity for logical clarity in achieving truthful outcomes suggests that scientists must be masters of sound logical reasoning if their work is to lead to the discovery of truths about nature. In fact, scientists are no more logical than others with similar educational backgrounds (Mahoney, 1976), and formal training in logic is not a routine feature of scientific training. Indeed, as this chapter notes, deductively fallacious reasoning is common, and to some extent unavoidable, in everyday science.

In other words, deductively valid reasoning is not a criterion for the truth of statements about events, in science or other walks of life. If someone accuses a speaker of illogicality as a basis for denying the speaker's argument, the argument may be unsound but not because of flaws in any underlying reasoning. The point is that reasoning is not what makes something true or false in nature. Remember, reasoning is just verbal behavior. It is not a variable that influences anything other than a listener's reactions. Yes, deductively valid reasoning about the world around us is often correct by other criteria, but its certitude is neither a reason for, nor guarantee of, correct conclusions about natural events. This perspective suggests that accusations of illogicality as a standard for the truth of a speaker's conclusion miss the point. The conclusion may be false and it may be supported by invalid reasoning, but the latter is not due to the former.

---

tempted to conclude that the initial assumption about that state of affairs is therefore true. For example, he might suspect that a particular dose of a drug has a certain kind of effect on behavior. If the experiment shows that behavior changes in that way when the drug is administered, it may be tempting to accept that the drug is responsible, thereby legitimizing the conclusion that the original premise about the behavioral effect of the drug is correct. We must hope, however, that the researcher is sufficiently well trained to recognize that the assumed state of affairs might still be false because other factors (the characteristics of the behavioral preparation used to generate responding) could have caused the experimental results instead. Eliminating these alternative explanations always takes more research.

It is also important to retrieve reasoning and logic from its traditional interpretation as a mental activity because this explanation supports other misunderstandings. For instance, it is tempting to view reasoning, and by extension all verbal behavior, as symbolic activity that involves private subjective meanings that exist in a logical mentalistic realm (Moore, 1981). Once verbal behavior of any sort is viewed through the lens of mentalism, the opportunities for a scientific approach to behavior, and the challenges behavior presents in daily life, are greatly diminished.

Finally, the interpretation of the culturally based view of reasoning in terms of a science-based understanding of verbal behavior is intellectually illuminating, but is it practically useful? In the process of freeing reasoning from its customary mentalistic context, this analysis deconstructs it in a way that highlights verbal practices that are certainly valuable in everyday life. For example, there is no question that some people are more skilled than others in solving problems, analyzing situations in which they find themselves, or persuading others to agree with a certain position. It is certainly the case that this skill can be beneficial to both speakers and listeners. Might this perspective aid practitioners such as Bridget in the vignette at the beginning of this chapter to teach the skill to children who are falling short? Could it serve as a foundation for a general educational curriculum for teaching effective reasoning skills? Or even a specialized curriculum for those planning careers, such as the law, in which the skill is especially important? These questions have yet to be answered in the ABA literature. There is no apparent barrier to this research agenda, so perhaps it is a matter of sufficient demand from the marketplace for ABA services.

This brief summary of a behavior analytic perspective toward reasoning shows how it can be analyzed in terms of its core features as verbal behavior. It would be easy to feel that this perspective diminishes this most impressive feature of our verbal repertoires. Indeed, that might be a fair complaint for all of the topics in this chapter. Consider what we have learned from scientific explanations of other natural phenomena, however. Sacrificing everyday notions about a phenomenon allows us to see what is really there and to put what we learn in the context of what has already been scientifically established. Reasoning and the other aspects of our verbal repertoire discussed in this chapter that seem special among our capabilities, not to mention impressively complex, are unavoidably just part of our verbal repertoire. This acknowledgment allows us to approach these issues with established and effective experimental methods for studying verbal behavior, as well as a scientific literature that provides a broad and secure experimental context for what we learn.

CHAPTER SUMMARY

1. Reasoning is no different than any other verbal behavior and involves the same response classes introduced by Skinner (1957).

2. The proposition is the core concept in reasoning—in common parlance, what we know, believe, think, judge, or assume. Propositions are complex forms of tacts, verbal responses that are consistently reinforced in the presence of a particular object or event. When propositions are connected with the assertive autoclitic, "is," they tact a relation between the two propositions. Tacts may relate verbal behavior to non-verbal features in the environment, but they may also relate verbal behavior to other verbal behavior, which is called an intraverbal.

3. The speaker's behavior of emitting a proposition may be considered effective when it produces reinforcing outcomes. This may involve a listener acting on it in some way (commonly described as accepting or believing it). The proposition may be considered effective (or ineffective) regardless of whether it is true.

4. This listener's behavior with reference to a proposition may also be effective or ineffective regardless of the truth of the proposition. If a proposition helps a listener respond effectively in the described situation, it may be considered true.

5. Uttering a proposition can therefore be defined as effective in two ways. If the listener acts on (accepts or believes) the proposition as a verbal stimulus, it has been effective for the speaker. If acting on it produces reinforcing outcomes for the listener, the proposition is effective again. In both instances, the proposition need not be true by other standards.

6. We learn to emit propositions in ways that increase the likelihood of a listener's accepting them. Patterns in our emission of propositions may be described as rules, in particular, the rules of logic.

7. Deductive reasoning refers to particular rules for arranging premises for which there is a high likelihood of a listener's accepting a series of propositions. Inductive reasoning refers to ways of arranging premises that do not conform to the rules of deductive inference.

8. For behavior analysts, the nominal distinction between deductive and inductive reasoning does not refer to distinct kinds of verbal behavior.

9. Deductively fallacious reasoning is often convincing. Scientists are often in the position of drawing conclusions that may be described as deductively fallacious.

TEXT STUDY GUIDE

1. In terms of Skinner's verbal response classes, what is a proposition and what are its typical components?

2. Describe the consequences of uttering propositions for both the speaker and the listener. What does it mean for a proposition to be effective?

3. From a behavior analytic perspective, what are the rules of logic?

4. What is deductive reasoning, from a verbal behavior perspective?

5. How does the text argue that deductive and inductive reasoning differ? How are they similar?

6. Why are scientists often in the position of drawing conclusions that may be described as deductively fallacious?

BOX STUDY GUIDE

1. Is it circular reasoning to argue that when a reinforcer occurs following responding and responding increases that it does so because the consequence is a reinforcer?

2. What is the problem with accusing someone of being illogical as a reason for denying the correctness of their argument?

DISCUSSION TOPICS AND EXERCISES

1. Defend the position that there is no functional difference between deductive and inductive reasoning.

2. Build an argument by proposing a sequence of premises that progress from those that might be easy for a listener to agree with to those that might be more challenging.

3. What applied research questions should be addressed in order to develop a technology for teaching reasoning skills to different populations?

SUGGESTED READINGS

Skinner, B. F. (1957). *Verbal behavior*. New York: Appleton-Century-Crofts. (Chapter 18: Logical and scientific verbal behavior).

Terrell, D. J & Johnston, J. M. (1989). Logic, reasoning, and verbal behavior. *The Behavior Analyst, 12*, 35–44.

Chapter 7

Behavioral Responsibility

Jen was a BCBA who worked for a public school district and was assigned to help teachers address behavioral issues with their students. She loved her job and got a lot of satisfaction working with teachers, who were usually desperate for her help by the time she was called in. Most of her referrals involved individual students who were presenting a particular problem in the classroom. The problems usually stemmed from some kind of "acting out," a description that for teachers often seemed to imply internal problems that were being expressed in the students' behavior. She wished teachers would more often worry about why some students were performing poorly on academic tasks, but sins of omission were not often considered a behavioral problem. She was thinking about this dichotomy between students behaving badly by omission versus commission when she met with her supervisor—Martha—in the district office to discuss scheduling issues. When Martha asked how things were going, Jen let loose.

"Why is it that teachers can't tolerate a student acting out but seem to accept the fact that the same student is struggling academically?" she complained. "I know they're aware of the academic problems, but they only want help dealing with the bad behavior, as if poor academic performance isn't a problem as well. I wish, just once, they would ask me to help them with the student's schoolwork."

Martha had been around long enough to know the answer, and she knew Jen did, too. "Acting out gets in the teacher's way. It can't be ignored like a bad score on a spelling quiz." "I know, I know," Jen conceded, "but it all comes from the same place. Sometimes I think teachers see disruptive behavior as something the student is responsible for but poor academic performance as something the student can't help."

"Maybe it's the teacher who can't help or doesn't know how," Martha suggested.

"Well, they usually don't know what to do in either case, but it's odd they're so willing to blame the student for one kind of behavior but not the other. Maybe it's because the reasons for learning problems aren't as obvious as the causes for acting out."

"Probably. I suspect some teachers assume that poor schoolwork means the student isn't all that bright, which they truly can't do anything about. Remember, teachers aren't trained to look at behavior the way you do."

Jen thought for a moment. "Yes, but the real issue is failing to look for ways of fixing either kind of problem. Whether you assume that bad behavior comes from the student's personality or that poor schoolwork stems from weak brainpower, you're missing the point. A teacher's job isn't to assign personal responsibility but to take the behavior that shows up and deal with it, not excuse it in some way."

"I agree, but be gentle," Martha cautioned.

"Don't worry," Jen reassured her. "I don't talk like this with teachers, but it's frustrating. I hope the day comes when teacher training prevents this kind of confusion, but I guess dealing with is my job at this point."

CREATIVITY

Where does creativity come from? Is the individual responsible for his or her creative accomplishments? To answer these questions, we must first be clear about what we mean when we label behavior as creative. Did you catch the subtle reframing in this agenda? Instead of accepting the question's implication that, as a noun, creativity must be a thing that we seemingly possess a certain amount of, approaching creativity as a way of labeling behavior focuses our interest on behavior, which is all that there is in the first place. There simply is no evidence that creativity is a physical phenomenon. Insisting that creativity is anything more than a matter of how we label behavior under certain circumstances would mean this supposed quality must be approached as a mental event. As we have seen, such a strategy is not only unnecessary, it is methodologically challenging and fraught with conceptual pitfalls. Studying the behavioral basis for traditional mentalistic references provides much better possibilities.

We can further refine our agenda by rephrasing the reference to what we "mean" when we label behavior as creative. Chapter 2 made it clear that words do not have meanings in the vernacular sense. As we have already learned, what we "mean" when we "use" a word is no different from asking what we "mean" when we "use" (engage in) other behavior, such as walking or eating. The meaning of what we say is a matter of identifying the sources of control over our emission of particular verbal responses. Previous chapters have used this tactic to approach the meaning of everyday words from a behavioral perspective, which avoids the trap of mentalism and eases the scientific challenge of explaining the behavioral elements underlying mentalistic references.

So, what are the variables that lead us to say that someone is being creative or showing creativity? It is easy to appreciate that what seems creative or novel to you may seem familiar to someone else. If a friend shows you a painting he made, and you have little artistic background, you might be inclined to compliment his creativity. If you then discovered that his painting was a copy of one someone else had made, you might want to retract your assessment. Others with more artistic training and experience might bring a more sophisticated history to their evaluation. In other words, the behavior we label as creative depends on our experience with such behavior. If we are familiar with the behavior in question, we may be less inclined to label it as creative.

If we can identify the factors influencing the supposedly creative behavior, we may also be less likely to call it creative. For instance, if we learn that an author's newly published novel is based on a true story, we may be reluctant to praise her creativity. If a painter produces a series of paintings that feature the same design elements except for variations in their color, the effort might be seen as less creative than a series of paintings lacking such a systematic foundation. If someone solves a problem in a way we had not considered, yet we learn that their approach was prompted by information on a website, we would probably not say they had come up with a creative solution.

In other words, we tend to label behavior as creative when we are not overly familiar with what is "created" or are unaware of the influences involved. As a basis for labeling behavior as creative, being unfamiliar and unaware ensures considerable subjectivity, enough to limit the usefulness of this label in everyday conversations. Even efforts to define standards for evaluating creativity in artistic competitions fall back on vague generalities that leave much to the interpretations of judges. In other words, our conventional verbal practices fail to provide good reasons for supposing that creativity is a distinct quality of human nature.

Nevertheless, the fact that we are taught to tact behavior as creative suggests it may sometimes be useful for the verbal community to identify certain aspects of a person's behavior in this way. Were there not some benefits, the verbal community would arrange the instructional contingencies necessary to learn this kind of discrimination, however unclear or inconsistent it might be from one instance to another. So, what might we learn about behavior by considering "creative" responding in the context of what we already know about operant behavior? Does it help to talk about behavior as sometimes being novel, rather than creative? This substitution is tempting because, as with creative behavior, we tend to view novel behavior as responding that seems to lack an obvious reinforcement history, leaving us to wonder about its origins. Of course, operant behavior rarely lacks a reinforcement history, though faced with any particular instance, we can usually make educated guesses at how the individual's history contributed to a response.

The question is whether operant behavior can really be novel. If this term means only that no two responses are ever exactly alike, this might be true if we look closely enough. However, this view is misleading because of what we know about how operant behavior works. (This topic was first introduced in Chapter 2 in a discussion of verbal response classes.) Basic and applied research long ago showed that variations in otherwise similar responses tend to be tied together by shared features of the surrounding environment. For instance, when a child responds verbally to seeing a dog, the details of the response may vary from one occasion to the next. The child may say "Dog!" or "Doggie!" or "Bow wow." However, all such responses occur in the presence of dogs, and many are likely to result in similar social reinforcers. We call the result an operant response class or an operant, a phenomenon Skinner noted in one of his earliest papers (Skinner, 1935). The very nature of operant behavior means that behavior that might seem to be novel is likely to be part of an existing response class.

Take the example of a composer facing the task of writing a new musical composition. Although she may start out with little more than a snippet of a melody, her history includes countless experiences of listening to music others wrote as well as pieces she has previously written. As variations within a responses class, her previous compositions (responding) will likely involve certain similarities to this new effort, which is why we are often able to recognize a piece as written by a particular composer. Although the new composition may be obviously different from previous pieces, it may be more similar to her previous work than to the musical compositions of others. These similarities in melody, harmony, tempo, and so forth, are likely to be variations within certain compositional response classes. Although the resulting composition may be easily distinguished from her previous work, it might be misleading to describe her behavior of writing it as novel, given her extensive compositional repertoire and its history.

This analysis should also suggest that the question of where creative behavior comes from is misleading. Because it is not a special kind of behavior, its origin is no different than the origin of any behavior. It is simply the result of our history of behaving in particular ways under often similar circumstances, together with the present consequences for such behavior. Labeling a behavior as creative behavior should not suggest that it is fundamentally different from other operant behavior. Although a certain accomplishment may strike observers as creative or novel, they usually lack a full picture of the history of such behavior and all its variations. They also are unable to examine that history in the light of how operant behavior works. The nature of response classes, which are continually adjusting in concert with changing environmental variables, suggest that it might be difficult to defend the argument that a particular piece of behavior is truly novel in the sense of everyday language.

From this perspective, creativity is not a human quality that some of us necessarily have more of than others. This analysis suggests that creative behavior is the result of our individual reinforcement histories, which should mean that we can engineer those histories to encourage individuals to emit more (or less) creative behavior, however we may define it under different circumstances. To some extent, this seems obvious. Someone who has a long musical history is more likely to impress others with their musical "creativity" than someone who lacks a musical background. Viewing creativity as no more than a loose label for behaving in certain ways implies that we need only specify the creative dimensions we wish

BOX 7.1

The Emergence of Complex Behavior

Consistent with the book's theme, this discussion about creative behavior focuses on the conceptual issues embedded in how we talk about it, rather than what might underlie the origins of complex behavior that we might call creative. One line of research that seems to explain at least some aspects of how complex behavior emerges in the apparent absence of explicit training has been especially illuminating. A series of studies has shown that different skills acquired under different conditions can come together under the right circumstances to serve new functions, a process called contingency adduction (Andronis, 1983; Andronis, Layng, & Goldiamond, 1997; Epstein, 1987; Layng, Twyman, & Stikeleather, 2004). This research reveals that if two or more performances are trained under different stimulus conditions, they may be "recruited" by a new stimulus condition that in some way combines features of prior stimuli. The emergent performance, which combines aspects of the previously distinct performances, may then be directly supported by contingencies in the new situation.

This phenomenon has been explored in diverse circumstances. Epstein (1987) demonstrated a fascinating example by training four distinct component performances in pigeons, which were then confronted with a situation in which reinforcement was only available by combining the previously learned, simpler performances, though this new, more complex performance had not been directly trained. To observers, the resulting performance might seem "insightful," though it is more easily explained in terms of a learning history. Contingency adduction has been used in educational settings to establish key component skills, practice them until they are fluent, and then introduce circumstances that make it more likely that the skills combine into more complex, composite skills—an approach called generative instruction (Johnson & Layng, 1992).

to strengthen and arrange an appropriate reinforcement contingency if we wish to generate more of it.

In fact, this sort of thing has been done in both laboratory and field research, as well as in practical applications. As described by Baum (2005), Tony Nevin and his students gave rats access to objects such as a box, a ramp, a swing, and a toy truck and then reinforced only responding the rats had not emitted previously. Perhaps not surprisingly, the rats soon began to emit new responses to these objects. Similarly, Karen Pryor reported that when she and her colleagues at Sea Life Park in Hawaii made reinforcers available only for tricks that porpoises had never before exhibited, the animals began emitting new tricks within a few days (Pryor, 1999). Applied research has shown that generating more creative literary efforts in school children who previously demonstrated it is a matter of arranging effective reinforcers for particular features of their writing (Glover & Gary, 1976;

Glover, 1979; and Mahoney & Hopkins, 1973). In fact, there are a number of ways of inducing variability in responding that can then be the focus of practical reinforcement contingencies (e.g., Esch, Esch, & Love, 2009; Goetz & Baer, 1973; Grow, Kelley, Roane, & Shillingsburg, 2008).

Finally, the topic of creativity illustrates the benefits of replacing a colloquial view of behavior with a perspective rooted in established science. The everyday view implies that creativity is an inner quality that is present to varying degrees from one person to another. This perspective assigns responsibility for creative behavior to the individual, not the environment. What is encouraging about approaching creativity as a matter of environmental contingencies is that we can nurture this sort of behavior when we wish. We need not wait for happy accidents of just the right behavioral history to come along for a few individuals. If we want children to write stories that we call creative, for example, we can build the necessary skills and tendencies with the right kind of opportunities and reinforcement contingencies.

CREDIT WHERE CREDIT IS DUE?

When we find creative accomplishments, it is natural to offer recognition and praise. After all, most of us probably believe that people deserve credit for their accomplishments and successes, even small ones. You may even be criticized for failing to show appropriate appreciation for the efforts of others. It is easy to argue this social requirement on behavioral grounds as well. When we praise the accomplishments of others or offer other kinds of emoluments, these outcomes presumably function as reinforcers, thereby making such efforts more likely. And if we fail to compliment or praise, we risk weakening otherwise laudatory behavior. Given that the achievement is genuinely praiseworthy, why would we not want to encourage more of the same? Unless such behavior produces reinforcers automatically (without social intervention), its durability depends on reinforcers arranged by others.

However, acknowledging the importance of reinforcement contingencies in strengthening or maintaining desirable behavior by giving credit in some way masks a common misunderstanding about its origins. Praising someone for an accomplishment implies that the behavior of interest somehow originated in the person, rather than from an environmental history. As argued throughout this book, it is useful to assume that, aside from our biology, all behavior is the result of a history of particular interchanges with the environment. It follows that praiseworthy behavior does not come from somewhere inside us but from our experiences, no matter how obscure the evidence in each instance.

It should not be difficult to accept this point of view in general, but it is fair to question its practical value. After all, it is still important to reinforce desirable behavior, even if it did not mysteriously come from within the behaving individual

BOX 7.2

When Behavior Just Happens

We often observe behavior in ourselves or others that we describe as spontaneous, impulsive, impetuous, or uninhibited. In fact, we may celebrate such behavioral tendencies. Someone who is spontaneous is often seen as fun to hang out with, at least up to a point. You may have already guessed, however, that these descriptors are misleading because they encourage the idea that behavior can occur without cause. As discussed in Chapter 1, we tend to look for causes for behavior that immediately precede its occurrence. If plausible options are not found, we may label behavior in a way that suggests that it "just happened" and therefore does not have a particular cause. It may be understood that apparently spontaneous behavior must have some general history, otherwise we might not be capable of it, but the sudden appearance of some action in the absence of any obvious explanation suggests that it occurred for no immediate reason.

Of course, this assumption fails to appreciate that the influences on any particular behavior need not be immediate, at least in any obvious way. For example, positive reinforcement and other types of operant contingencies, the centerpiece of behavioral influences, usually occur only intermittently. This means we are unlikely to spot consequences for some action in every single instance that might help explain why it occurred. We may also fail to identify possible motivating operations and prompting stimuli, given that we do not know what to look for and are probably not trying to do so in the first place.

The challenge may be illustrated with a research preparation in which a pigeon's key pecking behavior is reinforced on some intermittent schedule in an experimental chamber. This kind of example may be helpful because the pigeon's limited repertoire, history, and circumstances help avoid some of the distractions of everyday examples with humans. At times, the pigeon will walk around the chamber, preen, or just look in the direction of the stimulus lights or the key. Then it will "suddenly" peck the key in some manner for a bit, but just as "suddenly" it will stop and do other things such as walking around or preening again. In considering the reasons the pigeon starts or stops pecking the key at any given moment, the role of the carefully arranged reinforcement history looms large, especially given what we know about the effects of particular schedules of reinforcement on particular patterns of responding (Ferster & Skinner, 1957). Even though the investigator may see no momentary event that seems to explain a specific bout of key pecking, that does not diminish the contribution of the reinforcement history. The trap lies in thinking that there must be a distinctive proximate cause—an assumption not required by a historical causal model for behavior.

The philosophical assumption of determinism, not to mention a lot of well-established science, provides a better alternative than assuming that spontaneous behavior can occur without any cause. It suggests that when we want to understand behavior that appears to be spontaneous, we should look more thoroughly for causes that may not be simple or obvious.

but from an environmental history. Perhaps the most important practical question concerns how one can go about strengthening existing tendencies to engage in credit-worthy behavior.

Taking creativity as an example, if you believe it is a particular quality that comes from a special place within the individual, rather than an environmentally based construction, it is tempting to also hold the view that some people have more of this quality than others. If so, it follows that efforts to encourage creative behavior would be more profitable if aimed at those individuals who have the greatest potential, which implies that such efforts would be less effective if directed towards those with lesser prospects. This means that individuals showing little creative tendencies might not receive the same encouragement as others. Such discrimination may have some undesirable side effects, particularly if our ability to pick winners and losers is less impressive than we assume.

Furthermore, this colloquial perspective provides no guidance for exactly how to encourage creativity. If it comes from within as a given quality, all that should be necessary for it to emerge is to ensure that the individual has access to appropriate opportunities. Even if we grant that creative tendencies require more than opportunity and time but can benefit from explicit development, it is not clear what protocol should be followed. If focused development is planned, what should be the target behaviors? After all, the traditional approach to creativity suggests that it involves more than mere proficiency. If it does not lie in particular skills but in some inner creative reservoir, what should teachers encourage? On what should reinforcers be contingent?

A common answer to this last question is to "reinforce" the individual as the font of creative output, a reaction that misunderstands the nature of reinforcement. The underlying science makes it clear that the notion of reinforcing the individual is not only strategically misleading but technically impossible. If you want to reinforce the individual, when should you deliver the reinforcer? If it is the individual you intend to change, why would it matter which behavior was reinforced? In any event, whatever moment you choose, the reinforcer will follow some behavior belonging to a particular class, thereby influencing the likelihood of that behavior recurring under those circumstances.

That is, regardless of anyone's intentions, what is strengthened by a reinforcement contingency is a particular response class under certain conditions, a finding that long ago attained the status of scientific law. Reinforcement contingencies do not strengthen the individual in a behavioral sense of that phrase. When we say that a person has learned something and is behaviorally stronger as a result, we are invariably referring to changes in the features of particular response classes. These changes may be quite noticeable to others and important in his or her life, but what has changed is the person's repertoire, not some inner quality.

Because it is impossible to reinforce the individual as such, attempts to encourage creativity as an inner quality typically result in reinforcement contingencies that are likely to yield scattered outcomes. With the individual (not particular behaviors) as the object of change, reinforcers may be offered in a general manner in an effort to strengthen vague creative tendencies. However, they will actually be contingent on different behaviors from occasion to occasion, thereby lacking the systematic focus that might achieve desired outcomes. This problem is a common side effect of misunderstanding how operant shaping works and thereby viewing the individual, rather than specific features of his or her repertoire, as the focus of intervention efforts.

In contrast, when creativity is viewed as a tact uttered by a speaker in the context of a verbal community, the task is to identify the specific features of behavior controlling such tacts. With this assessment, it becomes possible to focus reinforcement contingencies on these features and make optimal progress toward strengthening what the verbal community views as creative behavior. For instance, if the work of a graphics artist specializing in developing corporate logos is often deemed by others as especially creative, and we can identify the variables controlling this reaction, we may be able to help the artist produce successful logos more consistently, not to mention train others to be equally effective.

Moving beyond our example of creativity, giving credit to the individual for desirable behavior of any sort fails to appreciate the role of environmental history and the resulting procedures for maintaining or strengthening such behavior. For instance, it is not that we should protest the appreciation of good table manners by pointing out that the person does not deserve any credit because the behavior was an inevitable result of a reinforcement history. (Please assure me you will not do this.) Reinforcement is necessary to maintain such behavior, not to mention an important part of our social repertoire. However, it is only by recognizing the origin of laudatory behavior that we can target reinforcement in a way that will consistently have the desired effect of encouraging more of such behavior or improving its desirable features.

ARE WE THEN BLAMELESS?

Given the argument that the notion of giving credit is misplaced, does this mean that neither should we blame someone for their misdeeds? To be consistent, the same argument does indeed apply, and for the same reasons. As with desirable behavior, undesirable behavior results from the environmental history associated with each different behavior, not from a vague inner motivation. Attributing it to the person misunderstands the nature of operant behavior and, therefore, fails to take advantage of the power of well-designed contingencies to make undesirable behavior less likely. As well, this misunderstanding fails to recognize the role of culture in setting the standards for acceptable and unacceptable behavior.

In everyday language, we say that the person knew what he did was wrong (or should have known) and that he should be punished for such behavior. Although sometimes punishment is all about retribution, another topic entirely, it is at least designed to make the behavior less likely to occur again. The chances of this outcome depend on how well we understand the influences underlying the inappropriate behavior. If we fail to recognize the role of environmental history, and instead hold the mentalistic view that it somehow comes from within the individual (who is, at least in a momentary sense, therefore a bad person), we are unlikely to address the real variables that must be targeted in designing an effective intervention.

The answer to the heading's question turns on the pronoun. In fact, "we" *are* blameless, in the sense that "we" refers to our homunculus, that inner person seen as driving our behavior. "We" are no more than what we do, and everything we do (including behavior that may be aversive to others) comes from our environmental history, right up to our present circumstances. This distinction between the person, as conceptualized in our culture, and the nature and causes of behavior, as revealed by behavioral science, is the key to what might otherwise seem a contradiction.

The apparent contradiction, as with the notion of giving credit, is that while the individual is not to blame as the source of his or her behavior, the contingencies associated with blaming someone for their actions can be important in making it less likely that the individual will misbehave that way in the future. In other words, it is misleading and counterproductive to accept the everyday notion of blame. However, arranging discouraging consequences for undesirable behavior can be useful, even though to most people the contingency will look like the individual is being blamed. In fact, it is the history of reinforcing consequences that should be "blamed" and replaced by more appropriate consequences.

The topic of misbehavior and punishment, especially in the context of criminal misdeeds, often raises issues that are emotionally laden. If a drunk driver kills a close friend, it is easy to wish only the most severe punishment for the driver. Dispassionately acknowledging the discouraging statistics about the rehabilitative effects of prison for individuals convicted of drunk driving is hard to do under these circumstances. Emotional reactions aside, the real challenge for society is figuring out how to ensure that that particular individual never again drives under the influence of alcohol, not to mention the larger task of reducing the prevalence of drunk driving in general. This agenda requires clear-headed appreciation of the causes of such behavior and an apolitical approach to using them to fashion effective contingencies.

Sometimes our desire to blame others for their misfortunes results in political agendas that can stymie our ability to resolve challenging social issues. For instance, some might blame poor people for their plight, arguing that if they only chose better or tried harder along the way to strive for a better life they would be able to hoist themselves up by their own bootstraps. This is an unavoidably mentalistic view because it assigns the source of behavior to mental qualities or influences we call choosing or trying. It thereby tends to minimize the contribution of many factors that influence particular behaviors that may be tied to poverty, such as those behaviors that affect academic success. Poverty is indeed a major social

BOX 7.3

With Malice Aforethought

Many laws require that violations must involve intent on the part of the accused. It is one thing if you cause someone's death by accident, for example, but quite another if it can be shown that you did so deliberately. Convincing a jury that a defendant intentionally committed a crime can be a challenge for the prosecution, however, because "intent" is not a specific behavior that can be directly observed or documented. The only option is to provide evidence that "shows" intent by the accused, which means intent can only be inferred from such evidence.

This constraint suggests that intent is not a physical phenomenon but a cultural invention that assigns the causes of behavior to the individual's mental state. This does not mean it is not worthwhile to distinguish between the circumstances under which certain kinds of behavior occur, however. In the above example about causing someone's death, the nature of societal reactions to such an act might differ depending on its causes. Consider a driver who is texting instead of watching the road and plows into someone in a crosswalk versus a burglar who shoots a homeowner in the course of the robbery. Aside from any inferences about intentionality in these two cases, it may be useful to distinguish between them in order to arrange different culturally sanctioned consequences, even though both criminal acts resulted in injury or death.

Unfortunately, the challenge of unambiguously discerning intent when it seems important to do so is inherently impossible. Because intention is mental fiction, it cannot be documented in any scientifically acceptable way. Experienced lawyers can point out that even voluntary confessions can leave uncertainties. Any criteria developed to aid in discerning an individual's intentions supposedly underlying some action are doomed to a fair degree of ambiguity, which creates endless problems for law enforcement.

A way of avoiding such dilemmas is to focus not on intent but on the nature of the criminal act and its determinants in the individual case. For the driver who killed a pedestrian while texting, the question might be not whether the death was intended but what variables contributed to the tragic event. The question of what to do in order to reduce the chances that the driver will run down another pedestrian, as well as making such accidents less likely in general, may be more effectively addressed by considering the real causal variables. The second example can be approached in the same manner. Again, the question is not whether the burglar intended to kill the homeowner but how to identify the causes of this behavior and make it less likely in the future. With this agenda, different consequences may be appropriate in these two cases.

problem in many countries, but it will be challenging to address it without understanding how behavior works at the level of individuals going through their lives day by day, moment by moment. The conventional notion of blame makes it easy to misdirect our concerns.

IT COMES DOWN TO RESPONSIBILITY

As this chapter, as well as a discussion in Chapter 1, have made clear, the conventional view of issues such as creativity, credit, and blame assign responsibility for behavior to the individual, not to a history of contingencies associated with different behaviors. Nevertheless, personal responsibility is a colloquial concept that would seem important in maintaining an orderly society and upon which our legal system is founded. When we talk about our friend Liz as being a responsible person, it means she is generally aware of (can tact) her behavior and its consequences. She considers her actions in light of her previous experience in similar circumstances. If Roberto's friends, on the other hand, know that he often acts irresponsibly, this means he seems to act without considering the consequences, making choices that include problematic outcomes for him or others.

This everyday understanding of responsibility implies both a self-descriptive verbal repertoire (awareness) and the freedom to choose a course of action. Let us examine these two elements. Chapter 4 noted that awareness requires experience

---

BOX 7.4

It's Not My Fault!

Have you noticed that people tend to take responsibility for praiseworthy actions but avoid blame for behavior others might not like? We are often not bashful about accepting, if not claiming, credit when we do things others appreciate. After all, such behavior tends to produce social reinforcers, which we are not in the habit of turning down. In doing so, we seem to imply that we are personally responsible for our actions and that they came from who we are as a person. Acts of apparent creativity, such as writing, provide good examples of this tendency, as if the words and sentences come from within us instead of from an acquired verbal repertoire.

On the other hand, when our behavior is problematic in some way, we are quick to point to external environmental factors as the culprit. This implies that blame, and any associated consequences, should be focused on the environment, not ourselves. If we are late to a meeting, we are quick to identify the "reasons," which invariably involve factors we could do nothing about and should be excused for. If we have a close call when driving, the contributing factors we single out usually fail to involve ourselves.

There may be a just little inconsistency going on here. The sources of behavior implied by these personal versus environmental claims are not equally credible alternatives, of course. Putting aside the mentalism associated with personal attributions, the environment is always at the root of our behavior, whatever its social consequences. An entrepreneur may proudly point to her hard work that made her business successful, but a tendency to put in long hours is part of a repertoire that comes from a long reinforcement history, not from a store of unique personal qualities.

with a verbal community, which teaches a self-descriptive repertoire. Being aware means that you are able to describe your own behavior. You can acquire this skill only if others prompt and reinforce self-descriptive statements about your sensing behavior, a task complicated by the fact that they cannot be sure when those statements are correctly tacting your private events.

The colloquial notion of responsibility acknowledges this requirement by excusing individuals who unavoidably lack self-awareness. For example, we do not hold babies or even young children responsible for their own behavior. Other individuals who have not learned this self-observational skill (those with severe intellectual disabilities) or whose ability to exercise this skill is limited by mental illness or drugs are not usually said to be fully responsible for their behavior.

In addition to requiring awareness, the traditional concept of responsibility also assumes we are free to choose one course of action over another. When individuals apparently lack this choice, they are again less likely to be held accountable for their actions. For example, if a child darts into the street and is hit by a car, the driver is unlikely to be criminally prosecuted if he or she was otherwise driving safely. Without the culpability that comes from volition, the idea of personal responsibility loses its customary meaning. Although there are exceptions to this way of defining personal responsibility in different cultures (for example, in some cultures a woman who is raped is considered the responsible party), we generally hold people responsible for their actions only if they had a choice about how they behaved.

Our legal system recognizes the role of self-awareness and choice by allowing an elaborate array of qualifications. The greater the evidence of external causal factors, the less someone is seen as answerable for their behavior. For example, if someone engages in an illegal activity (speeding) but does so because of pressing circumstances (taking a family member to a hospital emergency room), the violation may be excused. If a man commits a crime but can be shown to be mentally ill or fails to understand right and wrong or the consequences of his actions, the law accommodates this situation with options for pleas and sentences that are different from those that would otherwise apply. In both cases, evidence that self-awareness and free choice were diminished weakens the burden of responsibility.

In contrast with this point of view, the discussion of free will and determinism in the first chapter should have left you comfortable with a working assumption that all behavior is determined, even though we may be unaware of its particular determinants moment by moment. With this perspective, it follows that the colloquial concept of personal responsibility is simply inconsistent with the nature of behavior. Even though we learn to be aware of our behavior and its consequences, there is no internal or private mechanism by which the individual is the ultimate source of his or her behavior. Whatever we do is influenced by our history and present circumstances, not a personal homunculus or a self or a mind. Because most people lack a science-based view of these environmental influences, not to mention the necessary evidence that would explain their actions at any moment, they are not usually in a very good position to manage their own behavior. Even when they do, the actions they take are themselves the result of the same influences.

As suggested by the discussion of credit and blame, the fact that the causes of behavior lie in the environment, rather than in a mental world, does not mean that the everyday notion of personal responsibility has no practical utility in daily life. These concepts, no matter how misdirected from a behavioral point of view, are everyday labels for contingencies between appropriate or inappropriate actions and their consequences. Giving people credit for their accomplishments or blaming them for their mistakes involves social contingencies that presumably nudge their behavior in directions sanctioned by the verbal community. Teaching children that they are responsible for their own behavior involves stating rules ("You should not say things that hurt other people's feelings") and describing the consequences for following or ignoring them.

Yes, it would be better if socially mediated management of each other's behavior was phrased in terms of operant behavior and its environmental influences. The mentalistic underpinning of everyday notions of credit, blame, and responsibility unquestionably limits their practical utility. Under the mistaken assumption that these are private qualities present in varying amounts from one person to another, we often fail to pursue the possibilities of behavior change as far as we might. Teachers who give up on a child who often misbehaves fail to come up with better management techniques because of the assumption that the child's behavior reflects personal qualities, not the outcomes of environmental contingencies. When we hold people personally responsible for their shortcomings, we are not inclined to identify or address the actual causes of their behavior.

CONSCIENCE

Just as we are taught that we are responsible for our own actions, we are taught to feel guilty or ashamed when our behavior falls short of cultural norms. We reference this history when we talk about our conscience. It is easy to recall the kind of parental training that results in what we conventionally refer to as our conscience. Our youthful misdeeds were often punished, verbally or otherwise, and certain kinds of behavior acquired a punishment history. For example, clobbering our little brother was likely to get us into trouble, as was denying that we did it, and a seemingly endless list of other misdeeds.

In addition to making us less likely to violate parental and cultural rules, punishment contingencies often generate largely private physiological effects. Getting whacked on the bottom hurts a bit, but it also produces some degree of autonomic nervous system arousal, as does being severely scolded. These events include changes in heart rate, respiration, perspiration, and a good deal more. We are able

BOX 7.5

Can Your Dog Feel Ashamed?

It is difficult not to say your dog is ashamed when you catch him sneaking a left-over pork chop from the kitchen counter and scold the poor pooch in your most disapproving tone of voice. He hangs his head low and tucks his tail as far under him as it will go, slowly edging toward the nearest exit. What else could canine shame possibly look like?

In fact, it can look like whatever we agree it should look like because we merely invented the notion in the first place. As a verbal response, "shame" is under control of a number of stimuli, whether we are tacting behavior in humans or dogs. In the case of dogs, our verbal community teaches us to tact dogs as being ashamed when we observe certain behavior under certain conditions. The offending actions are generally deemed inappropriate, and the subsequent shame-like behavior may involve the above responses. Lacking any alternative, we label the dog's behavior with the same vocabulary we use for humans.

The more interesting question is not so much what we mean when we say a dog is ashamed, but whether dogs even feel ashamed in the same way we do. This chapter describes our history of being punished throughout our lives for behavior that is socially disapproved. It points out that such behavior often encounters punishing consequences, which in turn may produce autonomic nervous system arousal. To the extent that we can detect some of these physiological events, we are taught by our verbal community to tact such sensations as shame or guilt in the context of misdeeds. However, we learn to tact these private sensations as a result of special contingencies arranged by our verbal community, as described in previous chapters. More generally, we learn to say we are ashamed of our behavior under certain conditions even when we detect no internal sensations but recognize the inappropriateness of our actions.

Dogs cannot share all of this history. When their behavior is punished, autonomic nervous system arousal also occurs. In contrast with humans, however, these sensations are not the focus of differential reinforcement on the part of a verbal community, and therefore dogs do not learn to respond to the sensations as humans do by tacting the sensations and circumstances in a particular way. They presumably experience these sensations, but there are no reinforcement contingencies that might lead them to act differently when they are present. These sensations are just there. They are not the basis for behavior that in humans we call shame or guilt, because there are no contingencies that would teach such reactions. Lacking a verbal community and, therefore, this skill, dogs cannot "feel ashamed." Their behavior of hanging their head and tucking their tail when caught with that pork chop is not "acting ashamed." That is merely our label for the natural behavior of a dog under those circumstances. The explanation for those particular actions lie in canine biology and their individual histories with punishment mediated by humans.

to sense at least some of these physiological changes, and some (blushing, for instance) may even be evident to others. These sensations are paired not only with the misdeed but with accompanying social stimuli, including the parent's facial expression and reprimand. With sufficient history, behavior that has been punished is likely to elicit these conditioned respondent reactions, which we are taught to label as feeling guilty or ashamed under certain situations. Even when these biological reactions are absent, we have learned to label behavior that has often been punished in certain situations as something we should feel badly about. We tend to call these feelings and related verbal behavior our conscience.

If this seems too simple an explanation for such feelings, remember that this history of being punished for misbehavior is made up of countless instances throughout our lives. As adults, we do not get a spanking for speaking to a friend in a rude tone of voice, but similar responses have been paired with social punishment in the past. As a result, they may elicit arousal responses such as blushing, and we are likely to say we feel ashamed about the way we spoke.

This analysis based on established science provides a way of acknowledging the very real feelings sometimes associated with emitting socially proscribed behavior. There is no benefit in inventing a mental phenomena called a conscience that is supposed to guide our decisions to behave well or badly. Once again, assigning the causes of behavior to mental causes only distracts us from understanding what is really going on and using that understanding to address practical behavioral issues.

CHAPTER SUMMARY

1. Creativity is not a physical phenomenon but a way of labeling certain kinds of behavior. We tend to call behavior creative when we are unfamiliar with what is created or when we are not aware of what might have influenced such behavior.

2. We sometimes think of creative behavior as novel, but variations in responding are one of the characteristics of response classes and part of the fundamental nature of operant behavior.

3. Creative behavior comes from a history of reinforcement for behaving in a certain way under similar circumstances. This means we can produce creative behavior by arranging the right kind of reinforcement.

4. The notion of giving credit for good behavior may misunderstand its origins. It implies that the behavior originated in the person, rather than from a reinforcement history. This misunderstanding might encourage the assumption that some people are more prone to certain forms of good behavior (such as creativity) than others. All that should be necessary is to provide opportunities for good behavior to emerge. Even if it is conceded that such behavior should be explicitly encouraged, it is not clear how this might be done if the behavior originates in the individual.

5. The notion of "reinforcing the person" misunderstands the nature of reinforcement, which has its effects on response classes, not the individual as a whole. Recognizing creativity or other laudatory behavior as a tact on the part of the speaker encourages a focus on targeted reinforcement contingencies.

6. If the idea of giving credit is misplaced, it follows that the same misunderstanding is associated with the idea of blaming the individual for their behavior. As before, however, it may still be important to arrange appropriate consequences for undesirable behavior.

7. The everyday understanding of responsibility implies a self-descriptive verbal repertoire and the freedom to choose a course of action. This latter requirement cannot be met, which must lead to the assumption that all behavior is instead determined.

8. Our sense of shame or guilt comes from a long history of being punished for misbehavior. This elicits some degree of autonomic nervous system arousal, some sensations of which we can detect. Our verbal community teaches us to not only discriminate these sensations but to tact them as shame or guilt under certain circumstances.

TEXT STUDY GUIDE

1. Describe a behavioral interpretation of creativity.

2. What are the problematic consequences of a mentalistic interpretation of creativity?

3. How does the science of operant learning help us explain apparently novel behavior?

4. What is the conceptual risk associated with the cultural notion of giving credit?

5. What is wrong with the everyday idea of reinforcing someone?

6. Why does it matter exactly when you deliver reinforcers?

7. If we should not credit the individual for good behavior, why should we give credit at all?

8. Explain why we should not blame someone for their misdeeds.

9. What are the two implicit requirements underlying the everyday notion of responsibility? How does our culture accommodate these two features?

10. How does our understanding of operant learning conflict with the everyday conception of personal responsibility?

11. How do behavior analysts interpret everyday definitions of conscience, shame, and guilt?

12. Explain the role of punishment and our autonomic nervous system in what we feel as shame or guilt.

BOX STUDY GUIDE

1. What is contingency adduction? How might it be related to creative behavior?
2. What are the implications of the everyday idea that behavior can be spontaneous?
3. Why is it difficult to appreciate the role of operant shaping history in explaining apparently spontaneous behavior?
4. What are the problems with the requirement for intent in our legal system?
5. What might be a more useful approach to undesirable behavior, including criminal behavior, than focusing on intent?
6. Why do we tend to accept credit for ourselves but focus blame on external factors?
7. Can a dog feel embarrassed? Why? What differs between humans and dogs that explains your answer?

DISCUSSION TOPICS AND EXERCISES

1. How is the concept of operant response classes important to understanding how behavior analysts approach the topic of creativity?
2. Some might argue that literary creativity often comes from the writer's unique life experiences and that merely training individuals to write creatively would not lead to great works of literature. How might a behavior analyst argue with this position?
3. Consider the example of a Wall Street trader charged with using inside information to make advantageous trades not otherwise available to others. His lawyer argues that his actions were unintentional and he is therefore not guilty. If this focus on intent was reframed to focus on behavior and its causes, how might the issue of guilt or the consequences of a verdict be different?
4. Consider the feeling of pride in the same context as guilt or shame. Explain what this vernacular reference means from a behavior analytic perspective. How is this feeling acquired?

SUGGESTED READINGS

Baum, W. M. (2005). *Understanding behaviorism.* Malden, MA: Blackwell Publishing. (Chapter 10: Responsibility, credit, and blame).

Goetz, E. M., & Baer, D. M. (1973). Social control of form diversity and the emergence of new forms in children's blockbuilding. *Journal of Applied Behavior Analysis, 6,* 209–217.

Chapter 8

Ethics, Rights, and Values —
Without the Heat

Tobin was employed by his state's Department of Human Services as the Regional Behavior Analyst for Region 4. He took the position straight out of school with a fresh BCBA credential. Unlike many of his friends in graduate school, he never wanted to work with children with autism. He really enjoyed working with people with intellectual disabilities, though his job called for spending most of his time dealing with provider agency personnel. He found plenty of challenges in bringing them around to his way of approaching each client's needs, but they almost always genuinely cared about the well-being of each individual, and that made his work easier.

As he drove to a day program run by one of the agencies, he was thinking about a discussion he had yesterday with a behavior specialist at another site. Tobin was concerned that although the agency had a variety of activities available to the clients in their day program, there was relatively little movement of clients from one activity to another over time. Slots associated with some of the activities such as working in a garden nursery or in the kitchen were filled with the same individuals year after year, even though it was clear that they had long since learned most of the skills that could be acquired in those settings. As a result, other clients who might benefit from these placements could not have their turn with the opportunities. The behavior specialist offered a familiar defense: These clients were given a choice about where they wanted to work and freely chose their long-standing placements.

Choice. If there was one topic that drove him crazy, this was it. His own department promoted this as a value by incorporating it in policies and departmental jargon, as well as through values-centered training given to agency personnel. Any position that seemed to violate the idea that clients can make free choices was automatically deemed disrespectful. It was as if all you had to do was utter the word, and any disagreements you had concerning some issue were supposed to fall away. In practice, however, the effects of this mantra took the form of staff deciding what clients wanted, which usually looked an awful lot like what the agency wanted. It had become a generic excuse for the status quo and was routinely thrown up as an unassailable reason for resisting change. It wasn't that he didn't know how to handle this argument one-on-one. In fact, it was usually not too difficult to work someone like yesterday's behavior specialist around to the behavior analytic approach to this topic. But the misunderstandings about free choice as a value in the intellectual disabilities culture seemed to take so many forms and to be so widespread within the state system that addressing them one staff member at a time was hopeless. What was needed was a change in the departmental culture, and that was a much bigger challenge.

ETHICS AND ETHICAL COMMUNITIES

Ethics concerns those contingencies sanctioned by a community that address how we behave. It is simply a label for behavioral practices within a community that involve how its members deal with one another. Ethical behavior therefore concerns how we influence each other's behavior. For instance, treating elders with respect is especially valued in certain communities, and such behavior, or contrasting behavior, is likely to meet with consequences that strengthen or weaken it.

Contrary to everyday assumptions, it is the contingencies that define ethical values, not values that drive the contingencies. Social contingencies create ethical standards, which are often articulated as rules that describe behavior the community deems appropriate or inappropriate. These standards usually reference how we behave toward each other. Although some standards are enshrined in governmental laws or other formal rules, many are more informally practiced. We codify laws stating that stealing from others is not acceptable and mete out preordained punishment accordingly. However, there is no law that dictates what we should do if we find a little girl in the supermarket who has become separated from her parents. Nevertheless, we have been taught that we should comfort the child and try to find her parents, rather than ignore her distress.

Ethical standards may also concern behavior that has only indirect effects on others. For example, cruelty to animals is viewed as a violation of these standards in many ethical communities. Although such behavior might not seem to concern how we deal with each other, witnessing animal cruelty or even learning about it in the media is aversive to most people, even as only observers, and is therefore the subject of social disapproval in various forms. Behavior that has important environmental consequences (air or water pollution, for instance) is another example of ethical concerns in which our behavior impacts others at a distance.

An ethical community is made up of members who share participation in contingencies that reinforce or punish certain behavioral practices. Each of us participates in a number of different ethical communities. The field of behavior analysis is one such community, for instance. Among other practices, its members tend to reinforce talking about behavior in terms of the science underlying operant behavior and to punish talking about behavior in terms of mental causes. We also participate in ethical communities defined by our extended family, our friends, our recreational interests, and so forth. In each of these communities, we exhibit a somewhat different repertoire. When you visit your parents, for example, certain features of your behavior are likely to differ from what your friends usually see. You might clean up your vocabulary, for example, or make your bed for a change.

RIGHTS

What Are Rights?[2]

By now, you probably realize that rights are just verbal behavior. Although the term serves as a noun in our grammar, rights have no physical status. When we talk about our rights in everyday language, we are making statements about how we or others or things are used to obtain reinforcement or avoid punishment. For example, if we announce that we have a right to eat unhealthy food if we like, we are saying that such behavior is reinforcing and that others may interfere with our access to unhealthy food only with our permission. If we insist that everyone wear seat belts, we are saying that it is reinforcing to us to know that the likelihood of injuries in car accidents (especially those in which we may be involved) will be minimized as a result. This is a rights statement because we assert that we must mediate our access to this reinforcing state of affairs.

In other words, when we make statements about rights, whether ours or someone else's, we are describing a circumstance that allows one to obtain reinforcement or avoid punishment. In addition, we are insisting that we control our access to these contingencies. If others wish to act in a way that involves these contingencies, they must at least obtain our permission. The widely held view that we each have a right to control the use of our own body is an especially clear example. If someone wants to obtain reinforcement from using our body, we expect to be able to grant or refuse permission. Rape is an example of the failure to obtain this permission, but risks to our health and safety in the workplace are other examples of ways this right may also be abridged.

It is easiest to think of situations in which our rights are being denied when aversive treatment is involved. The right to our personal possessions is obviously violated by a robber who steals our money at gunpoint. However, our rights may also be breached by people who care about us and otherwise treat us well. Just because someone feels kindly toward us does not mean they always ask our permission to obtain reinforcement from involving us in some way. For example, in interactions with a loving husband, a wife may feel her rights are ignored if she is not a full partner in the relationship.

---

[2]This discussion of rights is largely based on Vargas, 1975.

As verbal behavior, rights statements, and the meaning of any particular right, must be understood in terms of the controlling contingencies. Rights statements are often mands describing what others should do for the speaker. Rights statements suggest the conditions of deprivation or aversive stimulation experienced by the speaker and specify the consequences that will resolve these conditions and therefore be reinforcing. If you state that you have a right to enjoy going to a movie without others texting on their cell phones, you are manding that others not engage in such aversive activities. If you are successful, this rights statement is maintained by its reinforcing consequences.

Rights statements may also function as tacts, statements evoked by objects or properties of the environment. When you say that you have a right to go to a movie and not be disturbed by others, you are tacting your verbal statement. You are describing that it is a particular type of statement (a right) and that it is supported by an ethical community.

In understanding rights as statements about how we control each other's behavior, it should be clear that our assertions should not be viewed as inherently valid or superior to all others. Any statement of a right can be matched by a contrary statement. Even for rights that appear to be universal, circumstances can be found under which that right should not be practiced. One right always bumps into another in some way. For instance, the right to carry guns may conflict with the right to be safe from harm. The right of parents to discipline their children as they wish may clash with the rights of children to be safe from abuse. The right of businesses to maximize their profits may be at odds with the right of citizens to have access to safe working conditions or clean air and water.

And Where Do Rights Come From?

Although it might seem that rights statements originate with the individual, it is the ethical community that defines and sanctions the individual's rights. After all, we learn our verbal repertoire in the ethical communities in which we grow up, including our verbal behavior about rights. Within these ethical communities, as well as others in which we participate as we go through life, we gain experience with the contingencies that underlie our rights statements. As we experience working for pay, we learn about a variety of rights involving employment, for instance. We may exercise rights for ourselves, but it is the ethical communities of which we are members that defines what these rights are.

This means our statements and other actions concerning rights are fully controlled by our ethical communities, whether those rights concern ourselves or others. It is this control that defines our membership in these communities. This does not mean that we always agree with the influence of these communities. We may believe that we have a right to use our possessions as we wish, for example, but the ethical community defined by governmental interests limits the conditions under which we may do so. We may not drive our car wherever we want or as fast as we want. We may not play loud music and annoy the neighbors. We face constraints on what kind of structure we build on our property, what we grow in the front yard, or even where we park our car. By virtue of our history in certain ethical communities, however, their control usually leads to personal outcomes that are reinforcing or that avoid punishment.

It is only through an ethical community that we find support for our rights. Because an ethical community is defined by members who share contingencies that reinforce or punish certain behavioral practices, it is these mutual contingencies that constitute support for the rights designated by the community. When a local government passes an ordinance requiring dogs to be on leash when outside of the owner's yard, it does so because citizens have complained about problems associated with roaming dogs. The right to be free of such problems is established by this ethical community, and the ordinance, through its legal ramifications, constitutes support for this right. If the citizens of the town widely disagreed with such an ordinance, their elected representatives would likely share their views and not pass it.

VALUES

What Are Values?

As with rights, values are not physical entities, nor should we imagine that they have some sort of mental existence. When we talk about our values, we describe our behavior, or the behavior of others, in various environmental circumstances. If we say we believe in the Golden Rule, that we should treat others as we would like others to treat us, we describe not only desired behavior in ourselves and others but desired social reinforcement contingencies. In its countless applications to particular situations, this value identifies appropriate behavior sanctioned by an ethical community and its implicit reinforcing outcomes. If we find a wallet on the floor of a store, this value suggests we would find it reinforcing if someone found our wallet and turned it in to store personnel and that we should therefore turn in the wallet we found.

Is there a behavioral difference between rights and values? In colloquial dialect, the terms overlap a good bit. Both refer to morally acceptable or desired actions within a community. Both focus on preferred ways of behaving that are important and long-standing in our lives. Both imply a reinforcing state of affairs that would result from actions consistent with the right or value and, by contrast, aversive outcomes that would come from actions conflicting with it. Although we may sometimes raise distinctions between rights and values, these distinctions are not consistently evident in daily discourse.

There are also similarities between rights and values from a behavior analytic perspective. Both rights and values are verbal behavior about our behavior and the

BOX 8.1

Behavior Analysis and Religious Behavior

Some of the values with which we are familiar are associated with religion. Many of us grew up in households in which religion played an influential role, and for some it can be difficult to consider this aspect of our behavior from a scientific perspective. Nevertheless, it might not ask too much at this point to acknowledge that behavior we might call religious in nature is no more than operant behavior learned from our verbal communities. Behavior such as going to church, singing hymns, saying prayers, and putting some money in the collection plate should seem easy to accommodate from a behavior analytic perspective.

It can be more challenging to examine what we mean when we talk about our religious beliefs. Of course, they are, as Chapter 2 pointed out, "just verbal behavior." They are tacts of our own behavior, most often verbal behavior we learned through contingencies arranged by others. Religious beliefs may feel especially dear to us, but they are no different than other beliefs. Saying that you believe in God or in the power of prayer is not fundamentally different than saying that you believe you are a good tennis player or that it is going to snow tomorrow, as heretical as that might seem. As verbal behavior, such tacts need not have anything to do with physical reality. Just because we believe something is true does not mean it is, no matter how widely that belief may be shared in the culture.

A behavior analytic view of religious behavior can lead in pretty uncomfortable directions for some, and yet we must not carve out tempting exceptions to a scientific view of behavior. Some may find this topic fascinating, whereas others may wish to avoid it. Whether attracted or threatened, it is important to remain consistent in viewing even our most fervently held religious beliefs as operant behavior originating from our reinforcement history. That said, much of our everyday verbal repertoire is likely to remain largely vernacular. No matter how sophisticated our appreciation of the implications of the science of behavior analysis, we still talk to our dog as if she understands what we are saying and tell our family members we love them dearly. And some of us will continue participating in a religious life, all the while fully understanding such behavior for what it is.

behavior of others that more or less specifies the consequences for behaving one way or another. Both often involve statements, likely parsed as rules, describing behavior that leads to consequences that are reinforcing to the speaker. Both originate with and depend on ethical communities. Rights may more clearly specify the associated reinforcers, but the reinforcing circumstances associated with values are usually reasonably straightforward.

Are Values Beyond Science?

You have probably heard the argument that values are beyond science, that science cannot resolve questions about what is good or bad or what we should or ought to do. This prohibition is often offered in everyday conversations as obvious and beyond rebuttal. Approaching values as verbal behavior about behavior in particular contexts suggests otherwise, however. Remember that activities we call good are merely those that tend to produce reinforcers and that those we call bad tend to produce punishers. The functions of particular reinforcers and punishers are largely acquired via our history, especially our social history. The better we understand how our behavior evolves from our experiences, the easier it is to discern the origin of our values.

Statements involving "should" or "ought" are statements about reinforcers and punishers. When we tell a roommate she ought to wear a coat, we are tacting reinforcing consequences for complying. We are saying that keeping warm is reinforcing and that wearing a coat will accomplish this result. We can make the same translation into behavioral contingencies when the statement is more ethical in tone. If we say that you should not steal, we are saying that taking things that do not belong to you is aversive to others and may result in punishment. In other words, "should" and "ought" statements can be restated into questions about specific behaviors under particular conditions. With that, we can turn to the origin and maintenance of such behavior and the consequences for acting one way or another.

Translating value statements into behavioral terms greatly eases the scientific challenge of addressing values and their implications for individuals and society. We not only already know quite a lot about how behavior works, we know how to frame and pursue scientific questions about behavior. Consider some possible questions surrounding the issue of whether individuals who have terminal illnesses should be allowed to involve others in ending their life. This is a difficult topic for many, and values such as the sanctity of life and personal choice are often voiced in favor of contrasting positions. But what do "sanctity of life" and "personal choice" mean in behavioral terms? What are the sources of control over statements invoking these values? What about our reinforcement history leads us to articulate these values?

A scientific focus on this topic means we must determine the research questions that would help society to address this conflict in values. For instance, what might be the consequences for society if it passed laws allowing or prohibiting voluntary euthanasia under certain circumstances? How could society build support for resolving conflicting values in one direction or the other? Addressing these ques-

BOX 8.2

Questioning Religious Behavior

Given the pervasive role of religious behavior in the lives of many people, the introduction in Box 8.1 of what a science of behavior and its radical behavioristic philosophy might have to offer is teasingly brief. There are certainly many questions that might be considered, though the topic leads well beyond the focus of this chapter or even this book. As Box 8.1 suggested, the key is to examine this aspect of our lives as religious behavior, rather than as a special aspect of human nature, although this assessment is not meant to belittle in any way. The resulting questions concern how religious behavior in all its forms originates and how it is influenced throughout a person's life. The answers must be framed in the context of the science and philosophy of behavior analysis and should not be fundamentally different than those that emerge from examining other aspects of a person's repertoire. That said, you should not expect this approach to easily reveal all of the origins of and influences on such behavior.

Aside from the ritualistic features of our religious repertoire, perhaps the most curious aspect of religious behavior concerns the behavioral nature of religious faith. Although we view this topic as deeply personal, it is actually a subset of the general matter of what it means to "have a belief" about something. (This topic is first considered in Chapter 2, as well as in subsequent chapters.) Because of the importance of religion to many individuals and in various cultures, some might want to view religious faith as special or different compared to other beliefs. A scientific approach must put these traditional priorities aside. Our increasingly mature understanding of operant behavior has shown what other sciences learned long ago—that approaching phenomena as physical processes helps us explain how the world really works. This lesson suggests that there is no benefit in assuming that the behavior associated with what we call religious faith differs in any basic way from other instances of behavior.

In considering religious behavior, and especially religious faith, from a behavior analytic viewpoint, it is important to avoid being sidetracked by the temptation to address the content or meaning of our verbal behavior in its everyday sense. For behavior analysts, questions about religious behavior, much of it verbal, must be framed in the context of operant learning processes, as Box 8.1 suggests. However, everyday interest usually lies in the meaning or referents of religious verbal behavior, such as statements about the existence of a supreme being, the effectiveness of prayer, or other religious convictions. In a debate about the existence of a supreme being, for instance, the behavioral questions of interest concern the origin and maintenance of religious verbal behavior (e.g., what leads us to say, "I believe in God"), not on how the utterance comports with the physical universe. Discussion of whether there is a God, for example, is only more verbal behavior to be explained. Talking about religious beliefs in a conventional way, rather than as verbal behavior, falls into the trap of assuming that verbal behavior has meaning in the vernacular sense. As Chapter 2 first discussed, verbal behavior is no different from other operant behavior and does not "refer to" things or have meaning in some non-behavioral sense, a position that is inherently mentalistic. What is interesting to behavior analysts, for instance, is the learning history for religious statements that might explain its features, such as why this behavior tends to be so strong. These questions can only be answered within the context of our scientific understanding of operant behavior.

Finally, explanation of religious faith requires consideration of more than just our verbal behavior. Some aspects of religious behavior may involve emotions or feelings, intermingled with how we are taught to tact them. For example, we might describe a feeling of awe in contemplating the universe, an overwhelming sensation of peacefulness when lost in prayer, and euphoric joy accompanying some religious ceremonies. As Chapter 3 discussed, such physical correlates of our learning history may be quite real, though they are often difficult to localize and objectively describe. A satisfactory explanation of religious faith must incorporate the means by which such sensations come to be evoked by religious activities.

tions requires more than the within-subject experimental designs (e.g., Johnston & Pennypacker, 2009) that have proven so useful in discovering the details of behavioral processes and behavior change procedures. Some projects might be pursued by examining the evidence from other cultures that have already resolved this conflict. As individual states, provinces, or countries address this issue in different ways, their resolutions may provide opportunities to study different processes and outcomes, including both short-term and long-term effects.

The emotional tone of some arguments about conflicting cultural values might suggest that settling such disagreements is impossible and that engineering widespread cultural support for one position over another is unlikely. Cultural values are always changing, however, though never quickly enough for those pushing for change. Convictions about race and gender in the United States have changed substantially in recent generations, for instance, although it can certainly be argued that more change is still needed. Fifty years ago, cigarette smoking was widely accepted, though now, with broad cultural support, it is severely restricted. The means by which such values evolve can be studied in order to learn how other value conflicts might be resolved. (See Chapter 9 for further discussion of this topic.)

Arguing that science cannot address questions about values, or at least help resolve values conflicts, implies that values are something other than behavior or that behavior itself is beyond scientific understanding. Even if most people concede that values have something to do with behavior, many probably believe behavioral science is not up to the task of discovering where values come from and how to change them. It is true that neither behavior analysis nor related areas of science have yet developed the kind of research program required to answer the behavioral questions associated with a particular values problem, so there is no good example of such a scientific agenda. Viewing values as learned behavior makes this kind of approach feasible.

TAKING THE HEAT OUT OF ARGUMENTS

We have all participated in discussions about rights and values. In fact, it is hard to avoid them, especially with today's communication technologies and relentless 24/7 media. It often seems that values-based discussions degenerate into heated arguments in which failure to win on factual or rational grounds is supplanted by efforts to prevail on volume alone. Under these circumstances, useful discussion, much less resolution of differences, is unlikely.

One of the revelations of a behavioral approach to values is that it becomes possible to discuss values conflicts without all the heat. The key is to begin by getting all participants to agree that values statements are learned verbal behavior. This is easier said than done, of course. A straightforward announcement of this position is unlikely to be convincing, so it is usually necessary to lay some groundwork. It may help to recall the discussion of reasoning in Chapter 6. Your verbal behavior will often be most effective when you offer some preliminary premises that are likely to be accepted before proceeding to ask participants to agree with the challenging premise that values statements are no more than learned behavior.

It is a good idea to start by getting consensus that we begin learning to talk when we are very young and that even after we master a basic verbal repertoire it continues to be influenced by learning processes. Explain that we would not learn to talk at all without the contributions of a verbal community. It may be useful to point out that we not only learn to label things around us but the actions of others and our own behavior. It is especially important to focus on the development of verbal behavior associated with statements of belief and conviction. You need to be sure that your protagonists understand that such statements do not mean that beliefs and convictions are physical entities of some sort. It is important to use lots of examples of how this all works.

Our early verbal repertoire seems so limited compared to our mature verbal capabilities that it is difficult for people to make the leap between a toddler learning to talk and our participation in arguments about hot button issues of the day. In other words, it is important to make sure your conversational partners are buying what you are selling. Moving into a discussion of values-based issues before all participants have agreed that everything they say is learned will limit the problem-solving potential of the discussion. With this foundation, however, you are ready to wade into the values issue of interest. In general, your approach should be to keep others focused on the behavioral features of the issue. All along, you will have to be alert to inevitable backsliding into mentalistic positions.

What you can do with this foundation is focus discussion not on someone's convictions about their values on some topic but on the circumstances under which such verbal behavior was learned. That is, what are the influences on their statements about the values under discussion? What history led to their present repertoire on the topic? The objective should be to identify and then shift away from social influences toward more objective, if not scientific influences over what they say about a values issue. In any discussion of conflicting values, the most you can hope for is acknowledgement of any useful facts about the issue, as well as consideration of the possible consequences, both immediate but especially long term, of different courses of action. Values conflicts are not likely to be resolved simply by appealing to an organized set of facts, however. There are often many unknowns about what would happen if one course of action was taken by society instead of another. The point of such discussions should not necessarily be to get someone to agree with you but for all parties to agree about how to address the behavioral questions under discussion and how criteria for making decisions should be established.

Take as an example the issue of whether countries or states should include the death penalty among the sentencing options for individuals convicted of certain crimes. The issues likely to arise in such a discussion include where criminal behavior comes from, the influence of the death penalty on the likelihood of criminal behavior, the possibility that innocent individuals might be put to death, and the broader ramifications of this sentence for society, such as whether societal acceptance of the death penalty might influence treatment of individuals who might be viewed as less valuable to society because of age, infirmity, or disability.

First, it is important to figure out your own agenda in such a discussion. What are your own views about the death penalty, and where do they come from? Have you fully considered your opinions from a behavior analytic perspective? Are you familiar with relevant facts and evidence? In considering your agenda, it is important to ask whether you are merely trying to convince your protagonists that your views are right (or at least better than theirs) or whether you want a comprehensive consideration of how behavioral science can be useful in helping society resolve an issue for which there can be no broadly acceptable compromise (either the death penalty is an option or it is not). Informal discussions tend toward the former approach, but a scientist, especially a behavior analyst who understands where all this verbal behavior comes from, should be able to view any values issue with a neutral posture. This does not mean you should not have opinions on the matter, but you will be more effective in this kind of discussion if you are approaching the issues in the same way you are asking others to do.

You may, for instance, hold the view that the death penalty is a bad idea for a number of reasons, but you must be able to honestly consider contrary arguments. You should be willing to concede, for example, that the death penalty is undeniably effective in preventing individuals receiving this sentence from committing further crimes. It is also possible that the existence of the penalty reduces the occurrence of other capital crimes, though this argument must confront the evidence. In examining such evidence, which will often be behavioral in nature, it is important to assess its methodological soundness, regardless of whether you like what it suggests about the issue.

Focusing discussion on the kinds of evidence that might be useful in resolving the issue, rather than on who is right, may help recruit others to your interest in the scientific pursuit of useful evidence, perhaps even encouraging agreement that this is how matters should be decided. This approach tends to shift control over each person's verbal repertoire on the topic based on their long-standing history to new, scientifically based sources centering on methods and empirical evidence. Of course, it is unlikely that this shift will by itself lead to consensus on the underlying issues, but there is no better way to make progress.

CHAPTER SUMMARY

1. Ethics concerns those contingencies sanctioned by a community that address how we behave. Ethics is simply a label for behavioral practices within a community that involve how its members deal with one another. In effect, ethical behavior concerns how we influence each other's behavior.

2. Ethical contingencies define ethical values. Values do not lead to the contingencies. Ethical standards are often offered as rules that describe behavior the community deems appropriate or inappropriate.

3. An ethical community is made up of members who share participation in contingencies that reinforce or punish certain behavioral practices. Each of us participates in a number of different ethical communities.

4. Rights are statements about how we or others or things are used to obtain reinforcement or avoid punishment. Rights are verbal behavior and have no physical status.

5. Rights statements describe situations that allow us to obtain reinforcement or avoid punishment and that mandate our control over access to such contingencies.

6. Rights statements are often mands, suggesting the conditions of deprivation or aversive stimulation of the speaker and specifying the consequences that will resolve these conditions.

7. Rights statements do not come from the individual but from the ethical community, which defines and sanctions the individual's rights. Our statements and actions concerning rights are fully controlled by our ethical communities. It is this control that defines our membership in these communities. It is only through an ethical community that we find support for our rights.

8. Values are descriptions of our behavior or the behavior or others in certain environmental circumstances, as well as preferred social reinforcement contingencies.

9. Rights and values overlap in both vernacular usage and professional interpretations.

10. Approaching values from a behavioral perspective creates the opportunity to address values questions scientifically. "Should" or "ought" statements are about reinforcers and punishers, which means they can be restated into questions about specific behaviors under particular conditions. Arguing that science cannot address questions about values, or at least help resolve values conflicts, implies that values are something other than behavior or that behavior itself is beyond scientific understanding.

11. A behavioral approach to rights and values means that discussions about conflicting values can be held without emotional overtones. The key is getting everyone to agree that values statements are learned verbal behavior. With this foundation, it becomes easier to focus on objective evidence and consideration of the effects of different courses of action.

TEXT STUDY GUIDE

1. What is ethics from a behavioral perspective?

2. What are ethical communities? Why are they the origin of our ethics?

3. Explain the following point: "It is the contingencies that define values, not values that drive the contingencies."

4. What are rights from a behavioral perspective?

5. How is it that our rights can be violated by people who otherwise treat us well?

6. Explain how rights statements may involve both mands and tacts.

7. Why is it that our rights are defined, sanctioned, and supported by the ethical community?

8. What are values from a behavioral perspective?

9. Explain why there is little difference between rights and values from both a colloquial and a behavioral point of view.

10. How does a behavioral approach to rights and values make it easier to address such issues from a scientific perspective?

11. Describe the recommended tactics for discussing conflicting values in a way that avoids emotional arguments and leads to possible resolutions.

BOX STUDY GUIDE

1. Describe the approach to religious behavior outlined in this entry. Why must we avoid isolating religious behavior from our adoption of a behavior analytic view of all other behavior?

2. How can you applied the behavioral conceptualization of "belief" to the notion of religious faith?

3. Why is it important to approach verbal behavior about religious questions in the same manner as verbal behavior about other topics, that is, without interpreting its meaning or content in everyday terms.

DISCUSSION TOPICS AND EXERCISES

1. How many different ethical communities are you a member of? How are the practices of these communities similar or different?

2. Think of examples of rights statements that are mands and analyze the controlling contingencies.

3. Select a particular ethical standard and analyze its likely origins and maintaining contingencies.

4. Select a specific right and consider how it originated in your history.

5. With this same right, consider the contingencies that it implies.

6. Select a values conflict that is important in society. Develop a list of the questions that would be important in resolving this conflict that could be addressed scientifically.

7. Select a conflict of values in today's society that typically generates strong feelings. Detail how you might go about discussing this conflict in a way that avoids emotional arguments.

SUGGESTED READINGS

Hayes, S. C. (1984). Making sense of spirituality. *Behaviorism, 12(2)*, 99–100.
Skinner, B. F. (1953). Science and human behavior. New York: MacMillan. (Chapter XXIII: Religion)
Skinner, B. F. (1971). *Beyond freedom and dignity*. New York: Alfred A. Knopf.
Vargas, E. A. (1975). Rights: A behavioristic analysis. *Behaviorism, 3(2)*, 178–191.

Chapter 9

A Social Life

Jordan had been recently assigned by his agency to work with a 13-year-old boy who had a mild intellectual disability. He lived with his family and attended a public school special education program. Bobby's presenting problems were many, but what was most troubling was a pronounced tendency to resist compliance with requests by others and a history of aggressive and destructive behavior when things didn't go his way.

Based on his ABA training, not to mention his experience with similar cases, Jordan was familiar with the kind of contingencies that often led to these behavioral problems. For starters, because children with intellectual disabilities have difficulty learning, the parental lessons that might usually keep a lid on inappropriate behavior often don't work especially well. Parents are also not usually prepared to deal with aggressive behavior as their child grows older, and they typically learn to avoid episodes by not asking for desired behavior in the first place or caving in as necessary to minimize disruptive reactions. In other words, they unwittingly strengthen the kind of behavior they want to avoid.

As Jordan got to know the family, however, he observed that Bobby's siblings—one older brother and a younger brother and sister—showed the same tendencies as he did. Their penchant for ignoring parental requests and rules didn't usually progress to actual tantrums, but there was a surprising amount of aggressive behavior in the children's interactions. In trying to understand where this behavior was coming from, Jordan learned that the parents believed that corporal punishment was a necessary, if not desirable feature of childrearing. It was not evident that the parents were abusive, but it seemed that physical consequences for misbehavior, or failure to comply with parental demands, were frequent. In spite of this, the children were generally unruly, and it emerged that all had a history of behavioral problems at school. In watching the children during home visits, Jordan saw a lot of aggressive behavior.

Jordan's observations suggested that Bobby's problems were not merely the result of the parents' failure to limit disruptive behavior early on and teach a useful degree of self-control. The parents seemed to have created a family culture in which aggressive social interactions were typical and mutually practiced by all, and Jordan suspected that these practices involved the extended family as well. It was hard to tell, but it seemed that Bobby's siblings might have played as much of a role as the parents in teaching him how to deal with others. This assessment meant that a successful intervention would have to involve more than just helping the parents set up some appropriate contingencies for Bobby. Jordan realized he would have to figure out how to change the socially aggressive family culture.

CULTURE

Culture-free Contingencies

Absent the contributions of others, all humans participate in contingencies that are the result of our biology and its interface with the physical environment. The characteristics, capabilities, and limitations of our bodies intersect with the way the world around us works. No one can escape the pervasive outcomes described by gravity, the laws of motion, or any natural phenomena. The intertwining of our physical characteristics with those of our physical world results in culture-free contingencies that create the fundamental core of what it means to be human.

When we throw something to accomplish an effect at a distance, for example, what we pick up to throw and how we throw it is largely the result of non-social contingencies. Without anyone's help, we do not try to throw things that are hard to grasp, that have too little or too much weight, or that will not travel through the air with a useful trajectory. Although others may help us acquire this behavior, their assistance is not necessary. We would learn how to do this perfectly well if we had been raised on a desert island by sand crabs.

Much of our repertoire stems from such non-social contingencies. Our behavior is pervasively influenced, as well as constrained, by our senses, for example. The capabilities and limitations of our senses determine much of what we do, when we do it, or what we fail to do. We do not see well in the dark, and we are less active at night than during daylight hours. Our sense of smell is not especially impressive compared to that of some other species, and it is not a powerful influence on our behavior. We are comfortable with only a certain range of temperatures and respond by wearing clothes, finding shelter, and regulating our activities.

Our musculoskeletal system allows us only certain behavioral options and guarantees the same consequences for our actions, regardless of social influences. We climb trees or swim only with some difficulty and therefore spend most of our time on the ground. Our ability to cover ground by walking or running is sufficiently limiting that we find ways of going faster, such as riding horses, or minimizing the need to move quickly by, for instance, avoiding predators that are faster than we are. We share with all others of our species the same ability to balance, jump, lift heavy objects, or scratch our back. Perhaps most notably, lacking the contributions of others, we are unavoidably non-verbal in every way.

And the Influence of Culture

Add a social environment to this essential core and the impact on our behavior seems endless. These effects are what we call *culture*—everything that affects us that involves other people. This broad conception subsumes a more formal definition focusing on learned behavior shared by a group's members, acquired from their membership, and transmitted from one member to another (Baum, 2005). Our verbal repertoire is the most notable result of this social environment, and our verbal capability facilitates participation in all manner of cultural practices. We learn to behave in ways supported by our social circumstances and to avoid behavior that is unacceptable under those circumstances. We learn customs, manners, and values. We learn to adjust our behavior as we move from one social group to another and as society and our role in it change over the years. Furthermore, we are not merely passive recipients of social programming; we give fully as much as we take as members of the social environment of others.

Although no one would deny the ubiquitous impact of social experiences on their behavior, most people tend to interpret these effects in terms of their own private mental world. They may concede the contributions of our social history but typically assume these outcomes are modulated by mental processes that are uniquely our own. We admit that we learn the niceties of social interchange from our families and larger social community as we grow up, for example, but tend to believe we can choose whether to comply in one situation or another. We recognize that we trot out different repertoires with our friends at a ballgame than with our coworkers in an important meeting, but we hold that our convictions about social issues of the day are the result of our personal deliberations.

Nevertheless, our awareness of our of own behavior and our views about human nature and its qualities—indeed, most of the topics considered in previous chapters—come entirely from others. They come from each individual's social intercourse, moment by moment, throughout each person's life. What we interpret as our personal contributions—thinking about issues, trying to reason through problems, assessing the views of others, learning about a topic so we can decide for ourselves—are also fully the result of social influences. We cannot escape the influence of our culture by assuming we can reserve a role for personal deliberation and choice. After all, that conviction is also learned from others. In sum, were we raised by crustaceans on a desert island, most of the behavioral features that we have learned to think of as defining our species—the contributions of our social history—would be absent.

Furthermore, the mechanisms for this transmission from one person to another can be explained in a relatively straightforward manner by reference to operant learning processes. Although it might seem that this explanation is far too simple to stand up to the vast complexity of our repertoires, good scientific explanations are fundamentally simple, at least to all but the scientists who understand their underlying complexity. The general notion of gravity seems simple too, until a geophysicist begins describing the details of how it works. Operant selection is, after all, merely a description of how the relations between organisms and their environments work, and the basic processes involved are unchanged by whether the environments are social.

NATURAL SELECTION

B. F. Skinner observed that there are three ways that natural selection underlies behavior:

> human behavior is the joint product of (i) the contingencies of survival responsible for the natural selection of species, (ii) the contingencies of reinforcement responsible for the repertoires acquired by its members, including (iii) the special contingencies maintained by an evolved social environment (1981, p. 502).

It is this third kind of selection by consequences—selection of cultural practices— that is the focus of this chapter. Although selection involving an individual's operant behavior occurs in a relatively brief time frame that is easy to study (often minutes, hours, or days), selection of cultural practices occurs at a much slower pace, encompassing years, if not decades or longer. This makes it challenging to study the factors that modulate cultural practices. On the other hand, because the evolution of cultural practices involves no more than the collective behavior of individuals, we bring to the analysis a deep understanding of how behavior, including cultural behavior or practices, changes in orderly ways over time.

In explaining the evolution of cultural practices, the familiar elements of natural selection—*variation, transmission* or *replication,* and *selection*—are a necessary foundation. First, there must be variation in cultural practices for selection to be meaningful. We already understand the role of variation in response classes at the level of the individual. Each time we engage in a particular behavior, some of its features vary from previous instances, though we do not usually notice these small differences. What varies in cultural selection is also behavior, but as activities or practices of multiple individuals that serve particular functions within a group.

Styles of dress can be a good source of examples of both individual response classes and cultural practices. For example, an individual's behavior of wearing a hat is modulated by prompts from family members or friends, weather conditions, and a history of consequences involving both social and comfort variables. As a result of these factors, a person's behavior of wearing hats, including different kinds of hats, changes over time in orderly ways depending on the controlling variables. A person may consistently wear a certain type of hat in snowy weather or no

---

BOX 9.1

Phylogeny and Ontogeny

Throwing around these terms is guaranteed to impress your friends, but you should be prepared to explain them in case they call your bluff. Phylogeny refers to the evolutionary history of individuals. Phylogenic contingencies are those that operate during the environmental history of a species. Such contingencies select innate behavior that is characteristic of all members of a species because of its advantages under particular environmental circumstances in enhancing the survival of its members.

Ontogeny refers to the history of individual organisms during their lifetimes. Ontogenic contingencies involve interactions between an individual and its environment throughout its life and result in relatively flexible changes in its repertoire from one circumstance to another. Of course, these behavioral changes are what we call learning and are the focus of the science of behavior analysis and its technology.

An individual's behavior is a function of both phylogenic and ontogenic contingencies in proportions that are unique to each species. The contribution of phylogenic history to human behavior is less striking than the role of ontogenic influences. However, this does not mean that we can ignore the possible contributions of phylogenic influences in everyday human behavior. After all, unconditioned behavior is the substrate of all that follows as an individual's environmental history accumulates. Such behavioral influences are rooted in our biology and have a pervasive impact on how and what we learn.

---

hat at all in warm weather. A woman may regularly wear a hat in church but not at the grocery store. The selection of some forms of this behavior over others under particular environmental circumstances is determined by the different functions it serves for each individual. As a result, someone may consistently wear certain hats under certain conditions, the same kind of hat in multiple settings, or no hat at all.

As a cultural practice, wearing hats is also selected by its functions, though they may be largely social in nature. For instance, from the 1920s through the 1960s, as period photographs show, men very often wore a fedora style of hat in public, regardless of the time of year. (Interestingly, women originally popularized wearing a fedora.) The behavior of wearing fedoras was more likely on the east coast than the west coast of the United States, so the practice varied somewhat geographically. Given variations in weather around the country and throughout the year, it is hard to argue that the practice was consistently related to comfort, however, leaving social approval as the most likely controlling factor. Of course, men also wore other kinds of headgear during this period, but wearing a fedora was selected by social approval within broad cultural groups.

Selection of certain variations in cultural practices also requires some means of replication or transmission over time, particularly across generations. Cultural practices are necessarily transmitted from one member of a group to another. Of course, direct instruction by others, initially in the family but increasingly in school and other circumstances, is a primary means of transmission. Another way this occurs is through imitation, an underrated though powerful influence on our repertoire. Our imitative skills are finely honed at an early age, and they are invaluable in adapting our behavior to varying social circumstances. It has also been established that we have a tendency to imitate those behaviors that result in reinforcement for others. Such behaviors may well be those that are most common or frequent because they lead to reinforcing outcomes.

The tendency to imitate behavior that is frequently modeled by and successful for others may also underlie our tendency to follow rules that are often offered by individuals who are demonstrably successful in some ways. Parents routinely encourage children to behave in culturally sanctioned ways by articulating simple rules, such as "Don't talk loudly in public." However, adults may be only slightly less obvious when offering rules to each other that identify appropriate or inappropriate behavior. Such rules often point to contingencies that may directly affect health and welfare, such as "Wash your hands after you go to the bathroom." However, other rules we often refer to as social conventions are value statements whose consequences are predominately social in nature, such as "You should always thank someone who gives you a compliment" (Baum, 2005).

Finally, particular variations of a cultural practice must be selected if they are to continue and be strengthened, even as others fall by the wayside. In a general sense, all established cultural practices result in some degree of social reinforcement for compliance by members of the group. However, the underlying reasons for this cultural support for engaging in culturally sanctioned behavior often mean that other reinforcers may be encountered as well. For example, traffic laws describe culturally appropriate behavior that facilitates safe and efficient motoring. Staying on your side of the road and in your lane has its own rewards, aside from whether a passenger comments approvingly.

We must still ask why certain practices generate more social reinforcement than others. The answer to this question remains speculative. Baum (2005) approaches this issue from the perspective of biological evolution. He distinguishes between **proximate** and **ultimate reinforcers** for engaging in particular cultural practices. Proximate reinforcers often take the form of socially mediated consequences. When we behave in culturally approved ways, others may provide reinforcers. However, the efficacy of proximate reinforcers may depend on ultimate reinforcers, which have to do with health and reproductive fitness in the long term. A parent may praise a child who is finishing an ice cream cone at a city park for putting their dirty napkin in a waste can, but the reason for the parent doing so may have to do with the health benefits to the community of avoiding lots of trash on the ground.

WHERE CAN THIS LEAD?

A Role for Behavioral Science

You can see that behavior analysts approach the topic of culture based on the conceptual framework and science long established in the study of individual behavior. The behavior of individuals is, after all, the raw material of cultural practices. Perhaps the most pressing target for this approach is a scientific assessment of particular cultural practices. Can a science of behavior determine the implications of a certain cultural practice? Can it learn about its origins and why it continues to be supported? Can researchers identify both short-term and long-term consequences of the practice? How can they extend the effectiveness of the behavior analytic approach that has worked so well in resolving behavioral challenges with individuals to behavioral challenges widely shared in a culture?

If a science of behavior can answer such questions, will the answers be useful in guiding efforts to change cultural practices? The challenge lies in dealing

---

BOX 9.2

The Culture Doesn't Behave

Perhaps this far into the book it is not necessary to make this point, but you will always be surrounded by people who do not understand. There is no such thing as cultural behavior, in the sense of the culture as an entity that is doing the behaving. Behavior is an intra-organism phenomenon, the result of the interface between a living organism and its environment. Groups in any form are not organisms and therefore cannot behave, as Box 2.1 suggests. Cultural practices are not the behavior of groups but the collected result of the behavior of multiple individuals, each influenced by their unique histories. Even though we refer to cultural contingencies, those contingencies have their effects not on the culture as a whole but separately for each member of the culture. Even though the behavioral requirements of such contingencies may be widely shared, the effects are unavoidably individualized, although they may also share substantial similarities. Evolving cultural practices therefore result from the consequences for each individual's compliance, one response at a time (Glenn, 2004).

For example, for many Muslims, ritual prayer, or salat, is performed five times each day in the direction of the Ka'ba shrine in the city of Mecca. This cultural practice is widespread among Muslims, though it is certainly not adhered to by all members of that faith and certainly not across all circumstances. Although the social contingencies associated with this practice may be quite strong in certain Muslim communities, there is considerable variation in such behavior across individuals, and it is the consequences associated with these changes that lead to changes in cultural practices. For some, the traditional muezzin's call to prayer has been replaced by mobile phone apps, which send a reminder as prayer times approach.

with the fact that people often disagree about the advisability of various practices. When such disagreement is widespread, engineering cultural change can be difficult. Attempts to coerce changes that lack broad support may be effective for a while but will eventually fail unless support develops over time. In the United States, for example, passage in 1920 of the 18th Amendment to the Constitution prohibiting the manufacture, sale, or transportation of alcohol was notably ineffective, leading to its repeal in 1933. Remember that a cultural practice must be shared by a group's members, acquired from their membership, and transmitted from one member to another. These characteristics are likely to emerge only when members find a certain practice beneficial.

Cultural practices are always changing, so examples of cultural shifts are available for systematic study. For instance, not that many decades ago in the United States many people smoked cigarettes, cigars, and pipes in almost all social settings. There was almost nowhere a smoker would not have felt completely comfortable lighting up. Ashtrays were available in doctor's waiting rooms; in fact, physicians were used in advertisements encouraging smoking. Even Santa Claus was depicted in advertisements giving cartons of cigarettes as gifts. By the end of a movie, the smoke in a movie theater was often so thick that images on the screen were seen through a noticeable haze. Smokers were always nearby in restaurants and airplanes. For today's young people, all this is hard to imagine. Now smoking is generally culturally disapproved by most groups, and there are fewer and fewer settings outside of personal residences where it is even legal to smoke. Even the home is considered an inappropriate setting, given health consequences for family members. This is a dramatic cultural change, though it took almost a half century to evolve.

Although an anti-smoking industry gradually took form and eventually played a significant role, this transition in cultural support for smoking was not the result of an organized plan. Explicit attempts to change cultural practices are actually quite common, however. Governments establish laws and regulations intended to result in certain changes in the behavior of its citizens. Laws concerning taxation are often aimed at encouraging or discouraging certain practices. New businesses face the need to establish particular cultural practices for employees, and existing companies must continually modify their culture to compete effectively. Even relatively stable cultures such as religious communities evolve in response to changes in society.

The previous chapter's consideration of how the topic of rights and values might be approached scientifically hinted at the features of a behavior analytic approach to studying and engineering cultural change. Cultural practices are often described in terms of rights and values, and any interest in changing such practices must face conflicts between existing and proposed practices. For example, obesity is widely acknowledged as a serious health problem in the United States. There are many factors that contribute to this problem, which come together in ways we might describe as cultural practices. Food manufacturers are quite good at producing processed foods that appeal to consumers, and the advertising industry supports these interests with effective media campaigns. The restaurant industry is similarly effective in offering attractive menu items, serving large portions, and encouraging people to eat out instead of cooking at home. Most people are not well informed about nutritional matters (a fairly technical field, after all), and our busy lifestyles encourage us to eat foods that give us more calories than we need and discourage getting enough exercise to burn off the excess. The resulting problem of obesity is not merely personal. Government at all levels cannot avoid confronting the consequences of this health problem, especially in economic terms.

The challenge is that as individuals we often seem to be happy with what and how we eat. More technically, the different behaviors we engage in associated with food are maintained by reinforcing outcomes. When government tries to change such behavior in order to address the problem of obesity, there are many interests that tend to resist. The food industry fights regulations that encourage healthier eating because rules may hurt their bottom line. Consumers may welcome improved product labeling but draw the line at regulations that limit the foods available to them, such as what schools can sell in vending machines or what restaurants can put on their menu.

It is easy to frame these issues in terms of values and rights. Certainly many would argue that we each have a right to choose what we eat, even if we know it to be unhealthy, and we are likely to resist any constraints on our apparent freedom to determine our own diet. We value foods that taste good, which is at least partly related to food preferences learned in childhood. The phrase "comfort food" suggests that our food preferences may have little to do with the health consequences of what we otherwise find "comfortable." We also value the option of eating when we wish and as much as we like, even as we suffer the consequences of eating too much, too often.

Confronting such convictions in a systematic effort to change food-related behavior on a wide scale is a daunting challenge. Can a scientific approach to cultural practices as operant behavior help engineer change? What if we avoid mentalistic distractions and approach rights and values from a behavioral perspective, as Chapter 8 suggests, and focus on modifying particular cultural practices based on the established science of behavior? Might a science and technology of cultural change emerge? What would a science of behavior need to learn in order to guide a culture toward healthier eating?

The field of nutrition already offers a pretty good template for a healthy diet, though experts will always quibble about the details. Given a reasonably sound understanding of good nutrition, the overriding need is for behavioral science to develop recommendations for government, the food industry, and citizens that will lead to improved dietary practices that become accepted and passed on to future generations. It might seem obvious that government could simply pass laws and regulations that mandate desired actions by the food industry, but recall the government's failed experiment with Prohibition. Even if new laws and regulations could be counted on to change behavior effectively, which is unlikely, this approach presupposes that we know what kinds of governmental actions will be effective and what actions will be ineffective or even provoke resistance.

For example, government already requires informational labeling of some food products on the premise that this information will encourage consumers to choose healthier over less healthy foods. What can behavioral science tell us about this implicit prediction? Do some forms of labeling work better than others? How should labels vary among different food products, such as fresh meats or vegetables versus processed foods? What ways of including nutritional information on restaurant menus will encourage healthier food choices? What are the factors necessary to make product labeling effective? Do different consumer characteristics such as educational background require different approaches to labeling for it to be effective? What kinds of changes in consumer food purchasing can be expected from merely managing labeling practices? These are only a few of the many questions behavioral science must address concerning just food product labeling.

Monetary contingencies are another kind of influence on what we eat. They can be powerful ways of changing behavior, which is why governments often use such contingencies, already widespread in the food industry, to manage the behavior of its citizens. For example, the production of both raw and processed foods is affected by tax and price policies, and consumer purchases of food products are usually sensitive to cost. This relation between food prices and consumer purchasing behavior can certainly be bent toward the objective of healthier eating, but exactly how? What does a science of behavior already know about this relation and what remains to be learned? Is it just a matter of government intervening in ways that make less healthy food more expensive or healthy food less expensive? There are different ways such interventions can be arranged. Are some more effective than others?

The history of cultural change in the United States regarding smoking suggests that the use of media might also be an important way of influencing cultural eating practices. We are already inundated with information about what we eat that pushes our behavior one way or the other, but what can science teach us about using different forms of media to change behavior? The stop smoking industry focused its media dollars on making smoking broadly unacceptable, but is it a feasible objective to make obesity unacceptable? No one has to smoke, but we all have to eat, and some people naturally weigh more than others, even on a healthy diet. What might be desirable and achievable outcomes of using media to encourage healthy eating? Are there risks of promoting losing weight and looking thin? What types of media will be most effective with what kinds of messages? What density of messaging over what period of time is required for effectiveness?

Although these examples of scientific challenges often reference the role of government at some level, it is not the only mechanism for influencing cultural change in dietary practices. The food industry cannot help but play a major role, and there are endless interest groups that could certainly contribute as well, including those associated with health fields, educational interests, and citizen groups.

The collective challenge is not just to engineer cultural changes associated with eating, but to do so in a way that does not provoke **countercontrol**. The attempt by the federal government to prohibit drinking alcohol generated so much countercontrol that this remains the most well-known feature of this unhappy experiment.

BOX 9.3

Who Is In Control?

It is the nature of operant behavior that it both controls and is controlled by the environment. The relation is unavoidably reciprocal. Our behavior results in environmental changes that in turn have an impact on the likelihood of our engaging in particular behaviors in the future. This is especially clear in social interactions. When we pay someone a compliment, their reaction is likely to reinforce our behavior of offering the compliment, and when we say something rude to someone, they may respond in kind or just not interact with us as much. This back and forth between behavior and environment is what makes our repertoires flexible and adaptive.

Countercontrol is the term that generally denotes this kind of reciprocity in social relations. More narrowly, however, this term is most often used to describe the actions of one party that specifically counter or at least react to the control exerted by another party (Skinner, 1953). Countercontrol may be exercised by an individual or by groups of individuals. Examples of situations that might involve countercontrol include those in which the actions of a controlling party result in either a loss of reinforcers or aversive circumstances for others, who then engage in actions that push back against that control. The reactions of the controllee may thereby change the consequences of the controller's behavior, possibly leading to alternative actions that are more acceptable to the controllee.

Countercontrol in response to coercive or exploitive relationships is easily found in all spheres of life, including government, business, marriage, and other interpersonal relationships. A political party may be thrown out of power by voters because of their actions or their failure to meet societal needs. Employees may revolt against management policies with a strike, a work slowdown, or even sabotage. A spouse may respond to a partner's unacceptable behavior by filing for divorce.

Behavior that generates countercontrol by others may sometimes be effective in the short run, but it is likely to be ineffective in the long run. Behavior that creates aversive circumstances for others tends to generate reactions that terminate or lessen those aversive conditions. In a situation in which someone is attempting to manage the behavior of others, the emergence of countercontrol suggests that improved management contingencies are necessary.

Not only were people more opposed to Prohibition than their elected representatives may have suspected, it was implemented all at once with inadequate preparation. Although Prohibition did lead to reduced consumption of alcohol, it also encouraged consumption under surreptitious circumstances (such as speakeasies) and widespread criminal activity (such as keeping speakeasies well stocked with alcohol).

It might be argued that smoking was no less popular some decades ago in the United States than drinking was during the Prohibition era, but the effort to reduce smoking did not generate substantial countercontrol. Note that the government did not attempt to prohibit smoking by law, at least initially. What unfolded instead was a gradual increase in the pace of cultural change, slow at first but then accelerating more rapidly over the years. By the time that governments, businesses, and other interests were restricting where people could smoke, there was little cultural support for this behavior and relatively little backlash to such restrictions. The problem of changing poor dietary practices is admittedly more complicated than the task of reducing drinking and smoking behavior, and the risk of countercontrol in response to ill-advised attempts to manage what and how we eat would seem to be substantial.

Cultural Engineering

It is tempting to talk about cultures as if they map neatly onto countries. When we talk about particular practices, we often unintentionally imply that one practice or another is characteristic of an entire country, region, province, or state. In fact, geographical and geopolitical boundaries have little to do with the definition of a culture. Although different native languages from one country to another might seem to ensure that citizens sharing a common language constitute a cultural group, it is not that simple. Populations defined in geopolitical or linguistic terms include many cultures.

Each of us is a member of multiple cultural groups, which may substantially overlap with what we call verbal communities. There are the different cultures of our family, our work, our friends, our avocational interests, and so forth. These cultures can be quite different in certain ways, and our behavior can adjust significantly as we move from one to another, even during the same day. The style of our social interchanges certainly changes between home, work, and recreational settings.

Let us consider the culture associated with our work as a way of appreciating some of the behavioral features of cultures and the challenges of **cultural engineering**. Our work culture is defined by those practices shared over time by those with whom we interact as part of our work. Assume you are one of a small number of ABA practitioners employed by a human services provider agency serving families and schools. This culture includes others employed by the agency, as well as families, teachers, and others outside of the agency with whom you interact as part of your employment. What might be some of the cultural practices in which you participate as an employee of such an agency?

It will help to focus on those practices that are learned through your involvement with the agency. This means some of the behavior you bring from your training and previous experience may not qualify as part of the culture of that agency. Some features of your professional repertoire (much of your technical knowledge and skills, for instance) were not learned from members of that particular culture and may be passed on to others by virtue of their membership to only a limited degree. The agency culture might include various features of social interactions (perhaps a certain social style peculiar to the agency), certain characteristics of interactions between supervisors and supervisees, particular features of relationships with client families and professionals outside of the agency, and so forth. Even such traditions as how co-workers celebrate birthdays might be included as a cultural practice. Features of your work for the agency qualify as part of that culture if they result from your involvement with the agency, are shared by co-workers, and are a long-standing practice within that agency. Protocols for interacting with clients and agencies, the use of certain forms and materials, ways of monitoring professional services, decision-making practices, and much more may constitute your work culture.

Certain practices are likely to be especially important to you and your ABA colleagues. For example, how the agency defines and directs various aspects of your work, including job responsibilities, required features of professional services, and even scheduling considerations will be relevant to professional and ethical standards. Furthermore, no workplace is without its problems, so the problem-solving culture of the agency is likely to be essential to your professional satisfaction as well.

If you had sufficient information, you might be able to trace the evolution of some of the practices within this work culture. Some may stem from an agency's business model or from long-established policies created by a board of directors or a chief executive officer. The origin of some practices may lie in economic contingencies associated with the agency's services. Others, such as an employee birthday tradition, may simply have been initiated by someone who is no longer with the company and yet continues to be passed on to new employees.

Perhaps a more intriguing question is how you might engineer changes in such a workplace culture. If you wanted to change some of your agency's existing practices or initiate new ones, how might you go about this? In figuring out your objectives, remember that in order for practices to survive over an extended period they must benefit the members of the culture and be passed on to new members. You might believe that establishing a certain practice would be easier if you were the boss, but the temptation to establish it by edict or even by example might only seduce you into promoting a practice that fails to outlast your tenure. This is a common problem in organizations, even when a reasonable analysis suggests that the practice is a good idea.

It will help to begin with an analysis of the contingencies already associated with the practice under consideration or that might be required. Some contingencies might encourage the practice and some might discourage it. What is the balance of these conflicting contingencies? What will be their collective effects in the long run? Why might the practice survive or eventually fall by the wayside? It will also be important to determine if the relevant contingencies are contrived or natural. Contrived contingencies require ongoing maintenance, which raises the question of what contingencies will ensure that ongoing support. The advantage of natural contingencies is that they may need little management over time. If a desired practice must benefit and be passed on by the members of the culture in order to be sustained, the supporting contingencies must not themselves require special ongoing efforts.

Let us suppose that you want to start a practice in which the agency's ABA professionals meet for one afternoon a month to discuss clinical and ethical considerations associated with their ABA services for the agency. More broadly, you want to establish a culture of peer review for the agency that might have a number of desirable outcomes, including encouraging ABA employees to keep professional aspects of their work from being overwhelmed by the agency's economic interests, providing a regular mechanism for reviewing each other's clinical decisions, and reminding agency administrators that you and your colleagues are members of a profession with best practice and ethical standards. You might be able to arrange such meetings, even with good administrative support, but the real question is whether they will become an established practice in that work culture and still be in place as employees come and go over the years.

What contingencies will be required to create this practice and make it a durable feature of employment for ABA professionals? Administrators will have to accommodate a monthly afternoon meeting, obviously, but why would they? An agency director might think this is a great idea but soon want to use the meeting to deal with administrative matters instead. It would certainly not be surprising if other events or needs were allowed to interfere with regular meetings. What outcomes would convince the current administrator, and the next one to hold the job as well, not only to tolerate, but enthusiastically support these meetings? The reinforcers for administrators often lie in avoiding or at least resolving problems. If the meetings serve these functions, administrators are likely to be supportive. If, as a result of these regular discussions, clinical issues are addressed that could have led to problems if not resolved, administrators should benefit. If ethical issues are discovered and resolved that could have caused the agency difficulties, administrators will be happy. If the meetings become a notable feature of the agency and lead to plaudits from families, school personnel, and other outside entities, administrators will be enthusiastic about the meetings.

What about your colleagues—will they regularly show up and participate? Everyone is already busy; who needs another meeting? What are the natural con-

BOX 9.4

Survival Value of Cultural Practices

B. F. Skinner (1953) observed that a culture is an experiment in behavior. This proposal follows from his argument that cultural practices are selected by their consequences in the same way that individual repertoires evolve (Skinner, 1981). From an evolutionary perspective, both the ebb and flow of an individual's behavior and the changes in a culture's practices are an ongoing experiment in which, as a result of differential consequences, some variants persist or grow stronger and others wither and disappear. The outcome at any point is an assessment of the usefulness of any behavior or practice. Some prove useful and persist, and some fail this test.

This perspective suggests the possibility of evaluating cultural practices in terms of their survival value—the extent to which they contribute to the survival of the culture. Survival value is a complicated criterion, however. Practices that might work well for a culture at one point in time might be problematic at another. For example, practices that result in a high birth rate might be valuable for a culture when it has adequate resources but risky when it does not.

Another challenge to assessing the survival value of cultural practices lies in deciding on a meaningful time frame. The eventual outcome of various cultural practices can be decades or even generations in the making. The mere existence of a particular practice at any point in time should not be taken as evidence that it will contribute to the survival of the culture in the long run. For example, the United Society of Believers in Christ's Second Appearing, also known as the Shakers, was a religious sect founded in the eighteenth century. Among other practices, celibacy was strictly observed, and the Shaker communities grew largely through conversions, indenturing children, and taking in orphans. By the twentieth century, however, their numbers dwindled to only a few older women, presumably in part because of the practice of celibacy.

tingencies that might be required to maintain their participation? Certainly some important contingencies are social. If the meetings are socially enjoyable, people are more likely to attend consistently. Of course, the substance of the meetings should provide reinforcers for attending as well. If participants learn things that are useful in their work and get help from each other on questions they face, they will be likely to make time for the meetings. If people find the meetings professionally important, they may even arrange modest aversive social consequences for anyone missing meetings.

Insuring that the meetings have these outcomes over the long term may be challenging. What if one member of the group tends to dominate discussion or another has a contentious style of interaction? What if a certain individual shows up but does not participate in discussion? What if your colleagues allow meetings to be continually interrupted by outside events? What if it turns out to be difficult to maintain a substantive focus on professional issues? How can problems like these, which will certainly come and go over time, be prevented from discouraging meaningful professional discussion?

It is unlikely that cultural practices evolve and are sustained on the basis of only a single benefit to their members. In order to survive over an extended period of time, they tend to have multiple benefits and sources of support within the culture. In the above example, it may be that the long-term survival of the practice will require support from both administrators and ABA employees. If an administrator comes along who is not as supportive as the last, the ABA professionals may carry the day by insisting that the meetings be given priority within the agency. If one of the ABA personnel brings a problematic personal style to meetings, others who find the meetings valuable are likely to intervene or at least tolerate the problem. If the meetings are too often interrupted by outside crises, its members may implement restrictive rules about interruptions. The key is that the function of the meetings results in reinforcers for the participation of its members and for the support of others necessary for its survival as a part of the agency's culture.

CHAPTER SUMMARY

1. A core of human behavior results from contingencies involving only our biology and the physical environment. These contingencies are free of the influence of culture and therefore are the same for all humans.

2. The impact of our social environment involves learned behavior shared by a group's members, acquired from their membership, and transmitted from one member to another.

3. Most people assume that the impact of our social experiences can be filtered through personal mental processes, including our choice about whether we are influenced by those experiences. In fact, the mental processes that appear to allow us to modulate social influences are either invented or are actually behavior that we fail to acknowledge as such.

4. Natural selection underlies behavior in three ways: through the contingencies of survival responsible for selection of species, through contingencies of reinforcement responsible for individual repertoires, and through contingencies established by our social environment.

5. The evolution of cultural practices is difficult to study because the pace of change is slow. The task is eased by our understanding of how human behavior works.

6. The selection of cultural practices involves variation, transmission, and selection.

7. There must be variation in cultural practices for selection to be meaningful. What varies in cultural selection are activities or practices of multiple individuals that serve particular functions within groups.

8. Cultural practices must also be transmitted from one member to another. Direct instruction by others is a primary means of transmission. Imitation is also one of the ways this occurs.

9. Selection of certain variations of cultural practices involves reinforcement stemming from natural contingencies, as well as social reinforcement for compliance.

10. The challenge for a science of behavior is to assess particular cultural practices in order to evaluate and predict their effects, understand the nature of their support, and provide guidance about ways of modulating these practices.

11. Engineering changes in cultural practices is difficult because people disagree about the need for or direction of change. Cultural practices are often described in terms of rights and values, and any interest in changing such practices must face inevitable conflicts between existing and proposed practices. Can a scientific approach to cultural practices as operant behavior help engineer change?

12. Cultures are not defined in terms of geographical or geopolitical boundaries. Each person is a member of multiple cultural groups, which overlap with the notion of verbal communities.

TEXT STUDY GUIDE

1. Explain how some contingencies experienced by humans can be the same across cultures.

2. How is culture defined in the context of this chapter?

3. How do most people interpret the impact of their social experiences? What is the problem with this perspective?

4. Describe the three ways natural selection underlies behavior.

5. What is the feature of the evolution of cultural practices that makes them challenging to study?

6. What are the three elements of natural selection that must be part of an explanation of the evolution of cultural practices?

7. Why are some cultural practices selected and strengthened and others not?

8. What is the distinction between proximate and ultimate reinforcers?

9. What are the tasks for a science of behavior in studying cultural practices and their evolution?

10. What is the relation between geographical or geopolitical boundaries and cultures?

BOX STUDY GUIDE

1. Explain the difference between phylogeny and ontogeny.
2. In the context of this chapter, what is countercontrol?
3. Describe the reinforcement contingencies for both controller and controllee in a situation that leads to countercontrol.
4. What is meant by reference to the survival value of cultural practices?
5. What are the challenges to assessing the survival value of a particular cultural practice?

DISCUSSION TOPICS AND EXERCISES

1. As a way of appreciating the impact of culture, try to inventory human behavior that is free of social contingencies.
2. Choose a specific cultural practice and consider how the three elements of natural selection operate in its evolution.
3. Choose an existing cultural practice with which you are familiar or one you would like to develop. Consider what you would need to learn about the practice and how you might go about engineering this change as a behavior analyst.
4. Choose a specific cultural practice and consider how you might evaluate its survival value for the culture.

SUGGESTED READINGS

Catania, A. C. (2007). *Learning*. Cornwall-on-Hudson, NY: Sloan Publishing. (Chapter 3: Evolution and Behavior).

Skinner, B. F. (1953). *Science and human behavior*. New York: MacMillan. (Chapter XXII: Government and law, Chapter XXVII: Culture and control, and Chapter XVIII: Designing a culture).

Chapter 10

Radical Behaviorism

Lynn was feeling pretty happy with herself. After all, she had just completed a grueling two-year ABA Master's program (the hardest thing she had ever done) and passed the BCBA certification exam. Not only that, she had recently accepted a position that looked very promising. She was employed by a large agency serving developmentally disabled children. The agency operated its own school, maintained a residential program, and contracted with area schools and families in providing off-site services. Most of the children were diagnosed with autism spectrum disorders. Chrissy was assigned to work with teachers in the agency's in-house school program.

In spite of having survived an intensive Master's program, she still felt awfully new. Some days she was brimming with confidence, but other times it seemed she kept running into things she realized she didn't know that much about. Her professors had cautioned her that she still had a lot to learn, and the more she interacted with other BCBAs at the agency, the more she realized that this was true. More often than not, it was her supervisor, Penny, who tactfully made it clear that her program had not taught her everything. Lynn liked Penny, and they were getting along well. Penny had graduated from a different Master's program only a few years ago, and it was clear that her training had covered some topics that Lynn's program had missed.

The other day, Lynn and Penny were talking about a child's classroom treatment plan. Lynn thought she was speaking carefully, but Penny politely turned the discussion into a bit of a tutorial. Penny was concerned about what she described as Lynn's "casual" way of expressing herself in talking about the case. She focused on a few phrases as examples, and Lynn understood her points as she explained them. However, it was apparent that Penny's concern went beyond the examples. She was worried about Lynn's tendency to speak in everyday phraseology except when she was talking about established treatment procedures. At first, Lynn didn't get it. She accepted the correction about not talking about what the child "wanted" and conceded that it was not necessary for the child to "realize" the focus of the treatment contingencies in order for them to be effective. However, Penny was arguing that Lynn's tendency to talk in everyday terms could affect her judgment about the direction and technicalities of treatment plans. This suggestion was more difficult to accept. Lynn felt that as long as she was seeing a child's behavior clearly and using established treatment procedures she was on safe ground.

Lynn appreciated that Penny was being constructive rather than confrontational, and that made it easier to try to see her argument. It turned out that Penny's Master's program had included a full course on radical behaviorism. Lynn's program had certainly touched on this topic but more in passing than as a major instructional focus. Penny was clearly enthusiastic about the value of understanding this material, but Lynn didn't quite see why it should be so important. Still, she respected Penny's supervision and agreed to do some reading Penny recommended. Maybe this would help her understand why Penny was convinced that this aspect of behavior analysis was so important for practitioners.

RADICAL BEHAVIORISM

The Philosophy of the Science of Behavior Analysis

Reduced to its essence, this book has argued for approaching behavior as an entirely physical phenomenon influenced only by other physical events. To most people, this may seem pitifully little substance to explain the glories of human nature and woefully inadequate as a conceptual framework for a science of behavior. To you, nearing the end of this discussion, this simple argument is rich with profound and pervasive implications. If behavior is entirely physical in nature and does not involve events that are said to exist in a mental universe, it follows that behavior is susceptible to influence only by other physical events, which means that "mental events" cannot explain behavior. There are no exceptions or compromises. Given the contrary implications of everyday language, this conception of behavior is a breathtaking proposition.

As noted at the outset, this point of view is called *radical behaviorism*. Skinner defined it as "the philosophy of a science of behavior treated as a subject matter in its own right apart from internal explanations, mental or physiological" (1989, p. 122). The far-reaching implications of this simple definition are not so simple, however, as you may by now appreciate. Let us pull together the key features of radical behaviorism.

First, it is important to be clear that radical behaviorism is not the scientific study of behavior. It is a comprehensive philosophy of that science, most particularly the science of behavior analysis. As such, it concerns the philosophical underpinnings and assumptions of scientific activities and findings, including issues such as scientific language, methods, explanation, and reasoning. Scientists working in the trenches every day probably do not often think about the philosophical implications of their actions, but it is the sum of those actions within a discipline that constitute its scientific philosophy.

Perhaps the most important feature of radical behaviorism as a scientific philosophy is that behavior analysts view verbal behavior—specifically including their own verbal behavior—no differently than any other kind of behavior. Aside from its biological foundation, all verbal behavior is fully explained in terms of the laws of operant learning. A researcher studying the acquisition of verbal behavior by autistic children views his or her behavior involved in framing experimental questions, designing study protocols, analyzing graphed data, and drawing conclusions as fundamentally the same as the verbal behavior under investigation in these children and fully subject to the same kind of explanations.

The continuity in this approach between the behavior under investigation and the behavior of investigators makes an epistemological statement—a statement about the nature of knowledge. What it means for a scientist to know something is inextricably wrapped up with his or her verbal behavior and how it can be explained as ordinary behavior. Rather than being viewed as a superior form of knowledge involving logical domains and mental processes, explaining scientific findings is accepted as behavior no different than the behavior being explained. This perspective is unique to radical behaviorism. Unlike other sciences, in behavior analysis there is no conceptual discontinuity between the subject matter of the science and the explanatory behavior of its scientists. As Moore (2008) has observed, it is the science of behavior analysis that serves as the basis for the philosophy of radical behaviorism, which is in turn the foundation for the science. In other words, it is our understanding of what behavior is and how it works, as revealed by the science of behavior analysis, that guides us to radical behaviorism as the necessary philosophy of this science.

This epistemology stems from radical behaviorism's intolerance for mentalism. Skinner's statement about studying behavior "as a subject matter in its own right apart from internal explanations, mental or physiological" refers to a long history in psychology in which behavior was investigated largely as a means for drawing conclusions about how the mind works. Behavior was seen as a kind of necessary inconvenience for accessing the more interesting intricacies of mental life, a point of view still dominant in psychology, the social sciences, and behavioral neuroscience. Taking the position that behavior is a subject matter in its own right is not only a statement about the importance of behavior as a focus of scientific study, it ignores the mentalistic agenda in its entirety, emphasizing that such inventions lack a physical foundation. In paraphrasing a discussion by participants at a symposium on behaviorism and phenomenology, following Skinner's presentation of his paper "Behaviorism at fifty," Wann quoted Skinner as saying "I am a radical behaviorist simply in the sense that there is nothing in his formulation for anything that is mental." (Wann, 1964, p. 106).

Radical behaviorism also holds that behavior is not merely a result of its underlying physiology. It opposes the view that behavior can be adequately explained by the physiology that makes it possible. Neither does it allow using biological variables to legitimize mentalistic explanations. This has always been a tempting explanatory approach, and advances in brain imaging technology in recent years have proved too seductive for many. It is now routine to read about imaging studies that imply that particular patterns of brain activity are fully responsible for the way we behave under certain conditions (Faux, 2002). Participants are instructed to behave in a specific way while an imaging technique measures some aspect of brain activity. These measures are often said to represent a particular cognitive process or phenomenon, and conclusions are drawn about the role of that process in guiding behavior. Aside from the gratuitous assignment of a causal role to cognitive or mental processes, such studies fail to consider the contribution of learning processes, not only on the behavior that is observed but on the physiological activity that is being measured.

Instead, radical behaviorism approaches behavior as a set of relations between the organism and its environment that stand on their own. These relations do not require further analysis in either mental or physiological terms for their validity or utility. Evidence of orderly relations between behavior and environmental variables may be supplemented by an understanding of what is going on at a physiological level, but that information cannot fully explain the laws of behavior. Indeed, as Skinner pointed out, the laws of behavior help set the agenda for neuroscience by identifying behavioral phenomena that must eventually be accommodated by our understanding of human biology (Skinner, 1969).

For many, this priority of behavior as the sole subject matter of the science is too limiting, but such an assessment fails to appreciate the implications of radical behaviorism for a scientific conception of behavior. We have seen that abandoning the distraction of mentalism leads to a definition of behavior that is more inclusive than most might suppose. For instance, radical behaviorism defines behavior as circumscribing far more than what is obvious to external observers. It accepts that we have real experiences that are private and not generally accessible to others. Rather than ignore these private events because they may be difficult to observe, it incorporates them into the scientific agenda. Events actually going on inside the skin, whether serving as independent or dependent variables, are viewed as real aspects of behavioral phenomena. It remains important, however, that when we speculate about the role of private events we restrict our interpretations to what we have learned about learning processes by studying directly observable behavior. This guidance imposes a kind of conceptual restraint that is important in preventing backsliding into mentalism.

One of the reasons radical behaviorism can accommodate a conception of behavior that includes private events lies in how it deals with the behavior of scientists. In early efforts to study behavior, researchers came to realize that scientific progress would be stymied if research methods incorporated unbridled speculation about mental life. This led to a general restriction that only publicly observable events

BOX 10.1

Behavior Analysis and Neuroscience

Behavior analysts have long been concerned about efforts to explain behavior that bypass environmental variables and appeal to physiological variables instead. This tendency is a form of reductionism, which holds that something can be explained by reducing it to the subject matter of another science at a "lower" level (see Reese, 1996). This maneuver raises questions about what we mean by causation in the first place and ignores abundant evidence about the causal role of interactions between an organism and its environment. One of the more insidious difficulties with attempting to reduce behavior to underlying physiological mechanisms is that it requires assigning some causal power or force to the mechanisms. That is, the underlying physiology is seen as a motive cause of the behavior at issue. In its most egregious form, this causal force is given mental characteristics. Although a study may measure some sort of brain activity, for instance, the source of its assumed power to cause behavior may be assigned to mentalistic qualities, such as anticipating, wanting, and so forth.

Behavior analysts have always acknowledged that a complete explanation of behavior requires understanding the necessary contribution of associated physiological processes. However, the question of how the organism's biology participates in its behavior is quite different from asking how the organism's behavior is a function of its environment. It may be revealing to address questions about what is going on physiologically when responses occur, but this approach cannot answer the question of why particular responses occur and why they occur exactly when they do. Physiological events accommodate and influence responding, but they cannot by themselves explain why it occurs at particular moments in specific contexts. It is the organism's learning history under different stimulus conditions, as well as present environmental features, that explains why responding occurs at any moment. This is why what we learn in answering the second question (how the organism's behavior is a function of its environment) guides how we frame the first question (how the organism's biology participates in its behavior). It is only by understanding how behavior works that we can know how to investigate the contribution of physiological variables and how to interpret the results.

However much we may learn about the biological accompaniments of behavior, scientifically established relations between organism and environment stand on their own. What the science of behavior analysis has learned about the laws of operant learning cannot be undone or depreciated by the discovery of how the organism's physiology participates in these relations. An understanding of what is going at a neurological or biochemical level when an organism engages in some action cannot by itself fully explain why that action occurred at that moment. What we already know about the role of the environment means that such an explanation is incomplete without reference to the laws of operant learning.

were acceptable as the source of objective data. For a while, some interpreted this view as fully eliminating from scientific consideration any phenomena that did not meet this standard. It did not take long for a more convenient solution to emerge, however. Unobservable "events" came to be viewed in theoretical terms (see Box 10.2) and thereby were incorporated into scientific interpretations and theories.

This approach is mentalistic in how it explains the behavior of experimental participants. Mental events or processes are proposed as explanations of behavior, but because they cannot be directly assessed, some ostensibly related behavior is measured instead. These indirect measurements are said to represent the mental phenomena and are then used as the basis for explaining the behavior of interest. For example, a mental state identified as anxiety may be said to explain certain actions. In the absence of a way to measure anxiety directly, it may be defined in terms of particular measurement operations, such as performance on a questionnaire intended to assess anxiety. Scores on this questionnaire may then be expressed in terms of mental qualities and are used to explain the behavior at issue.

It is less obvious that this tactic is also mentalistic in how scientists must thereby explain their own behavior of drawing conclusions about their participant's behavior. In arguing that the indirectly measured behavior (such as responding to a questionnaire) "represents" certain mental events or processes, these researchers are being mentalistic by accepting a view of their own behavior in which mental concepts are given a special logical status that underlies the researcher's behavior of explaining and drawing conclusions. That is, arguments giving this kind of explanatory role to mental events and processes signify that proponents are being mentalistic about the causes of their own behavior (Moore, 1981).

In contrast, by treating the scientist's behavior no differently than that of the participant, radical behaviorism provides an alternative approach to dealing with private events. The challenge of directly observing private events—a problem of accessibility—is resolved by calling for an operational analysis of the verbal behavior of the scientists. Instead of either ignoring private events or inventing mentalistic representations of them, radical behaviorism incorporates them into interpretative analysis by asking about the sources of control over such statements. Focusing on the environmental sources of control over scientific verbal behavior avoids the need to be mentalistic in interpreting the verbal behavior of the scientist. In the case of anxiety, this approach would focus on identifying the factors in our learning history underlying statements about anxiety as a cause of behavior. To what stimuli are we responding when we describe someone as anxious? What physiological or behavioral events are we tacting? This analysis focuses our attention on possible relations between behavior and physical variables that together prompt talking about anxiety, which can then be examined experimentally.

In sum, as the philosophy of the science of behavior analysis, radical behaviorism accepts behavior as a subject matter in its own right, regardless of the challenges of measuring it or the variables of which it is a function. It approaches behavior as a

BOX 10.2

Theory and Theoretical Terms

In the context of science, the term "theory" is often misunderstood by non-scientists. Scientists do more than simply accumulate facts. They also organize those facts in the form of theoretical statements that augment the generality of scientific discoveries. Scientific theories are not speculations about the way we think the world might work but summaries of what researchers have already established, perhaps with limited inclusion of statements that are not yet facts but are reasonable predictions based on substantial evidence (see Moore, 2010, for additional discussion).

Skinner had no concerns with this approach to theory, which is widely respected in the physical sciences. The approach to theorizing that drew his ire was to "any explanation of an observed fact which appeals to events taking place somewhere else, at some other level of observation, described in different terms, and measured, if at all, in different dimensions" (Skinner, 1961, p. 39). This kind of theorizing is common in the history of psychology and the social sciences, and its appeal to "events taking place somewhere else" unavoidably involves the use of theoretical terms.

The definition and treatment of theoretical terms has been much debated in psychology. They are generally considered as falling into two categories: intervening variables and hypothetical constructs (MacCorquodale & Meehl, 1948). As summarized by Moore (2008), intervening variables are explicitly verbal creations and do not refer to physical events. They serve a systematizing role in theoretical scientific statements, summarizing established relations in an economical manner. In contrast, hypothetical constructs reference events that may be inferred on the basis of some evidence to exist, although they are not observed. In principle, we could collect evidence about such constructs if measurement technology permitted. Some researchers view elements of memory as hypothetical constructs. The referents of both theoretical terms are unobservable. Intervening variables are unobservable in principle because they do not refer to things that exist, but hypothetical constructs are unobservable in practice because although they are supposed to refer to events that may exist, the supporting evidence is not complete.

Radical behaviorism's approach to scientific theory recognizes that theorizing is unavoidably verbal behavior. As such, theoretical terms must be considered in light of how this verbal behavior is influenced by environmental contingencies. In these exercises, radical behaviorism rejects theoretical terms that violate Skinner's above statement. Theorizing that "appeals to events taking place somewhere else, at some other level of observation, described in different terms, and measured, if at all, in different dimensions" inevitably appeals to logical or symbolic processes. As we have already seen, this verbal practice is inherently mentalistic and therefore problematic for a science of behavior.

In contrast, Skinner (1972) described an approach to theory with three stages. The first task is to identify the basic data, which is followed by describing orderly relations among the data. Only then is it appropriate to derive higher order concepts from those orderly relations. This last stage is the zenith of scientific theorizing. The terms at this stage are what Moore called "abstract tact[s] with a high level of generality" (1981, p. 68). Skinner was confident that vernacular terms, even those with mentalistic connotations, would be properly established if theory building was approached only in this manner. For instance, he noted Galileo's work studying the relation between the position of a ball on an inclined plane and the elapsed time since its release and the resulting concept of acceleration — a third stage concept. He argued that terms such as "wants, faculties, attitudes, drives, ideas, interests, and capacities" could someday be appropriate third stage concepts given the kind of experimental attention exemplified by research on physical phenomena.

primary phenomenon, not merely a consequence of physiology nor an epiphenomenon of a more important mental life. Radical behaviorism rejects invented internal dimensions and causes, as well as explanations that rely on a mentalistic view of the researcher's explanatory behavior. That is, it insists on conceptualizing the behavior of participant and researcher in exactly the same way by avoiding the assignment of special qualities to the verbal behavior of the researcher.

With the previous chapters behind you, the above paragraphs should seem familiar, perhaps even comfortable, so you might be wondering what is so radical about radical behaviorism. It is radical in contrast to other versions of behaviorism, which either ignore behavior that is not publicly observable or incorporates mentalism in some way. Although you might assume that the term "radical" means that this form of behaviorism is extreme, perhaps in some negative way, this is not the correct connotation. "Thoroughgoing" is a more appropriate synonym than "extreme." Radical behaviorism is thorough in addressing all features of human nature without relegating some aspects to the sidelines as not publicly observable or treating them only on a theoretical level. It is thorough in offering a comprehensive explanation of behavior that is conceptually consistent across all circumstances. It is thorough in rejecting all intrusions of mentalism into explanations of behavior, including mentalism implicit in the verbal behavior of those who do the explaining. It is thorough in how it approaches behavior and its controlling variables regardless of whether they are inside or outside the organism. Indeed, it is radical behaviorism's internal consistency—its thoroughness—that many find particularly appealing.

Summary of radical behaviorism

Historical Context

Another way to appreciate the implications of radical behaviorism as a philosophy of science is to consider its origins and contrasts with other forms of behaviorism. Scientific interest in behavior emerged well back in the nineteenth century, even before the development of psychology or other social sciences as recognized academic disciplines (see Boakes, 1984). These interests were understandably mentalistic in nature. After all, everyday language made it clear that our behavior was at the beck and call of mental processes. Any bit of behavior was framed in terms of how these assumed processes explained or at least contributed to it.

For those concerned about developing a sound scientific approach to the study of human affairs, however, questions about mental or subjective experience presented serious challenges. Throughout the nineteenth century and into the twentieth, philosophers and early psychologists struggled with how to characterize and pursue their interests. For some years, for example, personal introspection was promoted as an appropriate method of observing private experiences, though many worried whether it could be a proper basis for scientific discoveries about the mind. The young field of psychology was especially concerned with finding an approach that would bring it respect as a new science, divorced from its origins in philosophy. At the same time, American society was becoming increasingly interested in what of practical value psychology could offer.

What emerged from these issues was a movement that focused on behavior rather than mental phenomena. This movement, called behaviorism, is most often associated with John B. Watson, and it grew into the dominant frame of reference for psychology, remaining so for much of the twentieth century. Watson's 1913 paper, "Psychology as the behaviorist views it," is customarily taken as the beginning of the behavioral movement.

Watson's classical behaviorism was a major step forward. He insisted that psychologists study only behavior and that mental phenomena were fictional and in any case not acceptable for a science of behavior. His approach is labeled **classical S-R behaviorism** because of its embrace of the discoveries of Ivan Pavlov and others concerning conditioned reflexes. This research focus evolved into an early general model of how behavior seemed to work. A behavioral event was explained in terms of antecedent stimuli (S) that were said to elicit or call forth the response (R) under examination. The goal of classical behaviorism was prediction and control of publicly observable behavior (Moore, 2008; Todd & Morris, 1994).

Watson's position accepted some limitations that concerned later behaviorists, however. For instance, his narrow focus on publicly observable stimuli and responses did not seem up to the task of explaining some features of behavior, including its variability and apparent spontaneity. Furthermore, his account seemed to ignore behavior that was not always publicly observable, including what we call feelings, sensations, thoughts, and so forth. This constraint seemed unnecessary, given that the more established physical sciences seemed to be able to deal with unobservable phenomena in useful ways (Moore, 2008).

Watson's classical S-R behaviorism held sway until about 1930. Its inadequacies encouraged a new variant described as mediational S-O-R behaviorism

BOX 10.3

John Broadus Watson

John Broadus Watson was an influential and fascinating figure in early twentieth-century psychology. He was born in 1878 and raised in rural South Carolina. He entered Furman University at age 16 and completed his doctorate at the University of Chicago in 1903. By 1908, he was chair of the psychology department at Johns Hopkins University. However, in 1920 in the midst of divorce proceedings from his wife, an affair with his graduate student assistant, Rosalie Rayner, became front page news and the university asked him to leave. (He subsequently married Rayner, who died in 1935.)

Watson is best known for an article he published in 1913, "Psychology as the behaviorist views it." In this "behaviorist manifesto," he articulated an uncompromising focus on behavior as the sole focus of psychology and argued that mental states and processes had no place in an objective science. He emphasized Pavlov's discoveries about classical conditioning as the mechanism for behavior change, in spite of its limitations as a comprehensive explanation for behavior. He was elected president of the American Psychological Association in 1916 and was a powerful force in establishing behaviorism as a conceptual model for psychology.

He also wrote extensively in the emerging area of child development, publishing a best-selling book in 1928 titled, Psychological care of infant and child. He wrote in the popular press about childrearing, though his views have been widely criticized. He felt that children should be raised as young adults and treated with a certain level of emotional detachment, even to the extent of not allowing them to sit on a parent's lap. He stopped writing for popular publications in 1936 and later regretted some of the positions he took.

In yet another chapter of his life, Watson worked for many years in the advertising industry, where he was again quite successful. He retired from advertising at age 65 and died in 1958, having burned his papers and letters. (See Todd & Morris, 1994, for a review of Watson's life and influence.)

(Moore, 2008). This approach added inferences about things that might be going on inside the organism that could intervene between stimuli and responses. This form of neobehaviorism readmitted mentalism into the study of behavior in the form of motives, tendencies, purposes, moods, attitudes, and such that were assumed to modulate the effects of environmental stimuli. So, environmental events (S) were seen as leading to the organism's mental processes (O) that in turn led to behavioral outcomes (R). In an effort to rationalize the scientific legitimacy of this approach, there was considerable debate about the status of scientific concepts. *Operationism*, the idea that scientific concepts should be defined in terms of their measurement operations (see Box 10.4), was a particularly appealing point of view for psychology, given its interests in mental processes.

BOX 10.4

Operationism

The concept of operationism grew out of the physical sciences in the early twentieth century. Percy Bridgeman, in his book, The logic of modern physics, argued that "we mean by any concept nothing more than a set of operations; the concept is synonymous with the corresponding set of operations" (Bridgman 1927, 5). In its youthful drive to become a legitimate science, psychology embraced operationism in methodological discussions of how to resolve the challenge of addressing mental events in a scientific manner. Psychology's version of operationism did not quibble about the existence of mental events but instead focused on defining them in terms of the operations by which they might be measured in research projects. For instance, what an investigator meant in referring to a concept such as "fear" was defined by the procedures or operations used to measure it in a study, such as certain behavioral reactions to stimuli or a score on a questionnaire. These measurement operations and their results were publicly accessible and therefore avoided the problems of subjectivity.

However, this approach requires accepting the idea that the meaning of a term can be established by personal experience and might serve as the basis for logical entities. Fear, for instance, might be defined in terms of the sensations we can detect under specified environmental circumstances, and these sensations might be assigned formal roles in a theoretical account. In this manner, language is viewed as a symbolic activity in which personal experiences lead to private subjective meanings having their own existence. This approach to language as a system of references to the meaning of words goes beyond the physicality of behavior to a nonphysical realm in which language involves logical manipulations of the elements of private experiences (Moore, 1981). In other words, this interpretation of operationism retains the philosophical dualism involving mind and body that has always bedeviled attempts to establish an effective science of behavior.

Skinner disagreed with this approach, and he took the occasion of a conference on operationism to articulate his contrary views (Skinner, 1945). As has been discussed throughout this book, in this seminal paper he described an approach to operationism as a functional analysis of terms in question so as to evaluate the factors controlling the emission of a term as a verbal response. For Skinner, the meaning of a term lies not in a mental lexicon but in an analysis of the environmental variables that determine the emission of a verbal response. The question about what a term means involves identifying the discriminative stimuli functionally related to the verbal response, as well as the consequences for this response. Determining what a researcher means by fear therefore points in the direction of environmental stimuli surrounding the verbal response. Examining the contingencies associated with statements about fear thereby encourages questions about the physical phenomena (such as learning processes) associated with that bit of verbal behavior. The objective is that the scientist's verbal behavior come under control of nature, as revealed through experimental procedures and measurement, not under control of social or cultural traditions associated with the investigator's research.

B. F. Skinner was not impressed with this effort to incorporate mentalism into the study of behavior, however. He instead articulated the conceptual framework he called radical behaviorism. His thinking had many influences (see Moore, 2008, Chapter 3) but was partly based on the philosophical consequences of his scientific discoveries about behavior. His first book, *The behavior of organisms* (Skinner, 1938), described not only the results of his early research but his view that behavior should be studied as a subject matter in its own right, rather than as a way of pursuing physiological or mentalistic interests. The key to much of Skinner's emerging philosophy lay in his view of verbal behavior, which eventually resulted in what he described as his most important book, *Verbal behavior* (Skinner, 1957). A particularly important part of his argument involved an approach to private events and subjective terms that avoided mentalism by focusing on understanding the sources of control over the verbal behavior of the speaker (Skinner, 1945; also see Box 9.3). As explained in previous chapters, this approach involves dealing with statements as merely a form of behavior, rather than as having meaning in another dimension. The "meaning" of a term or phrase is therefore explained in terms of the factors that influence its emission as verbal behavior. Identifying these factors leads to a focus on behavior and its environmental influences. In this way, Skinner argued that the verbal behavior of scientists should be largely under control of experimental procedures and data, rather than under colloquial influences (Moore, 1981).

Skinner and his students directed a prolific laboratory research program. Its findings not only revealed the basic processes of operant shaping (e.g., Ferster & Skinner, 1957; Honig, 1966) but provided the foundation for the development of applied behavior analysis (Baer, Wolf, & Risley, 1968). The basic research agenda has continued over the years, and its findings still serve as the core of contemporary behavioral technology. However, much of Skinner's writing throughout his long career focused on conceptual issues associated with radical behaviorism (Morris & Smith, 1993). He eventually offered a detailed summary of his life and work in a three-volume autobiography (Skinner, 1976, 1979, 1983).

Radical vs. Methodological Behaviorism

It may also help your understanding of radical behaviorism to contrast it with another version of behaviorism called **methodological behaviorism**. Methodological behaviorism might be described as a way of thinking about scientific method that comes from conventional experimental practices and their underlying rationale. Moore, based on earlier arguments by Day (1977), has summarized these practices and assumptions as follows:

a. That scientific knowledge is different from, and is intrinsically superior to, common sense knowledge.

b. That scientific knowledge is to be gained by conducting carefully controlled experiments that test predictions from hypotheses and evaluate results by using impartial tests of statistical inference. Replication, reliability, and generalizability are the central issues in interpreting the meaningfulness of the results.

c. That scientific knowledge involves constructing logical domains, with which the logical properties of symbolic entities and mathematical formulae are to be established. Hypotheses derived from manipulation of these symbolic entities evolve into theories, theories evolve into laws, and deductions from the laws may be taken as explanations of the event under consideration.

d. That in order for the features of the scientific endeavor to be admissible into the body of science, the features must be publicly observable and tightly specified according to the procedures entailed in their measurement.

e. That causal processes are to be accommodated according to the model of antecedent, linear causation, where causal efficacy with respect to some dependent variable is fully vested in one or more preceding independent variables. (Moore, 1981, p. 64)

At first glance, these features might seem to be quite reasonable, even the essence of modern science. What gives them away, however, is the mentalism involved in the scientist's view of these methods. Although a researcher may avoid proposing that the participant's behavior is a function of mental phenomena, methodological behaviorism does not avoid the trap of implying the existence of a logical domain that allows the scientist to reason and draw conclusions about the participant's behavior. Scientists certainly engage in behavior we might call reasoning. However, the discussion in Chapter 6 of how we might describe such behavior made it clear that reasoning is not fundamentally different from other kinds of behaving and should not be viewed as special in any way. It is just behavior under environmental control, not a particular kind of mental process. This position contradicts the assumptions in item "c," among others, which place scientific reasoning in a mental domain.

In other words, the view of scientific discovery and methods represented by methodological behaviorism is inherently mentalistic because of how it accommodates mentalism in explaining the behavior of the researcher. Radical behaviorism, in contrast, is consistent in how it approaches the behavior of both the participant and the researcher. It is not acceptable to explain the behavior of either in a way that allows a role for non-physical influences. The key is the need to understand the sources of control over the verbal behavior of the researcher, not merely to reason in a logical manner. The researcher's verbal behavior will lead to sound descriptions and effective predictions when it is controlled by the variables in the experimental environment, not because of logical-theoretical features (Moore, 1981).

BOX 10.5

Varieties of Behaviorism

Radical behaviorism and methodological behaviorism are only two of many flavors or behaviorism. In addition to radical behaviorism and early and late forms of methodological behaviorism, Moore (2008) also discusses philosophical behaviorism, logical behaviorism, conceptual analysis, and metaphysical behaviorism—and this is not an exhaustive list. Each of these variants represents a distinctive argument proposed at some point in the twentieth century about how scientists should deal with the conflict between the facts of behavior and the rampant mentalism foisted upon investigators by the culture. Today these variations are important to a dwindling number of philosophers, psychologists, and historians of science.

In this history, however, one individual stands out for his articulation of an approach to behavior that was strikingly similar to Skinner's radical behaviorism. J. R. Kantor received his doctorate in 1917 in the Department of Philosophy at the University of Chicago and spent most of his career at Indiana University. He developed a conceptual approach to behavior that he called interbehavioral psychology, and it was the focus of his prolific scholarship throughout a long career. As described by Morris (1982), Kantor's approach emphasizes the continuous and reciprocal interactions between responding and the environment. However, in contrast with Skinner's focus on successive stimuli and responses, Kantor's orientation is more holistic, treating the entire organism as part of a field. He viewed distinctions between stimuli and responses in a behavioral sequence as an unnecessary contrivance and was less interested in laboratory preparations than in analyses of complex human behavior.

Early in his career Skinner had many interactions with Kantor, but they mostly went their separate ways over the years. For example, Skinner established a vigorous research enterprise, whereas Kantor's contributions lay in his scholarly works. However, they shared an unrelenting intolerance for mentalism in any form, and Skinner acknowledged a debt to Kantor for helping him exorcise the "spooks" in his thinking (Skinner, 1967).

A Matter of Opinion?

The function of radical behaviorism for behavior analysts who do research is to encourage them to ask good experimental questions about behavior and stick to experimental methods that identify the physical variables influencing the behavior of participants. Radical behaviorism is therefore not so much an argument to be proved as it is a tactic for creating better science by helping researchers avoid conceptual traps and interpretive confusions. It is justified in the long run by the quality of the field's science, which, in turn, might be operationalized as the usefulness of the science in producing an understanding of behavior that supports an effective technology. It all comes down to how well this way of talking about behavior improves our ability to resolve everyday behavioral issues because of the effectiveness of the underlying science.

If otherwise well-trained ABA practitioners are insufficiently effective in their services, the understanding of how behavior works revealed in the research literature must be weak, either because it is still immature or because it is misguided. Some might argue that the basic research literature in behavior analysis is increasingly mature, although it would be a pretty big stretch to describe the applied research literature that way, even after decades of diligent effort. There is much more to be learned, and we should be encouraged that our applied science continues to generate a growing record of demonstrable effectiveness in diverse applications. The productivity of this research is largely due to its respect for the experimental methods and interpretive practices established by B. F. Skinner and other early behavioral researchers (see Johnston & Pennypacker, 2009; Johnston, 1996; Sidman, 1960). This experimental approach has always been driven by radical behaviorism.

What this means is that if you are uncomfortable with certain aspects of radical behaviorism, you might be reassured that this point of view does not represent some unimpeachable truth. No one can prove all of its positions are true and those of other perspectives are false. It is merely a way of talking about behavior that seems to avoid long-standing problems with other conceptual approaches and has accumulated an impressive record in serving the scientific and practical interests of behavior analysts.

On the other hand, if you want to be intellectually honest with yourself, you should not accommodate any lingering discomforts you might have merely because radical behaviorism cannot be proven to be correct. If you disagree with a particular element of the radical behavioristic position and want to put it aside, what you must then reveal is the particular alternative position you find more comfortable. It is important to be clear about the substance of that alternative argument because that position is what you carry with you as a practitioner. You cannot avoid talking about behavior, after all, and what you say about it mirrors other aspects of your actions as a practitioner. If you talk with parents about their child's behavior in ways that reference a certain kind of mental "cause," you will also be talking about ways of resolving the child's problems that are different from those that might be consistent with radical behaviorism. In other words, what you say to the parents about behavior has implications for your effectiveness as a practitioner.

In sum, if you find it difficult to accept certain features of radical behaviorism, you owe it to yourself, not to mention your colleagues and clients, to candidly articulate the alternative details you find more agreeable. Furthermore, you should be willing to defend your position and explain why you find it more appealing. This includes explaining how the practical consequences of your position might make you a more effective practitioner than would the radical behavioristic position with which you are uncomfortable. In other words, what you should not do is disagree with a certain argument but fail to confront the rationale and consequences of the alternative conviction you hold.

Selling Radical Behaviorism

As we arrive at the end of this book, it may be useful to recall the arguments in the preface about why practitioners need to understand this conceptual framework:

a. Because they work at the interface between science and society and must bridge the gap between scientific and everyday understandings of how behavior works;

b. Because everyday convictions about how behavior works often conflict with established scientific findings;

c. Because they must be able to convince clients and other professionals to support objectives and procedures shown to be effective in the ABA literature;

d. Because their understanding of radical behaviorism helps ensure consistency between the field's science and the resulting technology; and

e. Because their understanding of radical behaviorism helps avoid conceptual backsliding that might be encouraged by everyday language

At this point, you should appreciate these rationales but find them unnecessary as a means of convincing you to make radical behaviorism an integral part of your professional repertoire. As you have become familiar with this philosophy of science, you should have discovered it is intellectually appealing on its own merits, aside from its practical implications. It avoids or resolves apparent mysteries created by everyday language and focuses on real variables that are useful in managing behavior. Instead of getting trapped by phrasing that implies mental sources of control, it helps you focus on behavior and environmental variables. And you can explain to others why it is important to avoid mentalistic distractions and adopt this focus.

Some of you will especially like the fact that this conceptual framework helps you talk in an internally consistent way about behavior. Many find that learning about radical behaviorism is like working a jigsaw puzzle. The pieces begin to fit together, and a clear picture of behavior gradually takes shape. You are not stuck with pieces that do not fit, metaphorically akin to saying things about behavior that contradict your other convictions. You are not tempted, for instance, to say that someone is behaving "as if" she is expecting a certain outcome. You realize that even hypothesizing that an implied mental process might be going on and could explain behavior is problematic because it involves creating a logical domain for your own interpretive behavior, which is an insidious form of mentalism. More practically, this phrasing is likely to be accompanied by a clinical repertoire that is different than that of a colleague who knows to avoid this particular mentalism. What matters is the clinical efficacy of these differences.

Of course, you may also be discovering that learning about radical behaviorism often makes you the only one in the room who has thought through the thorny issues hidden behind colloquial dialect. This will mean you often have things to say others will find interesting and, some might say, impressive. Your observations will reveal a coherent perspective on behavior that is novel to others and remarkable in its perspicuity. Yes, radical behaviorism will make you seem smarter than first impressions of you. Respect, if not fame and fortune, will accrue, though the price is that you will not quite fit in the way you used to.

But can we sell radical behaviorism to everyone else? In your excitement at discovering this way of talking about behavior, you may have neglected this nagging question lurking in the shadows. You may now find radical behaviorism reasonably comfortable, but getting to this place presumably required some struggle and came after other course work in behavior analysis. How can people who see no problems with everyday language—and lack a background in behavior analysis—ever be attracted to this view of behavior and the complexities and awkwardness of this dialect? After all, in spite of our enthusiasm, we still use colloquial dialect most of the time, even among colleagues. Though it has problems we can easily point to, everyday ways of talking have evolved because they work well enough for daily communication and no special effort is required.

In answering this question, it might help to consider how other sciences have fared as their discoveries and special dialects have seeped into the culture. Their histories seem to be related to the extent to which their subject matter has something to do with human behavior. Geology has had a pretty easy time of it, for example. You do not encounter people debating geological discoveries, such as plate tectonics, over breakfast. It is not as if these discoveries have no implications for human affairs, of course, but we seem undisturbed by them. Astronomy had a tough start until we got over not being at the center of the universe, but since then most people have increasingly accepted its discoveries and, more recently, been entertained by the gorgeous pictures. Physics and chemistry have likewise not faced much of a struggle selling their findings, though it is not clear many people are overly interested in the details. In any case, these fields have not generally asked us to change the way we talk. Biology has a different story to tell, however, because the implications of its centerpiece—evolution—have firmly shaken our view of ourselves. More than 150 years after Darwin's publication of his ideas about evolution, our culture, among others, has still not fully come to grips with this view, even though its scientific consequences directly benefit everyone.

Although these sciences have dramatically influenced humankind, they have not generally asked us to pervasively change our view of ourselves as individuals. (The only part of evolution that seems to trouble some people is the idea that our species arrived at its present condition by evolving.) Scientific concepts and technical terms have made their way into daily discourse, but the intrusion has been

---

BOX 10.6

Of Squirrels and Birdfeeders

How can you watch a squirrel dining at a squirrel-proof bird feeder and not figure out shaping and all its nuances? These rodents are amazingly capable, no matter the challenges imposed by bird feeders designed to save a few seeds for our feathered friends. A newly placed and freshly filled feeder establishes contingencies that will in no time shape an impressive repertoire in these wily creatures. Any self-respecting behavior analyst cannot observe the developing repertoire without seeing the orderly interplay between responding and consequences, almost as if it was happening in slow motion.

Everyone else, not so much. Your sister, for example, may well watch with you and appreciate that some responses earn sunflower seeds and some do not and that the squirrel is learning the trick to getting a snack, but that is likely to be the extent of her conclusions. She will probably not see any similarity between what is going on in the backyard and the behavior of her two-year-old child and of herself as a dispenser of reinforcers. Even if she was inclined to tolerate your explanation, would you really expect her role in childrearing contingencies to change? Would she now stop reinforcing the very behavior in her child that she would love to get rid of?

Our reaction to the cluelessness of "civilians" may be like that of a local who is giving directions to a confused stranger. How to get somewhere is perfectly obvious if you already know. If you understand operant contingencies, what is going on with the behavior of a squirrel, or a two-year-old child, is really quite simple, at least on the surface. Perhaps what should also be obvious is that divining the principles of operant learning is not simple at all, even to someone who has good reason to pay close attention. If it was easy to learn how behavior works by merely observing, the world would be a very different place.

Reflecting on the difficulty most people have in understanding operant contingencies in daily life, in spite of their need to manage behavior in practical ways, should make behavior analysts humble about the challenges we face in selling our field within academic and professional communities, not to mention the culture at large. Although we may justifiably complain about the burden of culturally ingrained mentalism, it is not clear that our challenge would be much easier in its absence. Although some of our basic principles might seem straightforward, at least superficially, matters get quite complex from there—a conclusion that might be affirmed by scientists in other fields.

---

fairly limited and more or less optional. Neither have these sciences required us to substantially revise how we go about our daily lives.

The science of behavior analysis, carrying with it a distinctive philosophy, has not been so timid. It asks people to abandon most of what they think they know about what behavior is and how it works. It takes away mentalism in all its forms and offers in its place a pervasive and unyielding focus on environmental influences. In doing so, it demands a substantially different way of talking about behavior, complete with tricky constructions and inelegant phrasing. Why would we think we could sell radical behaviorism to our friends, let along strangers? Have you tried explaining this to your parents?

Perhaps our goal should be more modest than getting everyone to talk like well-trained behavior analysts. It is unlikely that the discoveries of any science will extensively reshape the details of vernacular speech, after all, much less the verbal repertoires of colleagues who have other interests in behavior and its psychological underpinnings. Even when particular scientific findings are largely understood and accepted in the culture, they are not often reflected in technically correct everyday language. (We still refer to the sun rising and setting even though we learn in school that it is actually rotating on its axis relative to the sun.) Colloquial dialect reflects different contingencies than those that are most useful for scientists. Our conversations serve decidedly non-scientific functions, and making discoveries about the natural world is not one of them. Our dialect is what it is because of the balance between efficiency and effectiveness. These everyday verbal contingencies are unlikely to be substantially changed by the discoveries of the science of behavior analysis.

A more reasonable goal is for people to understand the fundamental nature of behavior as a physical phenomenon and how its basic features work. This is not a small challenge, especially in light of the track record of biologists in selling evolution. For instance, it might be enough that parents understand the role of behavior-environment contingencies when you are talking with them about their child. This is surely more important than their eliminating all mentalistic references and phrasing from their speech. It is not that mentalism in everyday language is harmless; it will always cause problems. If even the basic principles of operant shaping were understood and appreciated, however, life for behavior analysts would be much easier. With this foundation, it might be less challenging to gain the cooperation of parents in arranging the right contingencies for their child. They would be able to discuss the key influences on their child's behavior, though they would probably still use common parlance in their description.

So, perhaps the goal is not to sell radical behaviorism in all its glory but to encourage an understanding and acceptance of the basic features of how behavior works. Is the real problem phrases such as "I changed my mind" or "He seems really frustrated," or is it more important that people are able to follow such comments with a useful discussion of what is really going on with environmental influences? As with any science, real expertise requires a significant investment of focused study, so it is not realistic to expect most people to acquire more than a rudimentary appreciation of the role of environmental contingencies.

We have actually made modest headway in this direction over the years. It is no longer uncommon to encounter proper, everyday references to reinforcement contingencies, for example, though we may wait in vain to overhear a mention of discriminative stimuli in the grocery store checkout line. More importantly, selling the role of operant shaping in a particular sample of behavior seems easier than it did decades ago. Perhaps our salesmanship has improved. As a profession, school teachers certainly seem more prepared for these discussions than they used to be, for example, though few seem to understand enough to avoid needing our assistance. Cultural change of the sort we would like is slow.

A society fully consistent with the science of behavior analysis and all its implications is exciting to imagine. B. F. Skinner's vision, the utopian novel *Walden two*, is more than 60 years old and continues to be a fascinating exploration of what such a life might be like (Skinner, 1948). (If you have not yet read it, you are certainly ready now.) It is important for us to savor the dream of a society that works as well as our science allows. The discrepancy between this dream and pedestrian reality is so great that we must share this ideal from time to time to buoy our spirits. Meanwhile, we must be sure we can articulate the best our science and technology has to offer.

CHAPTER SUMMARY

1. Radical behaviorism is defined by Skinner as "the philosophy of a science of behavior treated as a subject matter in its own right apart from internal explanations, mental or physiological."

2. Radical behaviorism is not the scientific study of behavior, but a philosophy of that science. It concerns the philosophical underpinnings and assumptions of scientific activities and findings, including issues such as scientific language, methods, explanation, and reasoning.

3. The most important feature of radical behaviorism as a scientific philosophy is that behavior analysts view verbal behavior—specifically including their own verbal behavior—no differently than any other kind of behavior. All verbal behavior is fully explained in terms of the laws of operant learning.

4. Rather than being viewed as a superior form of knowledge involving logical domains and mental processes, scientific explanations are accepted as behavior no different than the behavior being explained. Unlike other sciences, there is no conceptual discontinuity between the subject matter of the science and the explanatory behavior of its scientists. This epistemology stems from radical behaviorism's intolerance for mentalism. Taking the position that behavior is a subject matter in its own right is not only a statement about the importance of behavior as a focus of scientific study, it puts aside the mentalistic agenda in its entirety.

5. Radical behaviorism holds that behavior is not merely a consequence of its underlying physiology. It opposes the view that behavior can be adequately explained by its biological underpinnings. Neither does it allow using biological variables to legitimize mental explanations. Instead, radical behaviorism

approaches behavior as a set of relations between the organism and its environment that stand on their own. These relations do not require further analysis in either mental or physiological terms for their validity or utility.

6. Radical behaviorism defines behavior as including far more than what is obvious to external observers. It accepts that we have real experiences that are private and not generally accessible to others. Rather than ignore these private events because they can be difficult to observe, it incorporates them into the scientific agenda.

7. Early efforts to study behavior held that only publicly observable events were acceptable as the source of objective data. This was too constricting for many, so unobservable "events" came to be viewed in theoretical terms and incorporated into scientific interpretations and theories. In this approach, mental events or processes are proposed as explanations of behavior, but because they cannot be directly assessed, some ostensibly related behavior is measured instead. These indirect measurements are then said to represent the mental phenomena, which is used as the basis for explaining the behavior of interest. However, arguing that the indirectly measured behavior "represents" certain mental events or processes is mentalistic because scientific behavior is given a special logical status.

8. With radical behaviorism, the challenge of directly observing private events is resolved by calling for an operational analysis of the verbal behavior of the scientists. Instead of either ignoring private events or inventing mentalistic representations of them, radical behaviorism incorporates them into interpretative analysis but asks about the sources of control over such statements. Focusing on the environmental sources of control over scientific verbal behavior avoids the need to be mentalistic in interpreting the verbal behavior of the scientist.

9. In sum, radical behaviorism accepts behavior as a subject matter in its own right, regardless of the challenges of measuring it or the variables of which it is a function. It approaches behavior as a primary phenomenon, not merely a consequence of biology nor an epiphenomenon of a more important mental life. Radical behaviorism rejects invented, internal dimensions and causes, as well as explanations that rely on a mentalistic view of the researcher's explanatory behavior.

10. Watson's 1913 paper, "Psychology as the behaviorist views it" is customarily taken as the beginning of the behavioral movement. Watson's classical behaviorism was a major step forward. He insisted that psychologists study only behavior and that mental phenomena were fictional and in any case not acceptable for a science of behavior. His approach has become labeled classical S-R behaviorism because of its embrace of the discoveries of Ivan Pavlov and others concerning conditioned reflexes.

11. The inadequacies of Watsonian behaviorism encouraged a new variant described as mediational S-O-R behaviorism. This approach added inferences about things that might be going on inside the organism that could intervene between stimuli and responses. This form of neobehaviorism readmitted mentalism into the study of behavior in the form of motives, tendencies, purposes, moods, attitudes, and such that were assumed to modulate the effects of environmental stimuli.

12. Skinner's emerging philosophy avoided mentalism by focusing on understanding the sources of control over the verbal behavior of the speaker. This approach involves dealing with statements as merely a form of behavior, rather than as having meaning in another dimension. The "meaning" of a term or phrase is therefore explained in terms of the factors that influence its emission as verbal behavior.

13. Methodological behaviorism is a way of thinking about scientific method that comes from conventional experimental practices and their underlying rationale. Its key flaw is that it does not avoid the trap of implying the existence of a logical domain that allows the scientist to reason and draw conclusions about the participant's behavior.

TEXT STUDY GUIDE

1. Define radical behaviorism and explain how it relates to the science of behavior analysis.

2. Explain how radical behaviorism requires viewing scientific behavior as no different from other behavior.

3. What is the view of radical behaviorism regarding the status and role of physiology?

4. How does radical behaviorism expand the scientific agenda?

5. Describe how mentalism works using the example of anxiety.

6. Explain how an operational analysis of the scientist's verbal behavior leads to a different conceptual and experimental outcome.

7. Summarize the features of radical behaviorism.

8. Describe Watson's classical S-R behaviorism. What were its limitations?

9. Define and explain mediational S-O-R behaviorism.

10. Summarize Skinner's argument about how we should approach the scientist's verbal behavior.

11. Summarize the features of methodological behaviorism.

12. How is methodological behaviorism mentalistic?

13. If you disagree with certain tenets of radical behaviorism, what should you be prepared to do regarding your alternative views?

14. Why might it be fruitless to try to sell radical behaviorism broadly within the culture? What might be a more realistic goal?

BOX STUDY GUIDE

1. What is reductionism? Why is it problematic as a way of explaining behavior?

2. How is the term "theory" used in science?

3. Distinguish between intervening variables and hypothetical constructs. How does radical behaviorism approach such theoretical terms?

4. Who was John B. Watson? What was the key argument in his "behaviorist manifesto?"

5. Describe conventional operationism. From Skinner's perspective, what is its fatal flaw? How did Skinner approach operationism?

6. Who was J. R. Kantor? Summarize his conceptual approach to behavior.

DISCUSSION TOPICS AND EXERCISES

1. Select a mentalistic quality or feature often offered as underlying and causing behavior. Discuss how you might approach it both verbally and experimentally from a radical behavioristic perspective.

2. Find a brain imaging study that purports to tell us about some aspect of behavior. Discuss possible conceptual flaws in the author's reasoning.

3. Identify the issue or feature of radical behaviorism that bothers you the most. Explain possible alternative views and defend how they might be more beneficial to the field and in your career than the radical behavioristic position.

4. Discuss how you think behavior analysis should present itself to the culture and encourage its support.

SUGGESTED READINGS

Day, W. F. (1977). On the difference between radical and methodological behaviorism. *Behaviorism, 11*, 89–102.

Faux, S. F. (2002). Cognitive neuroscience from a behavioral perspective: A critique of chasing ghosts with geiger counters. *The Behavior Analyst, 25(2)*, 161–173.

Moore, J. (1981). On mentalism, methodological behaviorism, and radical behaviorism. *Behaviorism, 9(1)*, 55–77.

Moore, J. (2008). Conceptual foundations of radical behaviorism. Cornwall-on-Hudson, NY: Sloan Publishing. (Chapter 1: Radical behaviorism as a philosophy of science; Chapter 2: History of behaviorism and behavior analysis: 1800–1930; Chapter 3: History of behaviorism and behavior analysis: 1930–1980; Chapter 4: Behavior as a subject matter in its own right; Chapter 17: Radical behaviorism and traditional philosophical issues)

Morris, E. K. (1982). Some relationships between interbehavioral psychology and radical behaviorism. *Behaviorism, 10,* 187–216.

Skinner, B. F. (1948). *Walden two*. New York: MacMillan.

Glossary

Assertive autoclitic: A verbal response prompted by other verbal behavior that asserts a particular state of affairs and encourages a listener to agree.

Autoclitic: A verbal response that is controlled by other verbal behavior and that changes the effects of that verbal behavior on others.

Behavioral functions: The environmental effects or outcomes of a behavior.

Behavior-consequence contingency: A dependent relation between responding and its environmental consequences, often involving a response resulting in a reinforcer. See contingency.

Category mistake: As proposed by Gilbert Ryle, a type of error in which things of the same kind are taken to belong to each other, such as mistaking a behavior as an instance of or caused by a particular capability or skill.

Classical S-R behaviorism: The label for John Watson's approach to behaviorism, which was partially based on Pavlov's discoveries of conditioned reflexes.

Contingency: A dependent relation between two events. With regard to operant behavior, most often a relation between a response and its consequence.

Contingency adduction: The process of behaviors independently learned under different conditions coming together to form a new behavior under a new condition that may combine prior stimulus features.

Contingency-specifying stimuli: Verbal stimuli that reference events such a stimulus, response or consequence and may thereby alter the function of certain stimuli. Rules may fit this requirement when their contingency-specifying stimuli cannot be explained in terms of discrimination training. See Function-altering stimuli.

Copy theory: The view that what we perceive are only copies of the world around us that are transformed by mental processes and thereby guide our reactions.

Countercontrol: Behavior that mitigates or eliminates aversive sources of control, especially in the context of social contingencies.

Cultural engineering: The systematic application of behavioral science to change targeted cultural practices.

Determinism: A philosophical position that generally holds that human behavior is entirely the result of physical influences.

Discriminative stimulus: A stimulus that as a result of its correlation with reinforcement has acquired the discriminative function of making a behavior more likely to occur in its presence than in its absence.

Echoic: A verbal response for which a vocal verbal stimulus sets the occasion for a corresponding vocal verbal response.

Fixed action patterns: A fairly consistent pattern of responding that occurs in the presence of releasing or sign stimuli and that cannot be attributed to operant learning.

Free will: A philosophical position that generally holds that human behavior can be free of physical determinants and result solely from an individual's decisions, choices, and mental activity.

Function-altering stimuli: Verbal stimuli that do not have a discriminative stimulus function but that can influence behavior by changing the function of other stimuli. Rules may often be examples of function-altering stimuli. See Contingency-specifying stimuli.

Hypothetical constructs: Unobserved but hypothetically real events used in scientific explanations that are proposed to play a role in physical phenomena.

Intervening variables: Processes or influences invented to summarize established relations in theoretical scientific statements.

Intraverbal: A verbal response that occurs to a verbal stimulus based on arbitrary contingencies established by the verbal community.

Learning history: The accumulated effects of contingencies between an organism's responses and their environmental consequences. See ontogeny.

Mand: A verbal response that specifies its own reinforcer.

Mental events: A way of referring to particular non-behavioral or mental activities, although reference to "events" should not imply that such activity necessarily involves physical phenomena.

Mentalism: Attributing the causes of behavior to events and processes said to occur in a mind or inner world that lacks physical dimensions.

Methodological behaviorism: The label for a version of behaviorism that characterizes conventional experimental practices and their mentalistic rationale.

Molar analysis: A perspective toward behavior that emphasizes the aggregate effects of a history, often involving different response classes, in explaining a particular behavioral outcome.

Molecular analysis: A perspective toward behavior that emphasizes momentary contingencies or temporal contiguity in explaining a particular behavioral outcome.

Motivating operation: Any operation or stimulus that changes the effectiveness of events as reinforcers or punishers or that changes the frequency of behavior associated with these events.

Ontology: The environmental history of individual organisms during their lifetimes.

Operant behavior: Behavior that is especially susceptible to modification by its consequences.

Operant learning: Relatively systematic and durable changes in operant behavior resulting from its environmental consequences.

Operant selection: The effects of contingencies between operant responses and their consequences that make some forms of responding more likely than others.

Operant shaping: Modification of operant behavior by its consequences. May refer to small changes in a specific response class, or more complex changes in a repertoire, resulting gradual shifts in reinforcement contingencies.

Operationism: The philosophical position that terms and concepts are defined by the operations or procedures used to measure them.

Parsimony: An approach to scientific explanation that emphasizes simplicity and reliance on well-established knowledge.

Phylogeny: The evolutionary history of individuals originating from contingencies that operate during the environmental history of a species.

Proximate reinforcers: Reinforcers mediated by the immediate and often social environment.

Quantifying autoclitic: A verbal response prompted by other verbal behavior that quantifies a tact in a way that modifies the listener's behavior.

Radical behaviorism: The philosophy of the science of behavior analysis, which focuses on behavior as a purely physical phenomenon.

Reductionism: In science, a philosophical position that a phenomenon can be explained by reducing it to its constituent parts. For behavior analysts, this approach is considered as problematic when the attempt is to reduce behavioral phenomena to biological phenomena.

Reinforcement contingencies: Dependent relations between operant responses and their consequences that strengthen responding in some way.

Response class/functional response class: A collection of responses that are similarly influenced by (functionally related to) environmental events that precede and follow them. Also called a behavior.

S-O-R: Acronym for Stimulus-Organism-Response, referring to an assumption that private organismic processes intervene between stimuli and responses that modulate the effects of stimuli on responding.

Survival value: In the context of behavior analysis, an evaluation of the extent to which particular cultural practices contribute to the survival of a culture.

Tact: A verbal response usually emitted in the presence of an object or event and the form of which is controlled by that object or event.

Teleology: An approach to explaining a phenomenon that depends on the contribution of final causes. With regard to behavior, teleological explanations attribute cause to future events.

Textual operant: A vocal verbal response whose form is under the discriminative control of a textual stimulus.

Ultimate reinforcers: Reinforcers associated with health and reproductive fitness in the long term, rather than more immediate social origins.

Verbal community: A social environment that maintains verbal contingencies for its members.

Bibliography

Andronis, P. T. (1983). *A novel form of aggression by pigeons: Contingency adduction.* Unpublished doctoral dissertation, University of Chicago.

Andronis, P. T., Layng, T. V. J., & Goldiamond, I. (1997). Contingency adduction of "symbolic aggression" by pigeons. *The Analysis of Verbal Behavior, 14,* 5–17.

Baer, D. M., Wolf, M. M., & Risley, T. R. (1968). Some current dimensions of applied behavior analysis. *Journal of Applied Behavior Analysis, 1,* 91–97.

Bridgman, P. (1927). The logic of modern physics. New York: MacMillan.

Baum, W. M. (1995). Rules, culture, and fitness. *The Behavior Analyst, 18,* 1–21.

Baum, W. M. (2002). From molecular to molar: A paradigm shift in behavior analysis. *Journal of the Experimental Analysis of Behavior, 78,* 95–116.

Baum, W. M. (2005). *Understanding behaviorism.* Malden, MA: Blackwell Publishing.

Boakes, R. (1984). *From Darwin to Behaviorism: Psychology and the minds of animals.* New York: Cambridge University Press.

Branch, M. N. (1977). On the role of memory in the analysis of behavior. *Journal of the Experimental Analysis of Behavior, 28(2),* 171–179.

Catania, A. C. (1975). The myth of self-reinforcement. *Behaviorism, 3(2),* 192–199.

Catania, A. C. (1984). Problems of selection and phylogeny, terms and methods of behaviorism. *Behavioral and Brain Sciences, 7,* 713–717.

Catania, A. C. (1986). On the difference between verbal and nonverbal behavior. *The Analysis of Verbal Behavior, 4,* 2–9.

Catania, A. C. (2013). *Learning, 5ᵗʰ ed.* Cornwall-On-Hudson, NY: Sloan Publishing.

Catania, A. C., & Harnad, S. D. (Eds.). (1988). *The selection of behavior: The operant behaviorism of B. F. Skinner: Comments and controversies.* Cambridge: Cambridge University Press.

Catania, A. C., Mathews, B. A., & Shimoff, E. (1982). Instructed versus shaped human verbal behavior: Interactions with nonverbal responding. *Journal of the Experimental Analysis of Behavior, 38,* 233–248.

Catania, A. C., Shimoff, E., & Mathews, B. A. (1989). An experimental analysis of rule-governed behavior. In S. C. Hayes (Ed.), *Rule-governed behavior: Cognition, contingencies, and instructional control* (119–150). New York: Plenum.

Cerutti, D. T. (1989). Discrimination theory of rule-governed behavior. *Journal of the Experimental Analysis of Behavior, 51(2)*, 259–276.

Chiesa, M. (1994). *Radical behaviorism: The philosophy and the science.* Boston: The Author's Cooperative.

Day, W. F. (1977). On the difference between radical and methodological behaviorism. *Behaviorism, 11*, 89–102.

Dennett, D. C. (1984). *Elbow room: The varieties of free will worth wanting.* Cambridge, MA: MIT Press.

Donahoe, J. (1996). On the relation between behavior analysis and biology. *The Behavior Analyst, 19*, 71–73.

Epstein, R. (Ed.). (1980). *Notebooks, B. F. Skinner.* Englewood Cliffs, NJ: Prentice-Hall.

Epstein, R. (1981). Of pigeons and people: A preliminary look at the Columba Simulation Project. *The Behavior Analyst, 4*, 43–55.

Epstein, R. (Ed.). (1982). *Skinner for the classroom.* Champaign, IL: Research Press.

Epstein, R. (1987). The spontaneous interconnection of four repertoires of behavior in a pigeon (Columba livia). *Journal of Comparative Psychology, 101*, 197–201.

Esch, J. W., Esch, B. E., & Love, J. R. (2009). Increasing vocal variability in children with autism using a lag schedule of reinforcement. *Analysis of Verbal Behavior, 25(1)*, 73–78.

Faux, S. F. (2002). Cognitive neuroscience from a behavioral perspective: A critique of chasing ghosts with geiger counters. *The Behavior Analyst, 25(2)*, 161–173.

Ferster, C. B., & Skinner, B. F. (1957). *Schedules of reinforcement.* New York: Appleton-Century.

Glenn, S. S. (2003). Operant contingencies and the origin of cultures. In K. A. Little & P. N. Chase (Eds.), *Behavior theory and philosophy* (pp. 223–242). New York: Kluwer/Plenum.

Glenn, S. S. (2004). Individual behavior, culture, and social change. *The Behavior Analyst, 27*, 133–151.

Glover, J. A. (1979). The effectiveness of reinforcement and practice for enhancing the creative writing of elementary school children. *Journal of applied behavior analysis, 12*, 487.

Glover, J. A. & Gary, A. L. (1976). Procedures to increase some aspects of creativity. *Journal of applied behavior analysis, 9*, 79–84.

Goetz, E. M., & Baer, D. M. (1973). Social control of form diversity and the emergence of new forms in children's blockbuilding. *Journal of Applied Behavior Analysis, 6*, 209–217.

Grow, L. L., Kelley, M. E., Roane, H. S., & Shillingsburg, M. A. (2008). Utility of extinction-induced response variability for the selection of mands. *Journal of Applied Behavior Analysis, 41*, 15–24.

Guerin, B. (1994). Attitudes and beliefs as verbal behavior. *The Behavior Analyst, 17*, 155–163.

Hart, B. & Risley, T. R. (1995). *Meaningful differences in the everyday experience of young American children.* Baltimore, MD: Paul H. Brookes Publishing Co.

Hart, B. & Risley, T. R. (1999). *The social world of children learning to talk.* Baltimore, MD: Paul H. Brookes Publishing Co.

Harlem, P. & Miles, T. R. (1978). *Conceptual issues in operant psychology.* New York: John Wiley Sons.

Hayes, S. C. (1984). Making sense of spirituality. *Behaviorism, 12(2)*, 99–110.

Hayes, S. C. (1989). *Rule-governed behavior: Cognition, contingencies, and instructional control.* New York: Plenum.

Hebb, D. O. (1949). Organization of behavior, New York: Wiley.

Hineline, P. N. (1980). The language of behavior analysis: Its community, its functions, and its limitations. *Behaviorism, 80*, 67–86.

Hineline, P. N. (2003). When we speak of intentions. In K. A. Lattal & P. N. Chase (Eds.), *Behavior theory and philosophy* (pp. 203–221). New York: Kluwer/Plenum.

Honig, W. K. (Ed.). (1966). *Operant conditioning: Areas of research and application.* New York: Appleton-Century-Crofts.

Jacobson, J. W., Foxx, R. M., & Mulick, J. A. (2004). *Controversial therapies for developmental disabilities.* Mahweh, NJ: Lawrence Erlbaum Associates.

Johnson, K. R. & Layng, T. V. J. (1992). Breaking the structuralist barrier: Literacy and numeracy with fluency. *American Psychologist, 47*, 1475–1490.

Johnston, J. M. (1996). Distinguishing between applied research and practice. *The Behavior Analyst, 19*, 35–47.

Johnston, J. M. & Pennypacker, H. S. (2009). *Strategies and tactics of behavioral research* (3rd ed.). New York: Routledge.

Keller, F. S. & Schoenfeld, W. N. (1950). *Principles of psychology.* New York: Appleton-Century-Crofts.

Lamal, P. A. (Ed.). (1991). *Behavioral analysis of societies and cultural practices.* New York: Hemisphere.

Layng, T. V. J., Twyman, J. S., & Stikeleather, G. (2004). Engineering discovery learning: The contingency adduction of some precursors of textual responding in a beginning reading program. *The Analysis of Verbal Behavior, 20*, 99–109.

Lee, V. L. (1988). *Beyond behaviorism.* Hillsdale, NJ: Lawrence Erlbaum Associates.

Leigland, S. (1992). *Radical behaviorism: Willard Day on psychology and philosophy.* Reno, NV: Context Press.

MacCorquodale, K. & Meehl, P. (1948). On a distinction between hypothetical constructs and intervening variables. *Psychological Review, 55*, 95–107.

Mahoney, M. (1976). *Scientist as subject: The psychological imperative.* Cambridge, MA: Balinger Publishing.

Maloney, K. B., & Hopkins, B. L. (1973). The modification of sentence structure and its relationship to subjective judgements of creativity in writing. *Journal of applied behavior analysis, 6*, 425–233.

Marr, M. J. (1983). Memory: Metaphors and models. *The Psychological Record, 33*, 12–19.

McGill, P. (1999). Establishing operations: Implications for the assessment, treatment, and prevention of problem behavior. *Journal of Applied Behavior Analysis, 32*, 393–418.

Michael, J. (1982). Distinguishing between discriminative and motivational functions of stimuli. *Journal of the Experimental Analysis of Behavior, 37*, 149–155.

Michael, J. (1993). Establishing operations. *The Behavior Analyst, 16*, 191–206.

Michael, J. (2000). Implications and refinements of the establishing operation concept. *Journal of Applied Behavior Analysis, 33*, 401–410.

Michael, J. (2007). Motivating operations. In J. O. Cooper, T. E. Heron, & W. L. Heward, (Eds.), *Applied behavior analysis* (pp. 374–391). Upper Saddle River, NJ: Pearson Education, Inc.

Mill, J. S. (1973/1843). A system of logic. In F. F. McRae (Ed.), *Collected works of John Stuart Mill* (Vols. 7 & 8). Toronto: University of Toronto Press.

Moerk, E. L. (1983). A behavioral analysis of controversial topics in first language acquisition: Reinforcements, corrections, modeling, input frequencies, and the three-term contingency pattern. *Journal of Psycholinguistic Research, 12*, 129–155.

Moerk, E. L. (1990). Three-term contingency patterns in mother-child interactions during first language acquisition. *Journal of the Experimental Analysis of Behavior, 54*, 293–305.

Moerk, E. L. (1992). *First language: Taught and learned*. Baltimore, MD: Brookes.

Moore, J. (1980). On behaviorism and private events. *The Psychological Record, 30*, 459–475.

Moore, J. (1980). On the principle of operationism in the science of behavior. *Behaviorism, 3*, 120–138.

Moore, J. (1981). On mentalism, methodological behaviorism, and radical behaviorism. *Behaviorism, 9(1)*, 55–77.

Moore, J. (1984). On privacy, causes, and contingencies. *The Behavior Analyst. 7*, 3–16.

Moore, J. (1985). Some historical and conceptual relations among logical positivism, operationism, and behaviorism. *The Behavior Analyst, 8*, 53–63.

Moore, J. (2000). Words are not things. *The Analysis of Verbal Behavior, 17*, 143–160.

Moore, J. (2008). *Conceptual foundations of radical behaviorism*. Cornwall-on-Hudson, NY: Sloan Publishing.

Moore, J. (2010). Behaviorism and the stages of scientific activity. *The Behavior Analyst, 33*, 47–63.

Moore, J., & Cooper, J. O. (2003). Some proposed relations among the experimental analysis of behavior, applied behavior analysis, and service delivery. *The Behavior Analyst, 26*, 69–84.

Morris, E. K. (1982). Some relationships between interbehavioral psychology and radical behaviorism. *Behaviorism, 10*, 187–216.

Morris, E. K. (1984). Interbehavioral psychology and radical behaviorism: Some similarities and differences. *The Behavior Analyst, 7*, 197–204.

Morris, E. K. (1988). Contextualism: The world view of behavior analysis. *Journal of Experimental Child Psychology, 46*, 289–323.

Morris, E. K., & Smith, N. G. (1993). Bibliographic processes and products, and a bibliography of the published primary-source works of B. F. Skinner. *The Behavior Analyst, 26*, 41–67.

Newton, M. (2002). *Savage girls and wild boys: A history of feral children*. London: Farber and Farber.

O'Donnell, J. M. (1985). *The origins of behaviorism: American psychology, 1870–1920*. New York: New York University Press.

O'Donohue, W. & Kitchener, R. (Eds.). (1999). *Handbook of behaviorism*. San Diego, CA: Academic Press.

Place, U. T. (1993). A radical behaviorist methodology for the empirical investigation of private events. *Behavior and Philosophy, 20–21*, 25–35.

Place, U. T. (1999). Ryle's behaviorism. In W. O. Donohue & W. F. Kitchener (Eds.), *Handbook of behaviorism* (pp. 41–68). London: Kluwer.

Pryor, K. (1999). *Don't shoot the dog*. New York: Bantam Books.

Rachlin, H. (1985). Pain and behavior. *The Behavioral and Brain Sciences, 8*, 43–83.

Rachlin, H. (1994). *Behavior and mind*. Oxford: Oxford University Press.

Reese, H. W. (1996). How is physiology relevant to behavior analysis? *The Behavior Analyst, 19*, 61–70.

Schlinger, H. D. (1993). Separating discriminative versus function-altering effects of verbal stimuli. *The Behavior Analyst, 16*, 9–23.

Schlinger, H. D. (2008). Listening is behaving verbally. *The Behavior Analyst, 31*, 145–161.

Schlinger, H. D., & Blakely, E. (1987). Function-altering effects of contingency-specifying stimuli. *The Behavior Analyst, 10*, 41–45.

Schnaitter, R. M. (1978). Private causes. *Behaviorism, 6*, 1–12.

Schnaitter, R. M. (1980). Science and verbal behavior. *Behaviorism, 8*, 153–160.

Schnaitter, R. M. (1984). Skinner on the "mental" and the "physical." *Behaviorism, 12*, 1–14.

Schnaitter, R. M. (1987). Knowledge as action: The epistemology of radical behaviorism. In S. Moduli & C. Moduli (Eds.), *B. F. Skinner: Consensus and controversy* (pp. 57–68). Philadelphia, PA: Flamer Press.

Schneider, S. M. & Morris, E. K. (1987). A history of the term radical behaviorism: From Watson to Skinner. *The Behavior Analysis, 10 (1)*, 27–39.

Schoenfeld, W. N. (1993). *Religion and human behavior*. Boston, MA: Author's Cooperative, Inc.

Segall, M. H., Campbell, D. T., & Herskovits, M. J. (1966). *The influence of culture on visual perception*. Indianapolis, IN: Bobbs-Merrill Company.

Sidman, M. (1960). *Tactics of scientific research*. New York: Basic Books.

Skinner, B. F. (1935). The generic nature of the concepts of stimulus and response. *Journal of General Psychology, 12*, 40–65.

Skinner, (1938). *The behavior of organisms*. New York: Appleton-Century.

Skinner, B. F. (1945). The operational analysis of psychological terms. *Psychological Review, 52*, 270–277.

Skinner, B. F. (1948). *Walden Two*. New York: MacMillan.

Skinner, B. F. (1950). Are theories of learning necessary? *Psychological Review, 57*, 193–216.

Skinner, B. F. (1953). *Science and human behavior*. New York: MacMillan.

Skinner, B. F. (1957). *Verbal behavior*. New York: Appleton-Century-Crofts.

Skinner, B. F. (1961/1972). *Cumulative Record*. New York: Appleton-Century-Crofts.

Skinner, B. F. (1967). B. F. Skinner. In E. G. Boring and G. Lindzey (Eds.), *A history of psychology in autobiography (pp. 387–413*. New York: Appleton-Century-Crofts.

Skinner, B. F. (1969). Behaviorism at fifty. In B. F. Skinner, *Contingencies of* reinforcement (pp. 221–268). New York: Appleton-Century-Crofts.

Skinner, B. F. (1969). *Contingencies of reinforcement: A theoretical analysis*. New York: Appleton-Century-Crofts.

Skinner, B. F. (1969). An operant analysis of problem solving. In B. F. Skinner, *Contingencies of* reinforcement (pp. 133–171). New York: Appleton-Century-Crofts

Skinner, B. F. (1971). *Beyond freedom and dignity*. New York: Alfred A. Knopf.

Skinner, B. F. (1974). *About behaviorism*. New York: Alfred A. Knopf.

Skinner, B. F. (1976). *Particulars of my life*. New York: Alfred A. Knopf.

Skinner, B. F. (1978). *Reflections on behaviorism and society*. Englewood Cliffs, NJ: Prentice-Hall.

Skinner, B. F. (1979). *The shaping of a behaviorist*. New York: Alfred A. Knopf.

Skinner, B. F. (1981). Selection by consequences. *Science*, 213, 501–504.

Skinner, B. F. (1983). *A matter of consequences*. New York: Alfred A. Knopf.

Skinner, B. F. (1989). *Recent issues in the analysis of behavior*. Columbus, OH: Merrill.

Terrell, D. & Johnston, J. M. (1989). Logic, reasoning, and verbal behavior. *The Behavior Analyst, 12(1)*, 35–44.

Thyer, B. A. (Ed.). (1999). *The philosophical legacy of behaviorism.* Hingham, MA: Kluwer Academic Publishers.

Todd, J. T. & Morris, E. K. (Eds.). (1994). *Modern perspectives on John B. Watson and classical behaviorism.* Westport, CT: Greenwood Press.

Tonneau, F. (2008). The concept of reinforcement: Explanatory or descriptive? *Behavior and Philosophy, 36*, 87–96.

Uttal, W. R. (1998). *Toward a new behaviorism: The case against perceptual reductionism.* Mahwah, NJ: Lawrence Erlbaum Associates.

Uttal, W. R. (2000). *The war between mentalism and behaviorism: On the accessibility of mental processes.* Mahwah, NJ: Lawrence Erlbaum Associates.

Uttal, W. R. (2011). *Mind and brain: A critical appraisal of cognitive neuroscience.* Cambridge, MA: MIT Press.

Vargas, E. A. (1975). Rights: A behavioristic analysis. *Behaviorism, 3(2)*, 178–191.

Wann, T. W. (1964). *Behaviorism and phenomenology.* Chicago, IL: University of Chicago Press.

Vaughan, M. E. & Michael, J. L. (1982). Automatic reinforcement: An important but ignored concept. *Behaviorism, 10(2)*, 217–227.

Watson, J. B. (1913). Psychology as the behaviorist views it. *Psychological Review, 20,* 1958–1977.

Watson, J. B. (1925). *Behaviorism.* New York: Norton.

Watson, J. B. (1928). *Psychological care of infant and child.* New York: Norton.

White, K. G. (2001). Forgetting functions. *Animal Learning and Behavior, 29*, 193–207.

White, K. G. (2002). Psychophysics of remembering: The discrimination hypothesis. *Current Directions in Psychological Science, 11*, 141–145.

Williams, B. A. (1986). On the role of theory in behavior analysis. *Behaviorism, 14*, 111–124.

Wright, A. A., Katz, J. S., & Ma, W. J., (2012). How to be proactive about interference: Lessons from animal memory. *Psychological Science,* online first, http://www.psychologicalscience.org

Zborowski, M. (1969). *People in pain.* San Francisco, CA: Jossey-Bass.

Zettle, R. D. & Hayes, S. C. (1982). Rule governed behavior: A potential theoretical framework for cognitive behavior therapy. In P. C. Kendall (Ed.), *Advances in cognitive-behavioral research and therapy* (Vol. 1, pp. 73–118). New York: Academic Press.

Zuriff, G. E. (1985) *Behaviorism: A conceptual reconstruction.* New York: Columbia University Press.

Author Index

Page numbers followed by "*b*" indicate material in text boxes

Subject Index

Page numbers followed by "*b*" indicate material in text boxes